NOËL COWARD

Clive Fisher

NOËL COWARD

Weidenfeld & Nicolson
London

First published in Great Britain in 1992 by
George Weidenfeld & Nicolson
91 Clapham High Street
London SW4 7TA

British Library Cataloguing in Publication Data:
a catalogue record for this book is available from
the British Library.

ISBN 0 297 81180 0

Filmset in Palatino by Selwood Systems, Midsomer Norton

Printed in Great Britain by Butler & Tanner Ltd, Frome and London

For my father

Contents

Illustrations

Arthur Sabin Coward (Weidenfeld & Nicolson Archive)
Violet Agnes Veitch (Weidenfeld & Nicolson Archive)
The young Noël Coward (Weidenfeld & Nicolson Archive)
Noël coward with his younger brother Eric (Weidenfeld & Nicolson Archive)
Noël Coward with Philip Streatfield in Cornwall on the eve of the First World War (Weidenfeld & Nicolson Archive)
Noël Coward, Lynton, 1917 (T. J. L. Wynne-Tyson)
Noël Coward in about 1925, wearing a dressing-gown (T. J. L. Wynne-Tyson)
Esme Wynne and Noël Coward, Kensington Gate, July 1917 (T. J. L. Wynne-Tyson)
The young Jack Wilson (Weidenfeld & Nicolson Archive)
Coward with Wilson and Gertrude Lawrence at Goldenhurst in about 1936 (Hulton-Deutsch Collection)
Coward at home in about 1927 (Hulton-Deutsch Collection)
Coward and Lawrence as Elyot and Amanda in *Private Lives* at the Phoenix Theatre in September 1930 (Hulton-Deutsch Collection)
The closing tableau of *Design for Living*: Coward with Alfred Lunt and Lynn Fontanne (Mander & Mitchenson Theatre Collection)
Coward with Princess Marina at the Actors' Orphanage garden party in 1937 (Weidenfeld & Nicolson Archive)
Coward: the incessant and glamorous traveller (Hulton-Deutsch Collection)
Coward with Gladys Calthrop inspecting costumes for *Operette* (Hulton-Deutsch Collection)
Coward auctioneering gifts from the Duke and Duchess of Kent in 1941 (Hutton-Deutsch Collection
Coward and Graham Payn in Bermuda in 1956 (Press Association)
Graham Payn, Cecil Beaton, Coward, Mrs Jack Wilson and Mrs Ian Fleming in Jamaica (Beaton Archive, Sotheby's)
Coward with Gina Lollobrigida, Margot Fonteyn and Roberto Arias in 1959 (Hulton-Deutsch Collection)

At Buckingham Palace, February 1970: Coward – accompanied by Gladys Calthrop and Joyce Carey – receives a knighthood (Hulton-Deutsch Collection)

Coward as he will be remembered: to an entire generation the paragon of style and effortless sophistication, in Las Vegas in 1955 (UPI/Bettman)

Author's Note

This biography was begun with the conviction that a writer stands or falls by his literary legacy, and that even a figure of such diverse accomplishment as Noël Coward should be subjected to literary scrutiny in view of the fact that it is as a playwright and lyricist that he commands lasting renown. This book, as originally conceived, accordingly took somewhat different form. I was to discover, however, that authors and literary estates often have discordant opinions concerning the claims of the dead and the nature of posthumous biography. The Noël Coward Estate, for whatever reason, disliked my account of the achievement it exists to represent, and refused me permission to quote from his work. Coward's words are therefore rationed; and I should like to apologize for the fact that there are occasions when I have had to act as an inadequate spokesman for someone quite capable of speaking, and with distinctive eloquence, for himself.

Happily, I have encountered kindness and co-operation as well as opposition. I must thank Hilary Laurie, Allegra Huston and Natalina Bertoli, the editors who have supervised this book's progress, and also Kathryn Dymoke at the Society of Authors for her help and advice. My agent, Jane Conway-Gordon, was always ready to listen patiently to the grievances of an inexperienced biographer. My old friend Candida Brazil, by commissioning this project, showed faith in me when it mattered, while Alex Sainsbury showed saintly generosity by giving me somewhere to live in which to finish my undertaking. Above all, I am indebted to Jon Wynne-Tyson, who wrote so often and so promptly from Sussex, and whose unstinting assistance has crucially shaped the ensuing narrative.

Simon: You're not particularly beautiful, darling, and you never were.

Judith: Never mind; I made thousands think I was.

Hay Fever

Introduction

Most biographies are about what people become, but a few – Noël Coward's among them – are about what people choose to be. Coward was the first to admit to the artifice his persona represented: 'One's real inside self is a private place and should always stay like that. I have taken a lot of trouble with my public face.'[1] Indeed, it was his life's observance, and although it may sometimes seem that it is the inescapable lot of the self-invented to put their genius into their life and only their talent into their art, Coward aimed to overcome the problem by singing songs and writing plays, by being filmed and being photographed, in ways which emphasized the personality he chose to project.

He liked to insist that he was first a writer rather than an actor, but Coward was above all a star. And just as he made numerous pronouncements about his self-invention, so he also regularly insisted on the nature of stardom. It had nothing to do with the easy celebrity of film acting; rather, it was the ability to attract large numbers of people into a theatre and control them, by singing or by acting or by simply appearing, with the force of one's own personality. Coward was seldom given to equivocation, and his faith in his own stardom was unshakeable. But he was equally certain that stardom, like royalty, was an estate that carried obligations as well as privileges. 'If you're a star, you should behave like one. I always have.'[2] The privileges were affluence and adoration; the obligations, those of dignified conduct, of 'behaving beautifully', to use his favourite commendation. And to this end, he developed an almost seamless carapace of urbane distinction which protected his inner feelings from fame's unforgiving glare, and allowed him to live in the public eye for so long without succumbing to the strain of curiosity and idolatry which he saw torment, among others, his close friends the Oliviers.

But if stardom was innate, rather than something to be earned, Coward knew that it also had to be proved. 'If I had to write my own epitaph, it would be: "He was much loved because he made

1

people laugh and cry."'[3] That was understatement. He swept to fame on the eve of his twenty-fifth birthday in 1924 and dominated the West End and Broadway until the end of the Second World War. He had a Rolls-Royce by the time he was thirty. He had been tipped for a knighthood by the time he was thirty-two. And he saw his first biography by the time he was thirty-three. In 1925, he had three plays and a revue running concurrently in London. Immediately after the Wall Street Crash, tickets for one of his productions were changing hands for $150 each. As the world fought, and Churchill and Roosevelt argued about the words of 'Mad Dogs and Englishmen', Coward wrote and starred in a film which made millions weep. In his post-war decline, he still managed to be one of the most highly-paid cabaret stars of his day, and an acclaimed, if occasional, cinema actor. And although throughout his life, English critics, ill at ease with apparent frivolity, wondered whether his work 'dated', Coward knew before he died that his vintage comedies had been recognized as classics of their type. These details, drawn at random from his career, vindicate Coward's claims of stardom and recall Dr Johnson's valediction to the actor David Garrick: 'His death eclipsed the gaiety of nations and impoverished the harmless stock of human pleasure.'[4]

The Poet Laureate, Sir John Betjeman, addressing the memorial service at St Martin-in-the-Fields, tried to capture the essence of Coward's popularity: 'He was a master because he bravely and brilliantly made use of the sentimental as well as the comic and because, under that clipped decision, there was tenderness, par- ticularly towards the unimportant, the bit parts and the failures.' Most tributes to Coward, including his own – 'I am related to no one but myself' – insist on his uniqueness. His theatrical compatriot Terence Rattigan said that he was 'simply a phenomenon'. His theatrical opposite John Osborne called him 'his own invention and contribution to this century'. But Betjeman was right to recognize the conflicting elements in his personality. All lives, of course, are reconciliations of paradoxes, but with Coward the component parts of his fame and his psychological complexion seemed unusually diverse. He was a cynic and a patriot, naïve yet a wit, a rebel who became conformity's champion, a relentless self-disciplinarian synonymous with frivolity, a homosexual masquerading in his plays as an unscrupulous womanizer, and an embodiment of sophistication born in the suburbs.

Introduction

Not all of these contradictions were known to his public (and Coward himself would have been astonished by charges of naïvety), but about one of them he was insistent: his modest origins. Most successful examples of self-invention either distort their beginnings or forget them. Beau Brummell, alert to resentment of his social success in the world which he outshone, thought to disarm his enemies with exaggeration, and insisted that his father, a prosperous civil servant, had been merely a valet. Kenneth Tynan decided that his origins were irrelevant to his career as a metropolitan theatre critic, and so discarded the memories of his Midland boyhood. But Coward differed from those arbiters of style: he scorned fiction and forgetfulness, and was proud of his background because he was proud also of having escaped it. Thus, in 1965, he wrote:

I have never yet, in all my years, outgrown the childish and perhaps egocentric pleasure of being able to say: This is I, myself, sitting on top of this alien mountain; in this ferry boat chugging across Hong Kong harbour; staring out through coco-palms at this coral sea. I, myself, who in my earlier days knew the grey drabness of provincial lodging-houses, the oppressive gentility of English suburbia, who so often trod hot, unyielding pavements between various theatrical agents' offices in my midsummer search for an autumn engagement. Look at me now! My spirit crows, lying on the deck of a swaying ship gazing up at the crowded tropical stars.[5]

This conviction that one should remember one's beginnings and be true to them was so strong in him that in 1950, when a fascination with such matters was increasingly condemned, Coward wrote a comedy which revolves specifically around the folly of embellishing one's past. Earlier, at the meridian of his fame, he had presented a pair of plays, one of which celebrated the class which bore him, the other his own stardom. But it was a measure of the strength and attractiveness of his persona, and the perfection of his self-invention, that commentators overlooked the transformation in Coward's circumstances which these plays represented. As though an enormous imaginative leap had been involved in its creation, they applauded the sympathy and incisiveness they detected in his depiction of lower-middle-class suburban life, and forgot that it was the result primarily of romanticized recollection. And by the time of his death, the fallacy was even more established. Marvelling at the fullness of his subject's life, Coward's obituarist in the *Daily*

Telegraph, W. A. Darlington, seemed almost convinced that Coward had been born in a silk dressing-gown, with that improbably fault-less accent: 'His life was lived so much in the public eye that his early years of obscurity seem hardly relevant.' But Coward did not appear in the world fully formed, like an antique deity, because even sophistication must have its apprenticeship. He appeared instead single-minded, ambitious and certain: 'When I was young, all I wanted was to be a star.'[6]

PART ONE
OBSCURITY

Chapter One

Noël Peirce Coward said that he was determined to travel through life first-class. For the inter-war and post-war generation of England and America, his way of life seemed the acme of glamour, not least because so much of it appeared to be spent in travel. Numerous photographs survive of Coward boarding aeroplanes, or dutifully involving himself in the organized revelries of ocean liners, or emerging from limousines, with a retinue in train, and journalists and the star-struck looking on. This apparently unceasing motion was often necessitated, especially in his later years, by business. But all his life, he had a strong wanderlust. 'I go away,' his autobiography insists, 'not to get anywhere, nor even to return, just to go.'[1] Sightseeing, however, bored him: 'The Coliseum stands there, you know, suffering from too many centuries of appreciation. The seven wonders of the world have a way of looking smug and grand at the same time, simply because it is expected of them.'[2]

Given this indifference, it is an irony of sorts that Coward's most famous song, arguably his most famous achievement, is a comic evocation of time, place and custom:

> Mad dogs and Englishmen
> Go out in the midday sun.
> The toughest Burmese bandit
> Can never understand it.
> In Rangoon the heat of noon
> Is just what the natives shun.
> They put their Scotch or Rye down
> And lie down.
> In a jungle town
> Where the sun beats down
> To the rage of man and beast
> The English garb
> Of the English sahib
> Merely gets a bit more creased.

> In Bangkok
> At twelve o'clock
> They foam at the mouth and run,
> But mad dogs and Englishmen
> Go out in the midday sun.[3]

But when he tried seriously to establish atmosphere and the peculiarities of place, in his short stories and, to a lesser degree, in his verse, there is a flatness which suggests that he was writing only to fulfil a duty or to conform to a tradition, rather than because he was interested. (In the case of the stories, it was a tradition which he had seen in the work of his sometime friend Somerset Maugham.) Critics were often perplexed by this apparent inadequacy: it was assumed, after all, that writers existed to observe and report, and very few writers before him were ever as exposed to diverse experience as Noël Coward. Thus, Ivor Brown, attempting an assessment during the Second World War:

Coward remains a puzzle. He sees so much – and so little. He has travelled far more than most men of his age and yet, when he writes, it always has to be of the same little world. Dump him anywhere, on any island of the seventeen seas, and he would certainly at once run into somebody known as Tim or Tiny, Boodles or Bims, and be dining with an Excellency or an Admiral twenty minutes later. If there were natives on the island he would hardly notice. God put them there, no doubt, to serve dinners to Excellencies.[4]

Of course he saw little: stars were supposed to be observed, rather than to observe. But even if he had not been born a cynosure, Coward would still have seen little of the life around him. Cecil Beaton damned him for his 'lack of interest in the world in general',[5] but Coward was defiant regarding the limitations of his vision: 'If I don't care for things, I simply don't look at them.'[6]

His maternal grandfather, Captain Veitch, was an enthusiastic amateur painter (a recreation Coward was to adopt in middle age), and his technique lay in pasting figures excised from the illustrated magazines of the time onto lovingly and fastidiously realized landscapes. His grandson reversed that technique in his drama: his characters are drawn, but their environments, whether the Brighton of the Regency, or the suburbs of the Depression, remain imprecise, irrelevant and unconvincing. Local colour was of no interest to Noël Coward, so it comes as no surprise to discover that his accounts of his childhood, and the south of London in which it passed, are less than haunting. For many people, the images of childhood retain a disturbing clarity until death. For others, they will be the subject of fanciful reconstruction. For Coward, they were neither here nor there:

> I cannot remember
> I cannot remember
> The house where I was born
> But I know it was in Waldegrave Road
> Teddington, Middlesex
> Not far from the border of Surrey
> An unpretentious abode
> Which, I believe,
> Economy forced us to leave
> In rather a hurry.[7]

It was not only the house where he was born that he could not remember. One looks in vain in Coward's autobiography for recollections of what he might have considered crucially formative experiences. And there are no lyrical descriptions of the villages, as they almost were, of Teddington, Sutton, Clapham and Battersea, which he knew before they were overrun by lilac and privet and swallowed by the city. His memory begins only with the theatre; and he often lacked literary curiosity and the urge to record. Moreover, he lacked illustrious forebears or relations whose activities were newsworthy, and if anyone thought to gossip about the Cowards, or form judgements about the way in which they lived, they did not commit their observations to paper. We can know nothing of Coward's first years except what he, and his mother, chose to relate, so one is thankful for V. S. Pritchett's account of respectable poverty in Camberwell at the end of the nineteenth century: 'The south of London has always been unfashionable and its people have stuck to a village life of their own; they were often poorish, but poverty or rather not having much money yet managing on it has its divisions and sudivisions of status. Respectability, the dominant trait of the English and certainly of the two-faced London mind, prevailed.'[8]

Violet Agnes Veitch settled in Teddington, Middlesex, in 1883, with her widowed mother, her sister Vida and an obscure relation called Borby. (Two other sisters had already married, and two brothers had died.) At that time still a quiet stop on the Thames,

9

Teddington's main attraction for the Veitches may have been connected with the presence of members of the exiled French royal
family. (There must have been a strong tendency towards royalism
in Coward's background, since his own fascination with royalty,
particularly with the present Queen Mother, verged at times on
idolatry.) But if that was the case, it was small compensation for
the remaining members of the Veitch family. Husbands had to be
found for Vida and Violet, aged, at the time of the move, twenty-
six and twenty respectively, and appearances had to be maintained.
Neither of these imperatives can have seemed easy with no money;
and Coward later admitted his suspicion that they devoted a lot of
energy to 'making over last year's dresses'.[9] Violet had to wait until
the age of twenty-seven before she married, in 1890. Vida (perhaps
because she spurned suitors, or perhaps because her lack of a
dowry combined unfavourably with her six years' seniority and
disqualified her from marriage when she arrived in Teddington, or
perhaps because she was simply disagreeable) was to die a spinster
aged ninety.

The Veitch sisters must have been inclined to apply high standards where suitors were concerned, for the fact was – and it is one
of the most important facts of Noël Coward's life – that his mother's
family felt that it had come down in the world, and that further
social decline was to be resisted. Violet and Vida took pride in the
fact that their father, Henry Veitch, had been a naval captain: a
photograph of Noël Coward at five, in sailor suit, conforms not
only to the fashion of the times, but also proclaims the brine in
his Veitch background. Furthermore, Violet and Vida knew of a
patrilineal connexion by marriage to established Scottish money;
and Noël Coward remembered that as a child he saw pictures of a
supposedly ancestral home in Scotland which served as a poignant
souvenir of lost prosperity. Vida appears to have been particularly
nostalgic for this bygone glory, as she was known to correspond
with genealogists about her Veitch patrimony.

Either because Noël Coward was closer to his mother than he
was to his father, and therefore found her more interesting, or
because he too was quite proud of his maternal antecedents, he
remembered Violet Coward's early circumstances and detailed
them carefully: 'My mother came from what is known as "Good
Family", which means that she had been brought up in the tradition
of being a gentlewoman, a difficult tradition to uphold with very

10

little money in a small suburb, and liable to degenerate into refined gentility unless carefully watched.'[10]

But Violet Veitch married either for love, or in desperation, for Arthur Sabin Coward, described as 'a clerk' on the marriage certificate, was a travelling salesman for a piano company. If she thought that he had prospects, she was to be proved wrong. They had been brought together by the social and musical activities generated by the parish church, St Alban's, Teddington (described with aggravating winsomeness by Sir John Betjeman as resembling 'a bit of Westminster Abbey that has been left behind further upstream').[11] Arthur Coward's family, we gather, was 'fiercely musical' (one of his sisters, Hilda, was known as 'the Twickenham Nightingale'), and Noël Coward remembered that his father sang well and that he could improvise respectably at the piano. Violet was less musically accomplished, not least because her hearing had been impaired as the result of an illness which she had developed while at convent school (the nuns, she remembered, did nothing more useful than pray). Nevertheless, during the earlier and more harmonious years of their marriage, she and Arthur used to accompany each other on the piano.

They went to live at 'Helmsdale', in Waldegrave Road, Teddington. They were there for over ten years, during which time Russell Arthur Blackmore Coward was born, and his younger brother, Noël Peirce. Violet, described by one of Noël Coward's earliest friends as 'an amusing, sharp-faced, brave little lady', and slightly discontented in suburban obscurity, was alert for her children from the outset. She equipped Russell with the most distinguished godparent Teddington could provide, R. D. Blackmore, since 1869 famous for his novel *Lorna Doone*:

My Dear Mrs Coward. What a peaceful and delightful baby! I shall be proud to have such a little godson; who deserves, and (I trust) will have a very happy life. With kindest wishes, I am truly yours, R. D. Blackmore.[12]

But whatever his deserts, Russell Coward died of meningitis, aged six.

He was apparently greatly mourned by his mother, but eighteen months after he died, on 16 December 1899, Noël Peirce arrived. In his early fame, less than thirty years away, Coward seemed an embodiment of twentieth-century style, so it was fitting that he was born, like a harbinger, as the nineteenth century expired. But it was

11

the imminence of Christmas, rather than the end of the age, which determined the baby's first name. (Peirce, which he detested, came from a friend of his mother's.) Not to be thwarted by Russell's death, Violet Coward tried once more to secure R. D. Blackmore's sponsorship. They were not particularly close friends (as the formality of their correspondence indicates), and this time Violet Coward failed. But Blackmore had his reasons:

My dear Mrs Coward. I have been thinking long & sadly over your kind and flattering wish; & the more I am convinced that I must not do as I should like. It must be more than mere mishaps, or casual fortune that attends my dear Godchildren. Four out of five have been taken already – one more since your dear little Russell was called away – & I think it is a warning to me that precious young lives must not be subject to the risk I seem to cause them.[13]

By the time Eric Coward was born in 1905, R. D. Blackmore was dead and there were no other promising godparents available. But the youngest of the Cowards seems generally to have been neglected, and his story can be finished even as it is begun. Noël Coward disposes of Eric fairly unceremoniously in his autobiography:

I think my relationship with Eric requires a little explanation ... I was reasonably fond of him but I cannot honestly say that we were ever very close until perhaps the last sad months of his life. Perhaps this five-year difference in our ages was either too long or too short. At all events I have to admit, a trifle guiltily perhaps, that I never found him very interesting. It is possible that I might have been subconsciously jealous of him and resented his intrusion into the cosseted 'only son' pattern of my life, but in fairness to myself I don't think that this was so. I tolerated him, was occasionally irritated by him and, engrossed as I was by my crowded and exciting career as a boy actor, paid very little attention to him.[14]

As his elder brother's theatrical inclinations began to emerge, Eric was useful as a supporting actor and audience. And as it began to seem during his teens that Noël might become a successful actor, Eric must have thought that his only destiny lay in his brother's shadow. He clearly decided that if he was to secure any life of his own, it would have to be away from Noël's, and accordingly he went to Ceylon to become a tea planter. (In the days of Empire, planting was a third option traditionally open to the young or restless sons of large families. It was theoretically safer than a career in the army and potentially more lucrative than one in the church. Laurence Olivier's elder brother was a planter.) When Eric returned to England, it was for good. He had cancer and died, aged twenty-eight, in 1933.

Yet somehow, Noël Coward seems always to have been an only child, an only child, moreover, with only one parent. Although he inherited many physical characteristics from Arthur Coward, and although it was from his father that he took his musical aptitude, he seems never to have cared for him, and confided as much to Cole Lesley, his servant turned secretary, friend and biographer. Like Eric, Arthur Coward is conspicuous only by his absence in Coward's writings, though he was on his son's mind when he was writing his short story 'Aunt Tittie', which was greatly admired by Somerset Maugham: 'James Rogers was a good man and a piano tuner at the time of his marriage, later he developed into a travelling agent for his firm, so that during my childhood in the house I didn't see much of him but he was mild-tempered and kind when he did happen to be at home and drank only occasionally, and then without exuberance.'[15] Arthur Coward was a disappointment to his wife and to his elder son. His job proved less and less prosperous; by the time the family had migrated north of the Thames, it had come to an end and he occupied himself with building model boats and sailing them on the Serpentine. Like his brother Jim Coward, Arthur in adversity took to drink,[16] and instilled in his elder son a horror of heavy drinking and of any form of dependency.

Coward never stated that his parents' marriage was inter-mittently strained, but it seems very likely that the dominant and ambitious Violet found it difficult to conceal her regret at the way life had turned out. Whether her son understood these tensions at the time, or merely absorbed them, to be interpreted later, the implications for him were enormous. Cole Lesley, remembering violent quarrels between the Cowards and between Violet and Vida, noted that the theme of the embattled family is one to which Coward's writing returned regularly. One might add that he excelled above all at capturing the distractions and bickerings of unhappy love, that he was a sceptic where romantic love was concerned (though like so many sceptics, he wanted to believe) and had been so for some time when he started writing plays: '"They were married and lived happily ever after" is an assertion that I have always viewed with distrust. Even as a child, admittedly a

13

theatrical child from whose eyes the scales of illusion had fallen at an early age, I remember wondering cynically what happened *after* Cinderella had tried on the shoe and married her Prince Charming.'[17] It was this romantic disillusion (compounded by the problems posed by his own sexuality) which informed Coward's best writing of the Twenties and Thirties, and which, coinciding neatly with the general social disillusion of the time, made him seem so poignantly true for his generation.

That, however, was all in the future. In the meantime, the boy and his mother established a bond of mutual love, support and expectation. As the family was not anchored by Arthur's work to any particular area, the Cowards, chased by rising costs and dwindling means, moved repeatedly after Noël's birth and before the onset of the Great War: from Teddington, to Sutton, to Battersea and thence to Clapham Common, where their house was called Ben Lomond. Thrift had become a vital discipline to Violet Coward; but however she tried to husband her family's slender means, finances continued to deteriorate. In Battersea, she was driven to the indignity of taking in 'paying guests' (they dressed for dinner, but they were lodgers nevertheless), sometimes even to letting the flat and taking her family with her into cheap and temporary exile in the country. Finally, in about 1917, after five years of struggling to survive in Clapham, she followed the example of her sister-in-law, Ida, and assumed the lease, lodgers, furniture and 'goodwill' of a boarding-house in the hinterland of Belgravia. Money was so scarce that she had to manage with little domestic help, and until her son's first success, Violet Coward's life at 111, Ebury Street was one of unremitting hard work.

Young Noël Coward 'was always very forward and amusing as a child', his mother was to remember.[18] Coward himself insisted that he had never known shyness and we gather that he was a prodigy of exhibitionism, and ready to perform for Violet Coward's friends at the slightest opportunity. As a boy he was self-confident, impertinent and rebellious, and his parents either could not or would not curb him. The maid-of-all-work the family was able to employ before finances became too desperate told young Noël, he remembered, that he was 'too sharp by half: you'll cut yourself one of these days'.[19] Coward himself gleefully admits to stealing, to pouring boiling water down the speaking tube into the porter's ear at the Battersea flat, and to biting the arm of a schoolmistress to the bone. As soon as he was considered old enough to travel alone on buses and the underground, he delighted, he later claimed, in scandalizing fellow passengers with sensational tales of domestic affliction – of beatings, fights and crazed intemperance.

If his parents ever wondered why Noël was so naughty, they could have considered his unsettled education. Financial difficulties, coupled with the family's itinerant state, ensured that the young Coward did not attend the same school for any fixed period (he thought nothing of playing truant anyway), and his formal education, such as it was, ended completely in 1910. Judging by his reading matter, he was not encouraged to take learning at all seriously at home. His earliest regular enthusiasms were boys' comics – *Chums*, the *Boy's Own Paper*, the *Magnet* and the *Gem* – and in his early adolescence he enjoyed the light fiction of the time: Phillips Oppenheim, William Le Queux, Stanley Weyman and the early novels of Edgar Wallace. He remembered in 1967:

No superior intellect being available to regulate my choice and steer me into deeper waters, I was left to splash about in the shallows to my heart's content ... the erotic social jungles of Miss Cynthia Stockley, the romantic 'cloak and dagger' bravuras of the Baroness Orczy, the somewhat ponderous and occasionally gory historical novels of S. R. Crockett, as well as his more whimsical excursions Sir Toady Lion and Sir Toady Crusoe, and the lighthearted adventures of Edgar Jepson's Lady Noggs and Baroness von Hutten's Pam. There seems to have been a preponderance of baronesses among the female writers of that period.[20]

This lack of education and discipline had several consequences. All his life, Coward showed a contempt for self-proclaimed experts generally, and intellectuals in particular. His lack of any grounding in serious literature forced him to become an autodidact in his late thirties; and his pride in his self-education shows in much of his writing. What also shows in his writing is a crude patriotism. As he grew older, a tendency developed for him to write and think about England with increasing pomposity, even chauvinism, and to display a xenophobia and insularity which evokes the tone of the boys' weeklies of his childhood, a tone so famously captured by George Orwell: 'The King is on the throne and the pound is worth a pound. Over in Europe the comic foreigners are jabbering and gesticulating, but the grim grey battleships of the British Fleet are steaming up the Channel and at the outposts of Empire the monocled Englishmen are holding the niggers at bay.'[21]

Orwell insisted that tens of thousands of Englishmen between 1900 and 1940 were taught such attitudes by the stories they read in the *Gem* and the *Magnet*. Many of Coward's pronouncements from the late Thirties onwards seem to corroborate his argument. More immediately, however, the consequences of this lack of formal education are apparent in his letters. Play-acting and attention-seeking were as natural to the aspiring star as one would expect; it is harder to detect the future writer in some of his early adolescent correspondence.

But Coward was not a believer in regret, nor was he ungrateful. His childhood was unusual, unsettled and without constraints, certainly by the standards of the time and his class, but it was also quite definitely a happy one. His autobiography mentions certain idyllic interludes – holidays in Cornwall and Southsea and prolonged stays in the country – as well as giving a general sense of early contentment. It is a commonplace that children from even the most unorthodox homes rarely see anything strange in their first environments. Noël Coward was a stranger to convention from an early age; but as far as he was concerned, everything was as normal, 'except perhaps that certain embryonic talents may have made me more ... difficult to manage'.[22]

Chapter Two

Violet Coward loved the theatre. She greatly admired a popular musical *comédienne* called Gertie Millar, and she adored the Terrys. Although money was always scarce, the theatre was a necessary luxury and, in the days before cinema, an affordable escape from surburban tedium. If her hopes for her son were bold, she loved also to indulge him, and he had scarcely learnt to walk, talk and listen, before the theatre had become a regular treat. At first, naturally, she spared him the melodramas and sentimental extravagances fashionable at the time in favour of more appropriate material. Noël Coward, she knew, was easily displeased:

The first time I ever went to the theatre was to see *Sinbad the Sailor* at Kingston. I was only about six, and very angry, because I thought it was all going to take place on Kingston Bridge, and as it wasn't I had to be taken out, because I made a scene. The next play I saw was called *The Dairymaid*, where a great deal of *churning* went on.[1]

After these initial disappointments, the theatre quickly took hold, and by his early adolescence Coward and his mother went to the West End whenever they could: 'Mother in a dust-coloured cloak over her evening dress, with a small diamanté butterfly in her hair, and me in a scrupulously pressed dinner-jacket suit (Lockwood and Bradley in the Clapham Road).'[2] But long before then, the young Noël Coward had been given a toy theatre, and long before then also his self-confidence and shameless urge to show off had persuaded his mother that he might perhaps be steered professionally in the direction of the stage. Besides, at nine years old, he was 'absolutely uneducated'.[3] Family precedent had led to his being made to sing in the choir of the local church (and he hated it, because congregations, unlike audiences, do not applaud), but he had still failed to get into the Chapel Royal school. The theatre seemed an obvious way to harness his flamboyant but untutored mind, and suggested also a means of releasing him and, vicariously, his mother from suburban confinement.

17

Happy coincidence was a feature of Noël Coward's early life and early success. At the time when the socially ambitious Violet Coward wondered what to do with her bright and adored son, the acting world was changing. Actors had been subject to shifting social esteem. William IV's mistress and the mother of his many illegitimate children, Mrs Jordan, may have been an actress, but even in her time the majority of her profession was still considered, as it had been in David Garrick's day, to be 'rogues and vagabonds'. But by the end of the nineteenth century, Henry Irving had determined to raise the theatre's standing. He himself was knighted in 1895 (Queen Victoria, beginning the process of polite acceptance, is said to have remarked, 'We are very pleased, sir'), but the accolade was as much a recognition of his business acumen as his thespian genius, since he was an actor-manager. The profession had to wait until 1934, and the elevation of Cedric Hardwicke, for pure acting skills to be recognized. However, by the time Noël Coward joined 'the gay mad world of powder and paint', as he liked to call it, it was principally a haven for middle-class failures – whatever their acting skills, they at least had the diction, and an idea of the bearing, which audiences required. At about the same time also, constraints were beginning to be placed upon the lives of child actors. The nineteenth century turned suddenly against the exploitation of minors, and one of the many, if less spectacular, areas of reform was the theatre. Growing public concern that child actors, used principally in pantomimes, were exposed to the notoriously laxer morals of the theatre, and that they were not only deprived of sleep but also plied with gin and vinegar, all in order to stunt them, led to the imposition of a series of controls. In 1903, it was made illegal to employ children under the age of ten; others, ten and over, were permitted to work after nine o'clock at night, but they had to be licensed for that work by juvenile courts.

In 1910, with his mother's encouragement, Noël Coward took a series of lessons at Miss Janet Thomas's Dancing Academy in Hanover Square, and just as they were about to come to an end, Violet Coward decided, on her son's behalf, to reply to an advertisement in the *Daily Mirror* of 7 September 1910.

SEARCH FOR CHILD ACTORS
'For many months past now I have been busy collecting my cast; as I want thirty or so bright children between the ages of ten and fourteen, this has

been far from an easy task. <u>To get suitable boys has been especially</u> <u>difficult. I have got sufficient girls at last, but am still badly in need of</u> <u>five or six boys. The Goldfish</u> ... will be the first play given ... I start rehearsing almost at once.' Miss Field has obtained more influential support for the Children's Theatre. Princess Dolgorouki, Princess Hatz-feldt, the Duchess of Norfolk, the Duchess of Marlborough and the Marquis de Soveral are among those who are supporting and taking a most active personal interest in it.

The underlining is Mrs Coward's: as though anticipating the needs of future biographers, she saved every piece of information about her son, every piece, that is, apart from that which related to his short career in the army in 1918. Cole Lesley, from whose book the advertisement is quoted, noted that the distinguished supporters were never heard of again, but the promise of their involvement must have swayed Violet Coward who, Lesley noted, 'dearly loved a title'. *The Goldfish* marked Coward's professional début. He was paid a guinea and a half a week (which very usefully augmented the cash in supply at home), and he was to work hard for his living until a few years before he died.

Whatever Coward's opinions of his qualifications at that time – 'I was born into a generation that still took light music seriously ... from the age of seven onwards [I could] play any tune I had learned on the piano in the pitch dark'[4] – it is most likely that his sheer confidence swayed Lila Field. Amongst the other children taking part in the production was Alfred Wilmore, who became the actor Micheál MacLiammóir, and who left a celebrated vignette of the young Coward:

He was ten years old and already in manner and bearing a young man. The face, of course, was that of a child but the eyes were already amused and slightly incredulous, the voice was as crisply *rubato* then as it is today, and when he spoke after a few preliminary boyish grins it was to ask me how much work I had done.
'Work?' I said aghast. 'Do you mean acting?'
'But you've had your audition, haven't you?'
'Oh yes, I'm engaged,' and then ... 'What are you going to be when you grow up?'
'An actor of course. Why, what do you want to be? ... You'd better make up your mind, you know. People should always be quite clear about what they want to be.'[5]

To Wilmore, Mrs Coward seemed 'immensely tall, very charming, very dignified' (of Arthur Coward there is naturally no mention). 'I remember her always with a fur hat on. It never came off in summer or winter, whenever I saw her, it was there.'[6] Young children – lacking the deliberate analytical faculties of maturity – rely on idiosyncratically selective, visual impressions, so Violet Coward survives in Wilmore's childhood memory as an imposing figure. But it was not only the undiscriminating young Coward's mother hoped to impress. She attached a great importance to appearances (an importance she bequeathed to her son), and it was a matter of pride to her that they should be maintained. But she was much more than primly respectable. She shared a birthday with Hitler (to the adult Noël Coward's amusement), and in the face of adversity she proved indomitable. Saddled with a retiring husband, it was she who worked tirelessly, who made the decisions, and who identified the gifted member of the family and cosseted his genius. If she had to struggle to be realistic with money, she cherished dreams for her son, and it is no exaggeration to say that with a more orthodox mother, and in the absence of the right sort of encouragement and tolerance, Coward's early life would have been very different, and he might easily not have gone on the stage at all. 'She was a great woman to whom I owe the whole of my life,' he wrote at her death.[7] He declared his debt to her – and began to try and discharge it – almost as soon as he began writing: nearly all of his early plays, *I'll Leave It To You*, *The Young Idea*, *The Vortex*, *Easy Virtue* and *Hay Fever* revolve round a strong mother. But before then, in the course of his adolescent acting apprenticeship, his mother may have felt that her faith was not misplaced, since in 1911 he was given a part, admittedly only one line long, in *The Great Name*, the latest venture to be put into production by Charles Hawtrey.

Hawtrey, who was knighted just before his death in 1923, was one of the great Edwardian actor-managers. He was to cast Coward in three other productions – *Where the Rainbow Ends*, in 1911, *A Little Fowl Play*, in 1912, and *The Saving Grace*, in 1917 (by which time the acute shortage of young men in the theatre worked in the still adolescent Coward's favour) – but in his jauntily-entitled memoirs, *The Truth At Last*, published posthumously and edited by Somerset Maugham, Coward, for a while his worshipping imitator, is given only one mention. Hawtrey sounds very appealing. Adored by his public, he was regarded as one of the most finished comedians of his time. He was anti-declamatory before Sir Gerald du Maurier, and dead-pan before the technique was appropriated by American comedians. The perfection of his comic timing was proverbial, and it was said that his witty lines burst in the auditorium like deftly-delivered hand grenades. Coward insisted that he learned everything he knew about performing comedy from him. Yet for Hawtrey, unlike Coward, the theatre was only a profession, and he owed other debts to pleasure: as Maugham put it, he 'was by passion a racing man and only by necessity an actor. I think that he forgot the name of half the characters he played, but never that of a horse he backed.' His extravagances were incessant and his finances intractable. Before opening in a play in New York once, he borrowed $15,000 from the management against his earnings, and lost it all on horses over the weekend; and in London, it was known that his favourite theatre was the Comedy, where three backstage exits allowed surer escape from creditors.

This roguishness was implicit in his stage persona (and like his young disciple, Hawtrey generally played a particular type). John Gielgud remembered him as being very fat and lethargic but very funny, and at the centenary of his birth, one reviewer wrote of Hawtrey, 'This lazy worldling had nothing but good manners to show for an expensive education; he always lied, it was observed, like an English gentleman.'[8] Almost all the plays in which he had established himself were no more than names by the time the twelve-year-old Coward met him. (Now, Hawtrey's name would mean nothing had it not been cheekily borrowed by George Hartree, aspiring actor, and skinny and bespectacled exponent of camp, later to become famous in the *Carry On* films.) But despite his lack of interest in the parts he played, Hawtrey must have remembered playing Lord Goring in the original production of Oscar Wilde's *An Ideal Husband*. The connexion with Wilde had begun in the early 1890s, when Hawtrey collaborated in the writing of a parody of the dramatist called *The Poet and the Puppets*, and had played the part of Wilde when it was presented. The dramatist is known to have attended rehearsals of his plays from time to time, and it would obviously be biographically satisfying to establish that he instilled in Hawtrey certain characteristics of comedy-acting that were ultimately passed on to Coward. While that can only be a matter for supposition, what is definite, and much less satisfying, is Hawtrey's part in Wilde's downfall. He gave evidence against the Irishman,

21

and attended a dinner of celebration given by Lord Queensberry on the night of Wilde's conviction.

When Coward was first working for Hawtrey, Wilde was virtually unmentionable in any context. Even later, when he knew about the nature of the Irish playwright's downfall, he never betrayed an awareness of his idol's part in it. In 1911, however, only Hawtrey's technique interested him, for Coward intended to learn. In later years, he was fond of recounting a story about the one line in *The Great Name* which he had been given: 'Stop that noise at once, please. In there they're playing *The Meistersingers*. Making such a horrible noise. We're used to good music here.'[9] (God knows what the rest of the play was like.) His mother rehearsed him so eagerly and so exhaustively in its delivery that when Hawtrey heard his histrionic and full-blooded rendition, he told his stage manager, Tarver, that he never wanted to see the young Coward again. But he relented, and the apprentice was made to speak his piece with a Cockney accent. One way and another, Hawtrey became a symbol of theatrical perfection in the eyes of his young imitator, and nearly twenty years after the relationship ended, Coward still looked back on it with gratitude: '[Hawtrey] knew how to bring out young talent ... He also knew that very youthful actors were frequently victimized by their own frustrated conceits, and that to deal harshly with them might crush down their small confidence.'[10]

In 1911, Coward appeared in *Where the Rainbow Ends*. He was earning useful money for his mother but, unconventional as Violet Coward was in some ways, she was pricked by her conscience when she thought that her son seemed to be committing himself to a notoriously uncertain profession. Furthermore, she was 'a good deal pestered by relations and friends about letting Noël be on the stage instead of at school'.[11] When a friend told her that a celebrated clairvoyant, Anna Eva Fay, was appearing in London, Violet Coward's curiosity got the better of her.

She had created a tremendous sensation in America and the Coliseum was packed. A man came round with slips of paper for you to write your question on. I was not going to ask anything but my friend persuaded me to. [The note, which survives, said: 'Do you advise me to keep my son Noël Coward on the stage? Violet Coward.'] Then there was a hush and Miss Fay came on the stage, with her male assistant. She spoke a few words, then sat on a chair and the man put a sheet over her. She held out her arms like a ghost, answered one or two questions and then called out, 'Mrs Coward, Mrs Coward' – my friend prodded me in the side and I had to stand up and she shouted, 'You ask me about your son. Keep him where he is, keep him where he is, he has great talent and will have a wonderful career!' I was entirely flabbergasted ... my feelings were beyond words, how could she know and *why* should she have answered me amongst so many people! When I mentioned my experience [to the relations] I was met with pitying smiles! So I did not say any more about it but I knew perfectly well that Anna Eva Fay was right.[12]

It is always easy to doubt or ridicule soothsayers, and one could conveniently argue that this was another case of lucky clairvoyance. What is interesting about the story, one of the most famous of Coward's childhood, is that Violet Coward's faith, either in the prophetess or in her son's abilities, allowed her to believe it. (She was Church of England, so it is difficult to guess how much of a sceptic she normally was.) Coward himself was to refer to spiritualism – and areas beyond the reach of science – in his comedies. The fact that he did not do so in a spirit of complete mockery must stem in part from this episode.

With all doubts removed, he was free to continue acting. In 1913, he was cast in *Hannele* by a rising young director, Basil Dean, who was later to stage some of Coward's plays, and for much of his second decade he committed himself to the consolidation of his reputation as a child actor. Apart from his work for Hawtrey, Coward appeared in or understudied in a number of now forgotten plays before he became liable for conscription: *An Autumn Idyll*, *War in the Air*, *Never Say Die*, *The Best of Luck*, *The Light Blues*, *The Happy Family*. Only one of the plays in which he acted during this apprenticeship has survived: *Peter Pan*, in which he played Slightly, (Micheál MacLiammóir remembered that he was 'too intelligent' to be good in the part) and earned the then not inconsiderable sum of £4 a week. In 1917, Coward made his first appearance on the cinema screen: impressively, his début was in *Hearts of the World*, directed by D. W. Griffith, one of the supreme figures of the Hollywood silent era, and Dorothy and Lillian Gish were in the cast. (While preparing material for the film, Griffith was taken to the French and Belgian battlefronts but was uninspired: 'Viewed as drama, the war is in some ways disappointing.')[13] *Hearts of the World*, though set in a French village under German occupation, was filmed in Worcestershire and was pure propaganda, made with the support of the Allied governments. Coward was only an extra, and although his involvement sounded at least like an impressive credential, it failed to instil any longings for cinematic stardom: the theatre continued to fascinate him, and when he wrote his autobiography, he admitted that without the mnemonic of stage work, he could not recall much of his adolescence.

If he was forgetful of the details of these years, however, Coward could recall their spirit, and many years later, at the end of his career, he evoked his theatrical pupillage in a short story:

Those were the days all right, days of glory for child actors. I think the boys had a better time than the girls on account of not being so well protected. I shall never forget those jovial wet-handed clergymen queuing up outside the stage-door to take us out to tea and stroke our knees under the table. Bobby Clews and I used to have bets as to how much we could get without going too far. I once got a box of Fuller's soft-centres and a gramophone record of *Casse-Noisette* for no more than a quick grope in a taxi.[14]

Not all young actresses needed chaperonage; and when Coward first met Gertrude Lawrence, in *Hannele*, she seemed very precocious and quite capable of looking after herself. She was fifteen at that meeting, *mondaine* and made-up, according to his autobiography, and with a repertoire of gently salacious stories. He was to change a great deal after that first encounter, in outward aspect at least, but Gertrude Lawrence had no time for self-invention, and stayed the same for the rest of her life. The assurance, however, was purely external and owed a lot to bravado, as her daughter, Pamela Clatworthy, implied: 'Her sophistication was always that of a little girl who dressed up in high heels and her mother's evening gowns: it was skin deep, and that perhaps above all was what made so many men ... want to protect her. She needed it, God knows.'[15]

Much has already been written about Gertrude Lawrence and her importance to Noël Coward. That she was a brilliant interpreter of his work, and the inspiration for Amanda in *Private Lives*, for the series of plays which comprise *Tonight at 8.30*, and, unofficially, for *Relative Values*, there can be no doubt. But the extent of their theatrical partnership is often exaggerated. They were to appear together only four times: in *Hannele*; in *Private Lives*, in 1930; in *Tonight at 8.30*, in 1936; and in *Tonight at 8.30* when it was revived, in 1948. They were kept from further, highly lucrative, collaboration by conflicting professional commitments; and Lawrence had effectively left England for good by the outbreak of the Second World War. Off-stage, it is hard to imagine that they had a great deal in common, or even a great deal to offer each other; and talk of their being lovers, physically, or in some obscure way, spiritually, is preposterous. There are enough surviving comments of Coward's to show that he found her disorganization, indecisiveness, profligacy and lack of self-discipline, in large doses at any rate, maddening in the extreme. Their perfect partnership existed only when they were made-up and spot-lit and applauded: beyond the stage-door, they were simply business associates.

Chapter Three

A fter his mother, Esme Wynne was the most important woman in Noël Coward's life. Had she followed her early ambitions and become an actress, and, better still, died relatively prematurely, like Gertrude Lawrence, her name and achievement might have reached a wider public. She was a remarkable woman, not least for the modelling of Noël Coward, but after writing several plays, novels and much journalism, she turned to books on philosophical and humanitarian subjects of acknowledged scholarship, and died a recluse.

Although they first met in 1911, their friendship did not blossom until 1913 (not 1914, as he claimed in his autobiography). Esme also came from London's unprosperous but then respectable southern suburbs, although Stockwell must have compared unfavourably with Clapham in the young Coward's eyes, because in *Present Indicative* he remembers it with brisk distaste. If he had already learnt from his mother that his family had declined in the strictly defined hierarchy of nineteenth-century England, it must have comforted the emerging snob to know that others also had suffered, and Esme Wynne's family, it seemed, had known better days. In particular there was a half-French grandmother who 'was what one calls "very comfortably off" with servants and carriage. Esme's family, except for a very respectable uncle, were what was known in those days as "Bohemians" – theatrical, given to over-eating and over-drinking.'[1] Esme cannot have been ignorant of this 'Bohemian' strain: both her parents drank enthusiastically, and her father overcame the scruples of his strict Christian upbringing and left home for another woman. However, although her family conformed only intermittently to Edwardian codes of respectability, Esme's childhood was conventional if not disciplined. Whereas Violet Coward merely laughed in blind adoration and disbelief whenever her son was accused of stealing, lying or playing truant, thus feeding his egoism, Esme's father attempted to inculcate in her his flexible but fervently-held moral code, and she grew up, by her own admission, 'a sincere and earnest child and from the age of six interested in Truth and truth'.[2] Her father hoped that his bright daughter would eventually pursue an academic career, and just before the Great War, Esme was sent to a convent in Melsbroeck in Belgium. Her mother, however, had been an actress when she first got married (she was never, as Coward later claimed, 'in the original troupe of "The Palace Girls"'), and even before adolescence Esme, drawn by the raffish glamour of the theatre, was determined to act and also to write.

Her determination must have been equalled by her abilities, because at only twelve years old, she had sufficiently impressed Charles Hawtrey for him to cast her in the leading part of Rosamund in *Where the Rainbow Ends*. Actors often resent competition and fear eclipse, and Coward seems at first to have disliked the star of the cast: *Present Indicative* reveals that he found her voice 'bleating' and her appearance 'podgy'. Even as a child, he made quick and often inaccurate assessments of others; and as an adult, he frequently subordinated truth to his desire to amuse. It is not therefore surprising that her account fails to correspond with his: 'A curious feature of his untruthfulness is that he continually ascribes to me what in fact belonged to him. I was NEVER a podgy child. When we met I was slim and he was like a spotted suet pudding in shape and colour.'[3]

Whatever their respective shapes at this time, Esme Wynne and Noël Coward had several important affinities: unorthodox mothers, similar backgrounds, theatrical ambitions, and in 1913 an intimacy began which Coward admitted influenced him 'profoundly' for several years and was to change the course of his life. They were inseparable, Violet Coward remembered, as teenagers; and with more interest in brevity than flattery, they christened each other 'Stodge' and 'Podge' (translated subsequently to 'Stoj' and 'Poj'). 'Stoj' later said that she 'adored his sense of humour, and his complete sexlessness (as far as females were concerned)',[4] and their friendship was able to develop without physical complications. If Esme is to be believed, Coward, precocious in all things, was well aware of his carnal inclinations by his mid-teens, and fully prepared to accommodate them. He tried to kiss her once, when she was thirteen and he was twelve, but neither could take the attempt seriously. Physical attraction was as absent from their intimacy as physical embarrassment, and *Present Indicative* reveals that they had baths together, if in the middle of some impassioned discussion, rather than resort to the dull decency of separation and the frustration of unresolved argument. For her part, she provided companionship that must have proved an important spur to the young Coward, who was intensely jealous and intensely competitive. She filled him, he later admitted, with 'competitive fervour', a crucial stimulus which most intelligent children discover amongst school friends. By then, Coward was not going to school, and his neglected brother, Eric, certainly did not offer fervour of any variety. Esme had already been given a leading part by the adored Hawtrey, a fact which must have roused Coward's jealousy; and by the age of thirteen, she had surpassed that achievement by writing a short play, *The Prince's Bride*, which Hawtrey himself had produced at the Savoy Theatre. Coward could not begin to match such triumphs; but he too was bright and determined, and inspired by Esme's example, he began to take an interest in literature.

In 1913, he was still reading comics and boys' thrillers; but she had the adolescent sophistication of her sex and was able to introduce him to George Bernard Shaw, Oscar Wilde, *The Rubaiyat of Omar Khayyam* and the Celtic Twilight. Coward said that the theatre 'had led us far in precocity'. They were certainly both deeply opinionated and, when not exploring literature, they found much to dispute. He was not remotely interested in religion, and had only had himself confirmed as a dutiful, if indifferent, son. Esme, however, was already eager to discover the deeper purposes of life and, although it was inaccurate of Coward to say that their friendship was constantly being interrupted by 'spiritual ecstasies' (which did not begin until after her marriage), she certainly tried to interest him in higher matters than his own future:

My interest in religion was tabooed. Noël was totally uninterested in the subject and didn't want to discuss it. He also felt that any doubts cast on Orthodoxy reflected on the intelligence of his adored mother who, like my own parents, was firmly, unquestioningly and irrationally Church of England. Eventually, to avoid the quarrels that resulted from any attempts on my part to speak on this fundamental interest, we drew up a Palship Contract, one clause of which forbade the discussion of religion.[5]

(Many years later Coward recalled this arrangement when writing *Private Lives*. Whenever Elyot and Amanda sense the imminence of an argument, they call a halt to their discussion with the formula of truce, 'Solomon Isaacs', or 'Sollocks!') Coward cared about the future but not about the hereafter. His interests were focused on the frenetic arena of the theatre; and Esme was not left in any doubt that his ambition to triumph within that arena was implacable from an early age:

I was with him when, during a country walk, he clearly formulated his desire in imagination and expressed it to me in the words: 'I am going to have the whole theatrical world at my feet.' At that time he was fifteen years of age, plain, with no financial resources except meagre earnings as an actor, a good ear for music, and an ability to play by heart but no knowledge of the theory; his chief asset being a brilliant sense of humour.[6]

She remembered that he was not only chubby and plain, but also slightly aggressive and quick to take offence. Nevertheless, there was something about Coward that seemed remarkable. 'Both his mother and I had every confidence in his talent and his humour; we knew that he could do whatever he wanted and it was all so carefully planned.'[7] As her acting career progressed, Esme was sent on tour with theatrical companies much more than Coward, whose mother did all she could to keep him in London and away from the indignity of lodging-houses and landladies' cooking. However, when they did appear together (and they both toured in *Charley's Aunt* in 1916), they occupied their free time in long walks and were not above naked frolicking in wooded places. If their fantasies were sylvan and literary in inspiration at this time, the work of George Bernard Shaw also continued to exert a strong appeal and Esme remembered: 'We were both pacifists of a kind; we neither smoked nor drank during our friendship, and were rooted in Bernard Shaw, who said that the majority are always wrong. We felt that about the war and we used to tell our friends who were old enough to enlist that they should be conscientious objectors.'[8] (When the time came, Coward did not claim conscientious objections to enlistment, despite the fact that he and Esme lost several young friends in the trenches; he found other means of escaping military service.) Shaw's polemical idealism clearly appealed to Esme, but Coward saluted his other achievements. He saw in the example of Shaw and Wilde a possibility of shaping his own ends which mere acting, however successful, could never guarantee. If he had the ability to amuse which Esme Wynne did not doubt, it made sense to record his comic lines, incorporating them in some story with a view to speaking them before an audience. He could become a playwright, and emulate Wilde in wit, and Shaw in social reform.

He experimented briefly with literary work involving 'Pan, and Fauns and Cloven Hooves', but Coward was not really interested in pastoral whimsy, and determined instead to write plays about people. He and Esme must have had faith in each other's abilities and literary values because they established a partnership, 'Esnomel', an ugly portmanteau of their names, which in 1917 produced its first play, *Ida Collaborates*. An opera, *Crissa*, was begun in that year or the next and 1918 saw the completion of *Woman and Whisky*. However, in 1918, just as the alliance had begun to prosper, it suffered two severe frustrations: he was conscripted, and she got married to Lynden Tyson. Coward got on perfectly well with her husband and did not at first see that marriage might alter Esme Wynne-Tyson's priorities. In any case, he was not one to let adversity overwhelm ambition, and he started to write with Esme in mind, convinced that having been Hawtrey's favourite child actor, she would gain the top of that profession. His first solo play, *The Rat Trap* of 1918, was about two writers, and he may have intended her to play the part of the compulsive bluestocking. He wrote the female leads in *I'll Leave It To You*, of 1919, and *The Young Idea*, of 1921, specifically for her. He valued her advice and inspiration, but the arrangement was nothing if not reciprocal, and a letter of the mid-1920s indicates the seriousness with which Coward took his duties as her self-appointed literary adviser and confidant, and the bluntness he was prepared to employ in those capacities. She had sent him her latest effort, a play called *The Supreme Folly*, and his response was characteristically opinionated. All of it apart from the beginning of Act 1 he considered 'dreary', with the last act 'interminable', and she received a caution: 'I tried in *The Rat Trap* to let two women have a long scene together in the last act but quickly realized my mistake and re-wrote it.' He applauded her sense of psychology, and some of her dialogue, but then: 'You do a thing we've *always* done and that is laugh at yourself – it's a bad habit and I'm swiftly getting out of it.'

Coward was famous in later life for reprimanding his friends. Esme Wynne was accustomed to his strictures at an early age, and the letter ends with two rebukes: 'You have a prose mind not a dialogue mind. Novelists can't write plays and Playwrights can't write novels – at least *very* seldom – Clemence Dane and Gals-worthy.' Also:

You and I need emotion before we can write dramatic scenes ... You're content and happy and becoming *'au fait'* with Christ. I won't say 'smug' because that would be unkind but may I suggest coming down to earth a teeny bit? Perhaps having a violent affair with The Fishmonger on Gosport Hard and then writing a play with some guts in it and firmly *minus* any spiritual uplift![9]

She bore his advice in mind, and shortly afterwards he was able to write and congratulate her on the progress her work was making. She may have had a more serious and better-educated mind, but he, this correspondence reveals, was instinctively a surer playwright. After *The Supreme Folly*, Esme dashed off *The New Elaine*, and his assessment of its merits revealed that he already had firm convictions about slenderness of plot and succinctness of dialogue. He reminded her: 'Keep the speeches short – and don't emphasize your points.' He felt that her psychological analysis was improving all the time, although 'I can see no reason for Elaine to be stodgy or unemotional at all – lots of men fall out of love with most attractive people.' He also considered her guilty of indulging in cheap slapstick comedy: 'It's insulting your Audience's intelligence and your own.'[10]

Mentor and pupil were changing places; but before the reversal of roles was complete, and to Coward's disbelief and fury, Esme renounced the stage, and their partnership, and *I'll Leave It To You* marked her acting swan-song. It seems that she felt incapable of reconciling the duties of marriage with the idle priorities of the stage. Furthermore, the religious upbringing she had received from her father had left a profound mark and, increasingly occupied with matters of the spirit, Esme Wynne became a Christian Scientist. For the rest of her life (which ended a year before Coward's) she devoted her life to this faith, though she later wrote books on education, ethics, religious history and philosophy which bore witness to a range of interest and curiosity far wider than that envisaged, still less attained, by Coward.[11] Meanwhile, they continued to see each other, though with diminishing frequency, and he was rebuked every time for what she saw as his relentless frivolity and spiritual indifference.[12]

Esme Wynne was married in 1918. She may have felt incapable

of being a wife and an actress, but she did not allow her new status to interfere with her writing career, and went on to produce several novels, two plays and a prodigious amount of journalism. She and Coward continued to see a lot of each other for several years and later they were frequent correspondents. However, things could not be the same, particularly after 1924, when the Wynne-Tysons had a son. Coward seems to have made some attempt to indulge Esme's new obligations: she remembered that he went to see her in the country shortly after her confinement, and told her 'that if he ever had to choose a religion, it would be Christian Science, having seen for himself how wonderfully it had helped me'.[13] But by the time that he came to write his autobiography in 1937, Coward breezily implied the irrevocable change in their relationship, and put the blame on Esme's religious conversion: 'This depressed me but apparently gave her a great deal of pleasure, a pleasure, I may add, that was not entirely free of superciliousness.'[14] It is impossible to say whether their partnership would have produced anything of worth or lasting merit, and whether it would have survived, without Esme's defection to religion. Coward's thirst for fame, glory and recognition would probably have sent him on a lone course sooner or later anyway. But he never doubted that Esme had sacrificed great talent to what seemed to him to be ludicrous objectives; and he hated waste as much as he feared failure. He could never quite forgive her decision; and many years later, he put his views about Mary Baker Eddy, the founder of Christian Science, into a verse (which Esme, to her credit, found amusing):

> By not letting thoughts of sin come
> You have made a handsome income
> Much larger than your friend the Nazarene.[15]

Chapter Four

It was not only his literary ambitions which began to stir at the beginning of Coward's adolescence. He began, then or shortly afterwards, to cherish social ambitions as well. In this, of course, he had his mother's example and encouragement. There was little practical assistance she could give, because there can have been few socially prestigious figures in her life at that time, but she could certainly ensure that all auspicious friendships flourished unhindered. Philip Streatfield, a thirty-year-old painter, somehow appeared in Coward's life in the spring of 1914. If Violet Coward knew the exact nature of this *amitié amoureuse*, she did nothing to stand in its way. (Esme Wynne, knowing that he was precocious in all things, suffered no delusions.) The fourteen-year-old Noël spent long hours in Glebe Place – now a millionaires' row; then, apparently, a suburb of Bohemia – watching the artist at work and wondering perhaps about the grandfather he had never known who was a painter as well as a sailor. Later that year, Streatfield went to the West Country in search of landscapes, and Noël Coward accompanied him. As usual, Violet Coward saved the letter which her son despatched shortly before the outbreak of the war which brought Victorian England to an end.[1] Children's letters are usually boring, and Coward's are no exception. But it is interesting to note that his epistolary style suddenly improved. His prose became much more fluent and began to contain fragments in French, and the diaresis began to be incorporated into his signature. At fourteen, Noël Coward was beginning to be aware that a writing style could not only suggest sophistication, but could also double as a powerful means of projecting a chosen personality. Perhaps already, after only a couple of months, Esme Wynne's more literary influence was beginning to tell; perhaps also Coward was absorbing the professional poise of actors. Other things do not change, however; and his early correspondence reveals that his love of sunbathing developed early, and that energy and extroversion continued to mark his behaviour.

With the outbreak of hostilities, he returned to London (a chance encounter led to his being escorted on the journey by the novelist Hugh Walpole). Philip Streatfield joined up, and fell in the trenches in 1916. Before he died, however, he performed one valuable service for his unfinished but clever companion: he wrote to a wealthy friend called Mrs Astley Cooper, who lived in Rutland, with the suggestion that she might be amused by the quick and ambitious young actor with literary longings. So Noël Coward received his first invitation to the country in 1915. It was obviously an important event, and Violet Coward at least knew that nothing should frustrate the opportunity. Coward's autobiography tells us that she went to see him off at St Pancras, and that disaster threatened when she

left her bag in the tube, with all the money she had scraped together for my return ticket ... Mother, however, rose above it as usual ... and asked a policeman the way to the nearest pawnshop. There happened to be one practically opposite and within five minutes she was back, without her only remaining diamond ring ... She stood on the platform waving as the train slid away, triumphantly pink in the face but with the suspicion of tears in her eyes ...[2]

Coward seldom wasted opportunities, especially social ones, and he made the most of Mrs Astley Cooper's valuable hospitality. After the convention and respectability of the suburbs, this was his first encounter with someone rich enough to indulge innate eccentricity, someone who can only have reinforced the young actor's growing conviction that there is a lot to be said for standing apart from the crowd. *Present Indicative* reports that his hostess could find no pleasure in her appearance, and that she had accordingly had all the mirrors in her house covered. But if her appearance dissatisfied her, her voice did not; and she apparently spent the evenings supine before the fire delivering herself of *bons mots*. (Regrettably, Coward did not record her wit; and if any of her amusing lines found their way into the mouths of his early characters, they went unacknowledged.)

Cole Lesley pointed out that this first stay in Rutland marked Coward's introduction to the hunting life, an experience he was to draw upon, without undue reverence, in his early comedy *The Young Idea*. The aspiring dramatist had little interest in the unspeakable pursuing the uneatable; but his eye for the luxury of Mrs

Astley Cooper's establishment was keen and appreciative, and his autobiography suggests that he took to life with servants (to light the fire in his room every evening, and lay out his dinner jacket) with relish. But he was also astute enough to realize that his own performance as a guest in the household must conform, and he remembered having to be 'very careful not to slip in my new patent leather shoes'.[3]

Cole Lesley maintained that Coward was forever at ease staying in grand houses after this early experience of Mrs Cooper's hospitality. But that assertion is contradicted by Coward himself. Like every performer, he needed his privacy; and his background had denied him the aristocratic assumption that he was welcome everywhere and would never get in the way. Noël Coward liked and needed hotels:

I do not care for the obligation of having to be considerate to other people's servants, nor do I care to experiment with other people's ideas of comfort which are so often widely dissimilar from my own. In an hotel I can ring the bell or raise the telephone and protest if there aren't enough pillows or the bedside lamp doesn't function properly. In a private house I cannot. In an hotel room I can put a 'Don't Disturb' sign on the door and sleep for as long as I like and capriciously demand a poached egg and a cup of tea at three o'clock in the afternoon, if I feel so disposed, without feeling that I am shattering an established routine and possibly causing my hostess's cook to give notice. To me the very idea of a round of country-house visits is anathema.[4]

Most of his early plays contain scenes in country houses of varying degrees of grandeur, and it was owing to Mrs Astley Cooper and her neighbours – after other doors had begun opening to him locally – that he was able to write them. If Philip Streatfield calculated that his protégé's social poise would be sharpened by the introduction, however, he cannot also have imagined that Mrs Astley Cooper's hospitality would lead, indirectly, to an important literary discovery. Later in the war, after Hambleton had been converted into a hospital for convalescent soldiers, Coward used to go and entertain the inmates with his songs, and it was on one of these visits that he serendipitously encountered the work of one of the most enduringly popular of Edwardian writers. Saki already occupied a prominent position in Esme Wynne's pantheon of writers, despite his apparent flippancy and blatant misogyny, but for some reason she had not introduced Coward to his work.

However, when the latter found *Beasts and Superbeasts*, his admiration was immediate and complete. He read it voraciously; later he was to say that the two most important literary influences on him were those of Saki (who died, like Philip Streatfield, in the trenches in 1916) and E. Nesbit (an unlikely pair: she wrote *The Railway Children*).

Coward was already setting Esme Wynne's verses to music and now, spurred on by her, he began to experiment with rhyme schemes, and to produce verse himself. His first, of which only a fragment survives, was comic:

> The Sinful AspaRAGus
> To Iniquity Will Drag Us.[5]

At about the same time (1917, according to Noël Coward's *Complete Lyrics*), he wrote his first song:

> Ordinary man invariably sighs
> Vainly for what cannot be ...
> Every peach out of reach is attractive
> 'Cos it's just a little bit too high,
> And you'll find that every man
> Will try to pluck it if he can
> As he passes by.
> For the brute loves the fruit that's forbidden
> And I'll bet you half a crown
> He'll appreciate the flavour of it much much more
> If he has to climb a bit to shake it down.

The young lyricist may have been fiercely ambitious, but at the same time, Coward thought sighing for what could not be a waste of time: he believed in getting on with the business in hand. But most lyrics – especially sentimental ones – are dishonest; this early effort merely followed a tradition.

The first stirrings of creativity usually please their authors at the time and Coward may well have felt proud of himself now. Indeed, his life was generally progressing well: he was continuing to act, he was beginning to make friends in the theatre, and in smarter social worlds. Much that he and his mother had longed for seemed increasingly attainable. But in 1917 he met Ivor Novello (possibly through Esme Wynne, who was a close friend of Novello's) and realized that he had a long way to go. Novello, the possessor of the most famous profile in England, and composer of 'Keep The Home

Fires Burning', was to remain a friend of Coward's until his premature death in 1951. During the Great War and the 1920s, his looks
particularly commanded fervent admiration, and the first encounter certainly made a great and lasting impression on Coward: 'I
envied thoroughly everything about him. His looks, his personality,
his assured position, his dinner clothes, his bedroom and bath and,
above all, the supper party. I pictured him sipping champagne ...
adored by everybody at the table ... I ... felt suddenly conscious of
the long way I had to go ...'[6]

He was right. Before he could get any further, however, real life
and the outside world intervened, and he was called up.

At fourteen, when the Great War broke out, Coward had no
thoughts for politics or patriotism. A later chapter of German expan-
sionism would leave him voluble on the subject of the Germans
themselves; but during the early stages of the First World War, it
is unlikely that he ever thought of the Kaiser except as a name in
music-hall songs. Later, when Esme Wynne had coaxed him into
seriousness, he became a rather emotional pacifist; but by 1918,
when he was conscripted, the war had become less an issue for
discussion than a dreary fact of everyday life. Four years of carnage
had soured initial patriotic fervour; and news from the trenches,
good or bad, but always horrible, was met increasingly with something approaching resignation. Whatever the intensity of his pacifism, though, there were other considerations involved in Coward's
reluctance to fight, not least the claims of his mother, who relied
on him quite as much as he did on her:

I depended on him perhaps more than I should, when he was young. He
always knew the right thing to do, his opinion was really law to me, for
he was always right. When I was at my wits' end and quite desperate ...
several times for money, he would talk and reassure me, and go off and
get money somewhere and bring relief and joy to me.[7]

With her need of support, and with ambition seething in his
mind, he could overlook his duty to king and country. *Present
Indicative*, published on the eve of another war, is forthright on the
subject, and coolly declares that although there were countless
young conscripts 'with far graver responsibilities', and 'millions of
mothers in far more tragic circumstances', it was still his resolute
priority to get out of the fighting in order to pursue his career and

make himself, and possibly his family, more prosperous, however 'reprehensible' such a policy might be.

Having had a mildly consumptive lung at the age of fifteen, he was pronounced unfit for active service, and languished in the Artists' Rifles. But he longed to extricate himself from the futility and boredom of lavatory-cleaning and formation drill: conveniently, while marching, he fell and hit his head badly. He took to claiming violent headaches which he later admitted were exaggerated; and Esme Wynne-Tyson remembered 'tremendous nervous breakdowns', but knew that Noël Coward was not an actor for nothing. There was a potion, the recipe of which was in circulation, which harmlessly induced the symptoms of severe fever, and Coward later admitted to Esme that he had drunk it. He was eventually discharged, and given a pension of seven shillings and sixpence for six months. It would be callous and dogmatic to condemn him for adopting these expedients. While, happily, almost all men are reluctant combatants, and averse to the regimented tedium of army life, most, in the event of national emergency, can be trained to adequate standards of soldiership. But Coward was the most unlikely conscript, and his spell in the army, which he described as 'brief and inglorious',[8] was a waste of his time and his country's money. For the would-be sophisticate, patriotism was to be a condition of middle age.

He returned to acting, to writing and to social-climbing. Mrs Astley Cooper proved a generous sponsor once again, and now decided to take her young and provincial friend on holiday with her to Alassio. Coward found the warm February sunshine they encountered there a blissful revelation, and ever afterwards, he was a restless sun-seeker. In the course of this holiday he also met Gladys Calthrop, the designer of all his productions between 1924 and 1950 and a lifelong friend. In London once again, and still under Esme Wynne-Tyson's sylvan influence, he began, but abandoned, a novel called *Cherry Pan*. He wrote three plays in 1918, and probably had the newly-married Esme in mind when completing *The Rat Trap*, a hysterical melodrama which pointed all too eagerly at the constrictions which matrimony imposed on aspiring writers. In 1919, he appeared as Ralph in Beaumont and Fletcher's comedy of 1613, *The Knight of The Burning Pestle*. At that stage in his self-education, Coward was still busy trying to assimilate and emulate modern masters like Shaw and Wilde. The past never greatly excited his imagination; and he may by that time have realized that he was not interested in acting in other people's plays, but in writing parts which would show off his own personality to the best advantage. He was inevitably unhappy in the production: he did not understand the play, and his appearance did not serve his self-invention. One reviewer complained that Ralph was 'a little too Mayfairish for a Jacobean grocer's son'.

The 'Mayfair' accent with which he had equipped himself would doubtless have pleased Violet Coward even if it did not strike the reviewer as appropriate. (It has been speculated that Coward developed his characteristically clipped manner of speech to accommodate her imperfect hearing. Whether or not that is true, there is no doubt that he knew that abandoning his suburban speech would help both his theatrical and his social ambition.) In other areas, however, he continued to make mistakes; and he later admitted that he presented himself at auditions in a navy suit, with a coloured shirt, tie, socks and handkerchief to match. Nor was it only his appearance that let him down. When his persona had crystallized, one of its chief aspects was its composure: it was essential that the type of humour he came to represent – arch, superior, insolent, but obliquely so – should come with an imperturbable, *dégagé* tone and cast of features. At this stage, Coward had a conspicuous chip on his shoulder and was still letting it show. Hawtrey had had to admonish him for 'giving himself airs'.[9] Constance Collier remembered that before he was acclaimed, he appeared 'a little bitter, as if aware that he had a much better brain than many of his more successful contemporaries'.[10] If he was quick-witted, he often resented references to the fact: Esme Wynne-Tyson remembered that he was always greatly annoyed when people said of him, 'He's clever and knows it.' 'He always logically commented: "How do they think I could be clever and *not* know it?"'[11] Yet at the same time, if he felt that his intelligence was being overlooked, he could also display irritation. Cicely Courtneidge, encountering him in 1916, had found that he was 'consistently airing his views, although he was never asked' and that he was 'difficult to like'.[12] The novelist G. B. Stern went on holiday with him just after the war, and remembered that he 'talked gaily and incessantly and wrote plays and read them to us and read them to us and read them to us' and that she could not imagine 'how he survived our irritation'.[13] Most revealingly, Esme Wynne's husband, Lynden Tyson, saw him in about 1919: 'As an actor he was up against it because he was very young and provocative, and the older stage people used to give him a good bit of hell. I remember him saying to me once, "They don't like me; they've got no time for me, but I'll have them eating out of my hands before I've finished."'[14]

Charm could not be learned, like a part: it had to be developed and polished to be successfully deployed, and that was particularly difficult with an awareness that one did not belong. As late as 1921, he had not quite got the measure of the smarter world on which he had set his sights. Invited by Lady Colefax to a house party outside Oxford, he encountered undergraduates: 'Their shirts and flannels were yellow and well used, against which mine seemed too newly white, too immaculately moulded from musical comedy. Their socks, thick and carelessly wrinkled round their ankles, so unlike mine of too thin silk, caught up by intricate suspenders.'[15]

He was not born to acceptance by the privileged world he had begun to see. Instead, he had to work hard for that acceptance, and there were inevitably moments when he fell prey to resentment of those who accepted their luck in life unquestioningly. However completely he later accumulated wealth, glamour, the trappings of privilege, he could never make up for the fact that he had been denied a smart education. The use of 'Bloomsbury' as a term of damnation, and the blind association of 'intellectuals' with all sorts of ills, lead one to the suspicion that there was something about those who were privileged by education which Coward begrudged. And his diatribes to the contrary – although they may contain elements of truth – have a strenuous determination about them which leaves one unconvinced. Many years later, he declared:

If mother had been able ... to send me to ... Eton and Oxford or Cambridge, it would have probably set me back years. I have always distrusted too much education and intellectualism ... There is something to me both arid and damp about dwelling too much among the literary shades of the past. My good fortune was to have a bright, acquisitive, but not an intellectual mind, and to have been impelled by circumstances to get out and earn my living ...[16]

But if Coward had been born without style, and if what he knew he had largely taught himself, he had determination, and it eventually bore fruit. His autobiography notes that between 1917 and 1919, he got to know thirty-four well-known people, amongst them Rebecca West, H. G. Wells, Somerset Maugham, John Galsworthy, Gerald du Maurier, Charles Scott-Moncrieff, Lady Carisbrooke, Lady Londesborough and Maurice Chevalier. Coward was primarily interested in what he later called people of achievement, rather than the merely grand, and the orbit of his social ambition was urban. (In this, he followed Wilde, for whom the drawing-rooms of Mayfair also held much more appeal than the stately homes of England.) As well as determination, Coward had the two qualities indispensable to successful social-climbers: shamelessness, and an ability to be in the right place at the right time:

On Armistice Day ... dined with Tony and Juanita Ganderillas ... After dinner we drove in a dark red Rolls-Royce through the Park and into Trafalgar Square, where we stuck, while hordes of screaming people climbed onto the roof of the car, the footboards and the radiator. ... I felt ignobly delighted in this moment of national rejoicing, to be in a tail-coat, a Rolls-Royce, and obviously aristocratic company.[17]

With the war over, and the Twenties dawning, he could return to the affairs which interested him. He had written *I'll Leave It To You* as a vehicle for himself and Esme Wynne-Tyson and in 1920 the play was staged in Manchester and then briefly in London. Although the production lasted for only a short time, and although it marked the end of his partnership with Esme, it still gave Coward some cause for self-congratulation. He was finally a produced playwright: he managed the publicity as though born to it and the fame he longed for inched nearer. Wilde, of course, had been famous for his curtain speeches, and Coward followed that example and spoke after his play's first night in Manchester. In London, there were press conferences and an early newspaper interview:

The success of it all is a bit dazzling. This may be an age of youth but it does not always happen that young people get their chance of success. I have been exceptionally lucky. I made up my mind I would have one of my plays produced in London by the time I was twenty-one, which will be in December. I hope to be a manager by then, too.[18]

He announced provocatively that he was related to no one but himself, and as though instinctively he fed reporters the sententious remarks on which they thrive: *I'll Leave It To You*, he declared, had been written in three days, 'whereas many of my plays take a week'. The critics were agreed that a playwright of promise had been born,

41

and some were even inclined to regard Coward as a prodigy, an assessment he himself would have been disinclined to challenge. An early sketch survives:

There is something freakish, Puck-like, about the narrow slant of his grey-green eyes, the tilt of his eyebrows, the sleek backward rush of his hair. He is lithe as a fawn; and if you told him with perfect truth, that he was one of the three best dancers in London, his grieved surprise at hearing of the other two would only be equalled by his incredulity.[19]

With Esme Wynne-Tyson married and the alliance officially over, Coward must have wondered for a while where he could go next. He formed a brief working partnership with Lorn Macnaughtan, soon to become Lorn Loraine, and for the rest of her life his confidante and secretary. Whatever else *A Withered Nosegay*, the fruit of this second collaboration, established, it is that the aspiring writer was no inspired parodist. The book comprises a collection of cameos of fictitious heroines from history. It was dedicated to Esme; and Lorn did the illustrations while Coward was responsible for the text. Looking back on this venture, he conceded that 'burlesque' was 'usually disastrous' for inexperienced writers, and the work now seems unreadably puerile. Coward manages to include his favourite historical periods, the French Revolution and the England of the Restoration, but the jokes are silly, the satire indelicate, implausible and ineffectual. The enterprise would not particularly have impressed a reasonably bright fifteen-year-old schoolboy. But he was not, and never had been, a fifteen-year-old schoolboy: he had to teach himself everything, from social grace to academic accomplishment. However, he somehow persuaded Christophers to publish it in 1922. Publication followed a year later in the United States, where the book was called *Terribly Intimate Portraits*.

His social horizons continued to expand and, at about this time, he met two young men who were both to play an important role in these still-formative years before fame: Lord Lathom and Jeffery Holmesdale. 'Ned' Lathom was rich, consumptive and stagestruck. He formed a company, The Ventures, dedicated exclusively to the performance of plays banned by Coward's future, and omnipotent, adversary, the Lord Chamberlain, and acted as a generous, if unofficial, patron towards the struggling actor and writer. Holmesdale, later Lord Amherst, was at that time a captain in the Coldstream Guards. He became Coward's travelling companion in his long expeditions of the Thirties, but their first trip together took place in 1921, when Holmesdale had to travel to Massachusetts to represent his family at a celebration at Amherst College. Coward, drawn by stories of New York's veneration of success, had already formulated a determination to cross the Atlantic. This seemed as good an opportunity as any. Ever mindful of his mother's belief that appearances counted for a good deal, he decided against travelling to New York within his means, which would have meant booking a passage in a small freight boat. Instead, he followed Holmesdale, and embarked on the *Lusitania*, having scraped together enough money to cross the ocean, if not to return.

His first stay in the city which was in many ways to become a second home to him was something of an endurance test. Owing to a combination of naïvety, slender resources and the optimism of the young and determined, he arrived in June with some manuscripts and only seventeen pounds in cash. Holmesdale went to New England, and then returned to London directly. Hopeful of earning something from his writings, Coward deposited some manuscripts with the Theatre Guild. But with July, the migration to Long Island and Maine began, and the few people of influence to whom he had introductions left the city. Worse still, the Theatre Guild closed until September, and his writings, the proof of his promise, were impounded.

Later on, he faced the summer heat and humidity penniless and alone. To begin with, however, there were diversions to excite and lessons to learn. He saw the mandatory sights. He stayed, briefly, at the Algonquin. He explored Broadway. He became friends with a memorably-named pair of artist-actresses, Gabrielle Enthoven and Cecile Sartoris, and when he could no longer afford to stay in a hotel, he moved into their studio flat in Washington Square. Cecile Sartoris worked with an expatriate Englishwoman called Irene Dean-Paul, or 'Poldowski', who gave recitals of Verlaine's poetry in the houses of the wealthy. She and Coward became allies in poverty and uncertainty; and he later remembered her artistic integrity, which, he felt, was 'not sufficiently swaddled in egotism to shield her from the irritation of failure'.[20] There were parties, expeditions to nightclubs, trips to Harlem, and half-hearted attempts at exploiting the rich. It all sounds very bohemian, very much of its time, and one half expects Carl Van Vechten and Hart Crane to appear. When all his friends left Manhattan, Coward lived on bacon bought on credit at an Italian delicatessen. He was tormented by cockroaches. In poverty and enforced idleness, he walked the long journey from Washington Square to Battery Park, to breathe the Atlantic air, and to stare wistfully at ships leaving for England, but even these pilgrimages were not without irritation: 'Unfortunately, owing to my carefully-conserved wardrobe, I was invariably asked for money by my brother paupers.'[21] But autumn finally arrived, and he became friendly with the actress Laurette Taylor, and her husband, Hartley Manners. Together, they held court every Sunday evening in their apartment on Riverside Drive; but all the guests had to earn their supper by participating in gruelling and humiliating parlour games.

Never one to waste time, Coward continued to write, and completed another play, *Sirocco*. He sold parts of *A Withered Nosegay* to *Vanity Fair*, and was paid to turn *I'll Leave It To You* into a short story. It was a matter of pride to Coward that he return to England showing a profit, and when he eventually secured a passage home, he was seven pounds richer. But the real gains which New York conferred were, predictably, intangible. To begin with, Broadway taught him that there was an alternative to the slow, deliberate and artificial stage delivery common in the West End at that time. Indeed, one of his credentials as the arbiter of modernity he was soon to become was his instinctive recognition of America's innovative spirit: 'In the Twenties and Thirties whenever I was about to do a new production in England I always used to go to New York for a fortnight and go to see every single play because the tempo and the wonderful speed and vitality of the theatre was far superior to the English then.'[22] He also learnt that as his persona developed and became more attractive and confidently unusual, he was able to charm other larger-than-life figures. The most interesting of these was perhaps the critic, Alexander Woollcott, who befriended Coward during this New York interlude and later claimed to have known him 'since he was a shabby youngster in his teens who either ate at the expense of some rich wage-slave like myself or didn't eat at all'. Modest gambling formed a bond between them, but later Woollcott decided that their friendship was one-sided: 'I know everything about Noël; he knows nothing about me. He is not even interested.' And after Coward's last stay with Woollcott, the latter told another guest: 'I hope he never comes back. He talks me to death.'[23] Tallulah Bankhead, the excitingly-named actress, also joined the ranks of Coward's friends in 1921, as did Alfred Lunt and Lynn Fontanne, who were later to become the darlings of Broadway, and one of the most celebrated acting partnerships of their time. (Their fame has faded considerably because they rejected the immortality of film stardom in favour of the applause of the theatre.) Struggling and obscure though they all were in 1921, the Lunts and Coward promised one another that they would all appear together in one of his plays when they were famous. And Alfred Lunt, like Esme Wynne-Tyson before him, was left in no doubt about the strength of Noël Coward's ambition: 'A gentleness and at times a deep sadness marked [his] character then, though the determination to succeed and preferably rapidly at that time was never far away.'[24]

Chapter Five

In the winter of 1922, Coward went to Davos in Switzerland at the invitation of his wealthy friend Lord Lathom. Micheál MacLiammóir, who had known him since they had appeared together in *The Goldfish*, was also there, though not in the same party, and was able to cast a slightly jaundiced eye on Coward's alpine progress:

Noël was with a very big, smart party ... I still thought then that he would do well ... he was always fond of fashionable, smart people ... I thought Wilde had already done everything that Noël could possibly do. I even used to run away and hide when I saw him, in case he recognized me.[1]

Lathom, convalescing after an attack of consumption, was passionately interested in the theatre, to the extent that he had backed *A to Z*, the most recent revue to be presented by the impresario, André Charlot. The revue – a series of disconnected sketches, satirical and sentimental scenes and choruses – was an extremely popular form of entertainment throughout the Twenties, and Charlot was the first manager in London to realize its potential. Coward, through the offices of Beatrice Lillie, had already tried to interest him in some of his songs and sketches, but Charlot had been unimpressed. In Switzerland, however, Coward rehearsed his newest compositions for Lathom, Charlot's patron, and so impressed him that the latter was immediately summoned to Davos. Coward had polished his talent since he had first met Charlot, and now he had the support and friendship of a rich and aristocratic admirer. The result of the summons, and of Coward's determined impromptu performing, was that a new revue was projected. Charlot returned to London, while Coward remained abroad to begin work on the project. It had been decided, at Charlot's insistence, that the inexperienced Coward should share the huge task of completing the revue with more experienced writers. Later, Charlot soured proceedings slightly when he used this arrangement as an excuse to try and pay Coward a reduced salary. However, the latter was heartily sick of financial embarrassment, and demanded, and eventually got, £40 a week: in those days, a generous sum. Once that financial disagreement had been resolved, the remaining preparations moved smoothly. Edward Molyneux, whom Coward had met in Switzerland, designed the costumes (as he was to do for all the leading ladies in all of Coward's plays), and Fred and Adele Astaire, friends from New York, offered choreographical advice. Such a concatenation of young talent virtually guaranteed some sort of recognition: and when *London Calling* opened in 1923, Noël Coward found himself confronting fame.

He saw his name in lights for the first time. The audiences were fashionable, and thronged backstage where, Coward claimed, he learnt to perform the 'little tricks' which he sensed were 'expected' of him.[2] His reputation as a lyricist began to grow, and one only has to listen to the songs Ivor Novello was producing at the same time to understand why Coward's work seemed so exciting and audacious. He was also extremely fortunate to have someone like Gertrude Lawrence to perform a song like 'Parisian Pierrot':

> Parisian Pierrot,
> Society's hero,
> The Lord of a day,
> The Rue de la Paix
> Is under your sway,
> The world may flatter
> But what does that matter,
> They'll never shatter
> Your gloom profound.

The idea of the song had come to Coward while he was watching an act involving a pierrot doll in a Berlin nightclub, and some time before the pierrot became a mascot of the Twenties, and of the art deco movement.[3] The song was immediately and lastingly successful, and he began to hear his music in restaurants and nightclubs for the first time. Gertrude Lawrence, it seems, could charm effortlessly, but Coward still had not learnt that to be seen to be trying to impress, whatever the nature of the audience, was a mistake: and *Present Indicative* reveals that, despite his 'perfect diction', and faultless white tie and tails, his rendition of the song 'Sentiment' fell completely flat, 'like pennies into mud'.

If he had not yet learnt the art of apparent casualness, the would-be man-about-town also knew nothing of subtlety, and *London Calling* became famous for a feud which was the direct result of his heavy-handed mockery: the feud between Coward and the Sitwells. He had first met Osbert Sitwell at the house of Mrs Beatrice Guinness when he was poor but already in demand as a houseguest. In 1923, Osbert, Edith and Sacheverell decided to give a recital at the Aeolian Hall, to be called 'Façade', to announce themselves, and the modern movement in poetry, to London. Shortly before it took place, Osbert had encountered Coward again, having heard about the plans for *London Calling*, and had invited him: 'It might give you some ideas.' It certainly did. During 'Façade', Coward was seen walking out 'a little more ostentatiously than perhaps he need have done', according to an eyewitness. Shortly afterwards, Hernia, Sago and Gobo Whittlebot appeared in Coward's revue, reciting so-called poetry:

> 'Your mouth is my mouth
> And our mouth is their mouth
> And their mouth is Bournemouth.'

The Sitwells, penetrating the flimsy disguise, were scandalized. (None of them stooped to attending *London Calling*, and it is doubtful that they would have accepted William Walton's verdict, that the Swiss Family Whittlebot was 'really not unfunny'.) According to their biographer, John Pearson: 'At the Duke of York's the Sitwells and modern poetry were being ridiculed themselves, and the philistines, instead of being laughed at, were now laughing in their turn. An actor from the London suburbs and the lower-middle classes had taken on *their* role of mockery – and at their expense.'[4] They reacted immoderately. Edith was so upset that she apparently developed jaundice, while the irascible Osbert made his position unequivocal. In an unpublished poem, he angrily analysed Coward's behaviour, and its cause:

> In one smug person, Coward sums
> Up both the suburbs and the slums;
> Before both, nightly boasts his race
> By spitting in a lady's face.[5]

And in case the upstart was in any doubt about the Sitwellian fury he had provoked, Osbert wrote to him:

We are delighted to have been the means of suggesting an idea to you. It is always as well to have one, even if it isn't your own; it must be a novel experience to you. All you want, now, is a little self-confidence – and, of course, to use your voice more. Insulting my sister is a fine beginning for you. We look forward to other triumphs. Have you tried cheating at cards?[6]

Coward insolently and disingenuously professed himself amazed and perplexed by such anger, a position he continued to maintain in *Present Indicative*. And if he felt any stirrings of contrition, he overcame them with the reflection that all publicity was good publicity. He redoubled his assault on the self-important arbiters of new form when he made his first radio broadcast, in 1924, with readings from *The Poems of Miss Hernia Whittlebot*; and in the following year, he published *Chelsea Buns*, which purported to be a collection of Hernia's latest poems.

One reviewer of the book considered that 'one almost feels sorry for Miss Sitwell, even though in the vernacular she has been "asking for it".' Whether that was true or not, the squabble reflected well on neither party. The Sitwells, faintly absurd at the best of times, reacted vaingloriously and without humour. Equally, after *A Withered Nosegay*, Coward continued to display a childish urge to tease. He also showed his resentment of those whose privileged background, and better education, led to claims to the right to adjudicate in matters of taste and opinion (only half flippantly, one of Hernia's lines ran: 'Oxford and Cambridge count for naught'), a resentment which was the other side of the coin of his famous snobbery. Sheridan Morley, in his biography of Coward, claims that the Sitwells annoyed because they violated form, which to Coward was supremely important. But at this early stage, he was not constrained by formal convention – as dancers, bewildered by the new rhythms in his revues, discovered.

The feud dragged on, absurdly, for years. In 1936, Osbert wrote petulantly in a newspaper that 'Mr Coward, with his frisky tea-shop dialogues, has gained among nitwits a certain reputation for wit – but who in England is really witty, whether rude or civil?'[7] And in 1947, Edith Sitwell was still complaining of the matter, in a letter to John Lehmann:

In 1923, Mr Coward began on me in a 'sketch' of the utmost indecency – *really filthy*. I couldn't have him up, as I had no money and didn't know how to set about it. Nobody helped me, and I had to put up with having *filthy* verses about vice imputed to me and recited every night and three afternoons weekly for *nine months*. They weren't just dirty, they were filthy.[8]

A reconciliation between Coward and Edith Sitwell had to wait until 1962.

The revue also brought him to the attention of another relentlessly ambitious, social-climbing homosexual with a long way to go: Cecil Beaton. Beaton went up to Cambridge in 1922: an early diary entry, written not very long after Coward's slightly embarrassed encounter with Oxford undergraduates, helps explain why the latter felt uncomfortable and excluded with more privileged contemporaries:

I've heard so much about Noël Coward – rather nasty things about his mother being a charwoman and he being very naughty. But he's clever and well-known since *London Calling* ... I just half wondered later if I wanted to get into that Ivor [Novello], Noël Coward naughty set. They're rather cheap and horrid and yet sometimes nice. If I got my start through them I should soon give them up and get on myself.[9]

Coward, meanwhile, was solvent for the first time. He went back to New York, and stayed at the Ritz. 'I remember thinking ... how sad it would be to have had Ritzes always and been denied the pleasure of earning them.'[10] He saw Beatrice Lillie, Gertrude Lawrence and Jack Buchanan – who had all been taken out of *London Calling* in London to repeat the best of the show in Manhattan – earn golden opinions. Many years later, in *Design for Living*, Coward would have Gilda remark: 'Perhaps your success has given you a little extra glamour.' She was echoing the young Coward's reaction on seeing his friends turn into stars: 'It invested them, for me, with a new glamour, as though I were discovering them too, and had never known them before in my life.'[11] Sailing back to England, he discovered that Douglas Fairbanks and Mary Pickford were booked on the same liner; and because the two-week confinement of Atlantic crossings allowed the socially ambitious many opportunities, Coward got to know them. Once in London, he established that his new friends had been invited to a party to be attended by the Prince of Wales, and through them he secured an invitation. Cecil Beaton could say what he liked, but the new name from *London Calling* was poised on the verge of a far greater fame and success.

The actor Bobby Andrews, a lover of both Coward's and Ivor Novello's, remembered encountering the former in Paris in 1920, and being struck by his saying that he would not, for anything in the world, have been born with a private income, as that would have taken away his determination to succeed. The only thing that seemed to matter was fame, and that was the reward of achievement and unrelenting hard work. Whatever the success of *London Calling*, it was Coward's aim to prove himself as a playwright, and had been since the end of the war, when he was still in collaboration with Esme Wynne. Years later, berating a new generation of playwrights, he would say that all dramatists should begin by writing about the class they knew best. But he did not. He borrowed situations with which he had some familiarity, and transposed them to other *milieux*. The early plays are today largely unperformed (and unperformable). But for all their faults they are important, because in them he wrote parts for himself which were not reflections of what he then was, but of what he wanted to become: the wit and the successful writer. As such, they are manifestos of his self-creation.

Coward's first independent attempt at playwriting had been *The Rat Trap* of 1918. It is about two writers. He is a banal playwright, while she has great, though uncommercial, prospects as a novelist. When they marry, she is forced to abandon her career in favour of running the household, and he prospers in mediocrity and smugness. As a compulsive writer, she must have been suggested by Esme Wynne, or G. B. Stern, without being based faithfully upon either. Keld Maxwell shares several of his creator's emerging preoccupations: 'If only all young playwrights would follow Mr Maxwell's brilliant example and introduce really natural dialogue on to the stage, they would be doing the theatrical profession and the public a signal service.' 'You literary people [Keld is told] never allow anyone to be epigrammatic but yourselves.' And just as Coward was reaching the conclusion that dialogue should always be subordinate to construction, we hear that Keld 'has a wonderful sense of the dramatic, which of course is most important, and his dialogue is exceedingly witty. He may fail a little in construction but that won't matter a bit if he shows real sincerity.' And for all those who imagine that Noël Coward was entirely devoid of political prejudices, an uncontested remark of Keld's indicates the conservatism that his creator inherited from his parents: 'Now that the labour classes are so firmly getting the upper hand, all the beauty of England is bound to be spoiled.'

'My faith in my talents remained unwavering,' Coward remarked at about the time he wrote his second play, *I'll Leave It To You*. Unlike *The Rat Trap*, which had to wait for production until 1926 when its author was much too busy to appear in it, *I'll Leave It To You* was produced almost immediately, in 1920, with Coward in the main role, which he had written for himself, of Bobbie. Although the idea of the play was suggested by an American impresario, Gilbert Miller, it could not have been more appropriate to the anxieties of its writer, since it took as its subject genteel poverty, the great preoccupation of Violet Coward. But rather than set it in the suburbs, or in a boarding-house in Ebury Street, Coward transfers the action to an indefinably smarter social environment. The action involves a family of young adult brothers and sisters brought up not to work. Their father has recently died, and the money is about to run out. Their mother is incapacitated by breeding from knowing how to maintain appearances without money. 'But, darlings,' she wails, 'you know you can't make money unless you're socialists and belong to Unions and things.' Coward shamelessly invents a rich childless uncle from Canada who promises his fortune to each of the children individually, if after a year they have established themselves in the career of their choice. 'What is the use of idling through life ... You, Bobbie, you are artistic, too, you might without undue strain become a world-famous composer, artist, actor.' It comes as no surprise to discover that the uncle has no money, merely common sense and an elementary understanding of human greed and the importance of motivation. But the aimless children become successes, and one reflects that the entire play is as clear-cut and didactically insistent as a Biblical parable.

When the play was produced, one reviewer complained, somewhat prematurely, that Coward's work preoccupied itself with the idle bourgeoisie. Another, recognizing the tradition in which Coward was instinctively at home, that of drawing-room comedy, suffered a spasm of inaccuracy and generosity, and declared *I'll Leave It To You* the best comedy since *The Importance of Being Earnest*, written thirty years before.

One character in the play remarks, 'The children are all so modern they become quite ungovernable', and it was not for nothing that Coward had referred to the early Twenties as being an age of youth.

It may be a simplification to insist that the wisdom of the older generation seemed suddenly and irrevocably discredited by the carnage of the First World War, but there was certainly a change in the air. As early as 1921, one finds Evelyn Waugh writing in the Lancing College magazine:

The men of Rupert Brooke's generation are broken ... what will the young men of 1922 be? ... They will watch themselves with, probably, a greater egotism than did the young men of the nineties, but it will be with a cynical smile and often with a laugh. It is a queer world which the old men have left them ... They will not be a happy generation.[12]

And less than a decade later, Waugh returned to his theme in the *Spectator*:

Until ten years ago it was nonsense to talk in any general way about 'The Younger Generation'. Youth and age merged together in a gentle and unbroken gradation ... But in the social subsidence that resulted from the War a double cleft appeared in the life of Europe ...

Every accident of environment contributed to make of [the younger] generation the undiscriminating and ineffectual people we lament today. For their elders, the War was either a shocking negation of all they had represented, or a reckless, rather thrilling, plunge into abnormality. For the younger generation it was simply the atmosphere of their adolescence ... The real and lasting injury was caused ... by the pervading sense of inadequacy. Everything was a 'substitute' for something else, and there was barely enough even of that. The consequence is a generation of whom nine hundred and fifty in every thousand are totally lacking in any sense of qualitative value.[13]

Waugh's complaint was typical of the press debate of the time. Coward, either sensing the imminence of this new and youthful age, or else giving it a shape and a name, wrote *The Young Idea* in 1921. One of its closing lines insists that 'the only thing that matters in the world is Youth'. The play was produced in 1922, the year T. S. Eliot's *The Waste Land* sang the lament for the ruined remains of European civilization.

The protagonists of the play, Sholto and Gerda, are cosmopolitan twins who return to England to try and persuade their remarried, and cuckolded, father to return with them to their mother. Coward had written the part of Sholto, another young sophisticate, with himself, naturally, in mind but had to fight to be allowed to play the part, as Robert Courtneidge, the producer, considered him too old. It is a bad play: Coward later decided that his favourite line was, 'I lent that woman the top of my thermos flask and she never returned it. She's shallow, that's what she is, shallow.' (The *Observer* critic, St John Ervine, recalled being surrounded by young clusters of Coward's admirers who relished every *mot*.) But it shows him using his experiences of the hunting shires, gained while staying with Mrs Astley Cooper in Rutland. And *The Young Idea* is rare amongst his comedies in suggesting that love and marriage can be reconciled. Wilde had celebrated youth ('Youth has a kingdom waiting for it'), but it was to the other Irish inspiration, Shaw, that Coward had turned in writing *The Young Idea*. Claims of being related to no one but himself were unsustainable. The play was noticeably derivative of Shaw's *You Never Can Tell*; but Shaw did not in the least mind. He saw the manuscript, and returned it to Coward covered with suggestions. He added: 'I have no doubt that you will succeed if you persevere ... never fall into a breach of essential good manners and, above all, never see or read my plays. Unless you can get clean away from me you will begin as a back number, and be hopelessly out of date when you are forty.'[14]

Coward did as Shaw advised; but he was still hopelessly out of date by the time he was forty-five. James Agate, meanwhile, was not uncomplimentary in the *Sunday Times*:

The Young Idea reaches after more than it can grasp – a good fault in a young writer ... It is unusual to find an actor sufficiently interested in plays to undertake the writing of them, and perhaps I may suggest that Mr Coward is not, primarily, a player ... He has spun this play out of his own wit and entrails, but hardly out of human nature. If he will only be content to observe a little more, and give observation back in his own way, he bids fair to become an admirable successor to Hubert Henry Davies and Harold Chapin.[15]

With that golden prophecy ringing in his ears, Coward wrote *The Queen Was In The Parlour* in 1922. This piece of romantic Ruritanian fluff had no part in it for its author, and had to wait until 1926 for production. Maudlin and trite, with a few bad jokes ('She's got sweetbreads instead of brains'), it revolves around the tragedy which can attend royal succession. Nadya is determined to prove that she is unworthy to become queen of Krayia:

Look at me – look at me! A fine Queen I should make – it's ridiculous. I've been to parties every night for the last month – some of them damned rowdy ones. I've been drunk several times – yes, drunk and noisy. I've had lovers, like any of the other women. I went to Deauville with a beastly little Italian last year; we used to have disgusting scenes in the hotel and the casino ...

The play was quickly forgotten. So when, fourteen years after Coward wrote it, the Abdication rocked the country, no one could remember that Coward's play, with a change of names and sexes, had been strangely relevant to its time. And by 1936, Coward's own attitudes towards the Windsors had hardened into contempt. There was no tragedy in their departure, as far as he was concerned. Indeed, he recommended that statues of Mrs Simpson be erected in every English town in recognition of a nation's gratitude for its deliverance.

PART TWO
FAME

Chapter One

While learning to appear poised, in his early twenties, and continuing to develop his persona, Coward realized that there was an art to being photographed, and knew that it was an art he must learn. Most people who pursue the limelight and are regularly subjected to the camera's gaze (actors are an obvious example) learn to attempt a difficult balancing act in which self-concealment and self-projection are evenly matched. It is an essential accomplishment of fame. In the early Twenties, Coward had not fully mastered that control: he was still concentrating on self-concealment, and the photographs of that time do not satisfy: 'There seems an emptiness somewhere, a blandness of expression in the eyes. There is little aggressiveness in the arranged smiles and no impatience apparent at all, and in this the cameras must have lied, for I have always been impatient.'[1]

As his persona was perfected, that impatience was curbed. The intensely neurotic young man eventually disappeared from view as well, although in 1924 it was still apparent that Coward was 'neurasthenic', in the parlance of the time. During his brief spell in the army, he had twisted lengths of string around his finger until he cut himself in order to try and control the nervous tension brought on by the claustrophobia of barracks life and his isolation in it. He suffered serious nervous collapses twice during his early adulthood; and intermittently throughout his life he was plagued by desperate stage-fright. By his early twenties, he had forgotten Esme Wynne's disapproval and started smoking, partly because everybody did it, and partly because it was 'at least an aid to outward nonchalance'. But however much he was prone to nervousness, Coward was suspicious of other relaxants: he tended to avoid anything that might induce loss of self-control in himself, and he deplored the use by others of anything which led to addiction or dependency. Drinking was fattening, it interfered with work, and it was the companion of failures like his father (and, as he later discovered, of moral cowards like Jack Wilson). Other drugs were in frequent and fashionable use after the Great War, but Coward can have been in no doubt about the dangers of their abuse: when he attended a ball given to celebrate Peace Day in 1919, he learnt the next day that one of his fellow revellers, a young actress, had died from an overdose. But if drugs were dangerous, they were also fascinating:

> The fact that we grab each new narcotic
> Can only prove in the end
> Whether our hormones jell or not
> Whether our cells rebel or not
> Whether we're blown to hell or not
> We'll all be round the bend
> From taking Benzedrine, Dexamil,
> Every possible sleeping pill
> To knock us out or knock us into shape,
> We all have shots for this, shots for that,
> Shots for making us thin or fat ...

That American version of 'What's Going To Happen To The Tots?' was written in the Fifties, but a fragment of a play survives from as early as 1918 to testify to Coward's ambivalence about narcotics. One wonders why he abandoned the project: he was not at that time afraid of controversy, as events had already demonstrated. Perhaps he had simply not seen enough then of their use and abuse: whatever his reasoning, he delayed his consideration of the subject for three years, and it was not until the run of *London Calling* that he felt sufficiently inspired or informed to return to the theme. The result, a melodrama which changed theatrical history, was *The Vortex*.

The play had a difficult passage to the stage. It toured several theatrical agents' and managers' offices, and while everyone liked it, no one wanted the young author in the lead part. Coward, however, was writing his way to fame and stardom; and his presence in the production was not negotiable. Finally, a producer called Norman Macdermott, who was eager to promote the work of young dramatists, offered to present either *The Vortex* or the recently completed *Hay Fever*. Coward decided on the former, because it contained a big part for himself, and looked forward to a brief season at Macdermott's converted drill hall in Hampstead. But the difficulties had only just begun. Playwright and producer quarrelled. Despite rigid economies – no actor was paid more than

£5 a week – insolvency was a constant fear and the venture was almost abandoned at one stage because finances were so parlous. Fortunately, a few years before, Coward had befriended a penniless author called Michael Arlen, and now he saw him translated to wealth and fame by the success of his novel *The Green Hat*. This was no time for pride, and he approached him for a loan. In any case, there was an appropriateness to the transaction, since Arlen's work had scandalized the older generation just as much as *The Vortex* was soon to do. With that financial obstacle surmounted, Coward was able to continue with the production. He now discovered, like all dramatists before and since, that leading ladies care little for the rules of team spirit: he wrote the part of Florence Lancaster for Kate Cutler but she took against the play at an advanced stage of rehearsals, thus forcing the author to look for a star to replace her. He was fortunate in persuading the famous Lillian Braithwaite to fill the breach.

Furthermore, there was the hostility of officialdom. At that time, under the Theatres Act of 1843, all new plays had to be approved by the Lord Chamberlain before they were granted a licence for performance, and in the first and more controversial half of his career, Coward was to find himself a regular supplicant at St James's Palace. His adversary for most of this period was the second Earl of Cromer, a former Equerry and Assistant Private Secretary to the King, who had been appointed to the position of Lord Chamberlain – at the recommendation of the Prime Minister, Bonar Law – in 1922. His accession was in many ways a fortunate one: as well as enjoying the trust and friendship of George V, he had a passion for the theatre and, for the times, a liberal conscience. However, when *The Vortex* was submitted to him for approval, his liberalism forsook him:

This picture of a wholly frivolous and degenerate set of people gives a wholly false impression of Society life and to my mind the time has come to put a stop to the harmful influence of such pictures on the stage. The scene in Act III of the drug-taking son upbraiding his mother for the immoral conduct of her life is revolting in the last degree and it is no palliation to the story that the play ends with both mother and son making vows to give up their evil habits ... I am inclined to ban this play entirely.[2]

Sir Douglas Dawson, Comptroller of the Lord Chamberlain's office, was equally implacable: 'Especially in these days the importance [of the stage as a vehicle for propaganda] is intensified when class hatred is preached, not only to the adult at the street corners, but to the children in the Sunday Schools ... a piece calculated to convey the worst possible impression of the social conditions under which we live today.'[3] The play's apparently seditious material clearly confounded the royal household, and Lord Stamfordham, Private Secretary to George V, revealed that the King had seen the manuscript 'and says evidently it is a disgusting play but unfortunately cannot be prohibited'.[4] In his autobiography, Coward claims that he finally secured a licence by persuading Lord Cromer that *The Vortex* was 'little more than a moral tract'. But the Lord Chamberlain may equally have been swayed by the opinion of his reader, who recommended that the play be licensed on the grounds that its motives were 'good', and 'There are certainly people like Florence Lancaster whom it would do good to see how they look to an observer.'[5] (The reviewer for the *Daily Graphic* would have agreed: 'There's some consolation in having grown up before the war. Some critics have complained that Nicky and Bunty are not true to life. I seem to meet them everywhere.')[6] Similarly, another adviser, Lord Buckmaster, defended Coward's social criticism: 'The reason suggested against it is that it holds up to unfair opprobrium the vices of the idle and rich ... The imbecilities of a ballroom and the follies and vices of prosperous and irresponsible people are just as fit a subject for the stage as the coarser vices of poorer folk.'[7]

One way or another, the licence was obtained, and the opening night went into theatrical legend. The young playwright had been sufficiently confident of the drama's cumulative emotional impact to dispense with the curtain-call which traditionally marked the end of each act, so that by the time the play ended – a play which trespassed far beyond the domains of contemporary dramatic acceptability – the audience was in a fever of excitement. Moreover, when sweeping some scent bottles to the ground in the final act, Coward had satisfactorily and conveniently cut himself. He acknowledged the tumultuous applause with bleeding hand and knew that he had a *succès de scandale* on his hands. It was the first night of a long run, with *The Vortex* there and then established as essential and fashionable theatre. The play transferred to the West End on the night of its author's twenty-fifth birthday, 16 December 1924.

The young Terence Rattigan was forbidden to see the play by

his parents, who considered it unsuitable. John Gielgud was not similarly constrained, and Violet Coward must have been delighted when this scion of the Terrys became her son's understudy in the production. He had not liked Coward at their first meeting, finding him 'dreadfully precocious and rather too keen to show off at the piano', but now he was all amazement:

The newspapers were full of Noël Coward's triumph in *The Vortex* at the Everyman Theatre in Hampstead, and so off I went to see it with my parents. In that tiny auditorium the atmosphere was extraordinarily tense, and the curtain of the second act, with Noël sitting in profile to the audience, his white face lifted, chin jutting forward, head thrown back, playing that infuriating little tune over and over, louder and louder, till the curtain fell, was one of the most effective things I ever saw done in a theatre ... after the performance, clattering back in the half empty tube on the long journey home to South Kensington, we all sat silent, in that rare state of flushed exhaustion that only a really exciting evening in the theatre can produce.[8]

Coward's former director, Basil Dean, followed the fashionable throng to Hampstead:

Not having seen Noël since he played an angel in my production of *Hannele* at Liverpool in 1913, I was astonished at his assured touch both as author, director and actor. Here was a formidable talent. His technique was as clear-cut as a diamond, although perhaps a trifle unrelenting. The big scene with Lillian Braithwaite in the last act surpassed in nervous intensity anything I had seen on the stage before.[9]

If Gerald du Maurier, the leading actor-manager of the time, was scandalized ('the public are asking for filth ... the younger generation are knocking at the door of the dustbin'),[10] James Agate, in the *Sunday Times*, was quite satisfied. He found the play's craftsmanship 'beyond reproach' and thought the dialogue 'taut and spare, and of an admirable *vraisemblance*'.[11] He also noted that Coward played on his nerves; and added the celebrated, if apparently irrelevant, caveat, that 'young ladies do not expel smoke through their nostrils.'

Suddenly, Coward was famous and did not stint himself when it came to being interviewed. Having demonstrated, with the production of *I'll Leave It To You*, that he needed no instruction when it came to dealing with journalists, he was now hungry for publicity, and editors did all they could to satisfy him. Inevitably, he was much photographed; one famous series of pictures was taken while the prodigy was making telephone calls in bed and looking singularly dissolute and disreputable, and resulted, as Kenneth Tynan later noted, in 'the myth that he wrote all his plays in an absinthe-drenched coma'.[12] Years later, the persona which crystallized in the Twenties, thanks to the publicity which he courted, became a liability, but now the suggestion of 'advanced degeneracy' which Coward and Fleet Street connived at caught a mood.

He certainly had no need of absinthe: champagne would have been more appropriate, as there was a lot to celebrate. From time to time, we all long to be rich and famous. To be rich, famous *and* young seems too much to ask, but Coward was now all three, and far from dissatisfied with his condition. After years of prudence, extravagance became legitimate, and in *Present Indicative*, he reveals that he spoiled himself with new suits, silk shirts, dressing-gowns and a car. He moved from the attic in Ebury Street to the first floor, and his dressing-room at the theatre, as recalled by Gielgud, glittered with scent bottles and a general impression of opulence. Sudden wealth is easier to get used to than sudden poverty, and it is axiomatic that luxuries can quickly become necessities. But Coward never took wealth for granted: he had been brought up in too much financial uncertainty.

Perceptive commentators like Agate, Basil Dean and Gielgud noted the quality of tension in *The Vortex*. This was partly explained by the tone of Coward's acting. Sybil Thorndike remarked that he could play 'nervous strange people, hysterical people', adding that 'only people who are hysterical can play hysterical parts': 'You see, he could scream!'[13] If Coward gave a performance of scarcely controlled neurotic energy, however, this play also demanded it, because it is a study of tension, its causes and solutions.

Briefly, it is the story, told over three short acts, of Florence Lancaster, an ageing society beauty, and her musically-gifted, highly-strung son, Nicky. She neglects her long-suffering husband, David, in favour of a succession of handsome younger men. The current one, Tom Veryan, is a dull hearty: 'One feels he is good at games and extremely bad at everything else.' When the play opens, Nicky has just returned from Paris, where he has been studying music, with the news that he is engaged to a young girl called Bunty Mainwaring, who turns out to be an old friend of Tom's. Florence is too absorbed in social engagements and Tom to be very interested, although she will inevitably feel jealous of Bunty's youth. A few other characters are introduced to propel the action or provide a change of scene: Helen Saville, ostensibly a cynic, but good-hearted; 'an elderly maiden gentleman' called Pawnie Quentin, one of the many banal homosexuals in Coward's writing; Bruce Fairlight, a dramatist 'the squalor of whose plays is much appreciated by those who live in comparative luxury'; and a singer called Clara Hibbert.

What made the play so sensational was its introduction of a 'drug-fiend'. Nicky, unable to come to terms with the futility of his life, and the emotional vacuum he senses at home, has not only become engaged to a girl he does not really love, but has taken to drugs as well; it was this, at a time when deviation or social defiance, in whatever form, rarely appeared on the stage, which had worried Lord Cromer. But drugs are really peripheral to the play. Although both Helen and Florence are appalled when they discover what Nicky is doing, Coward is not interested in launching an attack on a dangerous habit. He does not concern himself with an individual's right to destroy himself; he has no interest in the symptoms of addiction, and nothing to say about the immorality of drug-dealing, or the mentality of addicts, all matters any modern play dealing with drugs would explore. To Coward, Nicky's addiction is a symptom of, and a cypher for, much larger evils.

To begin with, the society Coward depicts, the society he was just getting to know, seemed somehow wrong. There is a vacuousness and a murkiness to it which he indicates in the detailed stage directions: Act Two, in Florence's house in the country, begins in an environment 'black with cigarette smoke and superlatives'. (Cigarettes, incidentally, are a vital stage accessory in Coward, as essential to his characters as swords are to Shakespeare's.) He is adamant about the futility of his characters' lives. Nicky knows that they 'swirl about in a vortex of beastliness', and resents 'the ceaseless din of trying to be amused'. The point is underlined by the dancing in Act Two, with the record playing at the wrong speed, and Nicky's discordant piano playing, and Coward's direction that 'everyone must appear to be talking at once'. Florence particularly embodies the vanity of it all. Nicky reveals that she

is terribly silly about being 'young' ... but she's been used to so much admiration and flattery and everything always she feels she sort of can't give it up ... And she hasn't anything in the least comforting to fall back upon, she's not clever – real kind of brain cleverness – and father's no good, and I'm no good, and all the time she's wanting life to be as it was, instead of as it is.

Florence also shows a refusal to feel, a fear of emotional commitment, which will later characterize a number of Coward's protagonists. This determination to live on the surface is made most apparent in the climactic scene:

Helen: It sickens me to see you getting back so soon.

Florence: Getting back?

Helen: Yes, to your usual worthless attitude of mind.

Florence: Helen!

Helen: A little while ago you were really suffering for once, and in a way I was glad because it showed you were capable of genuine emotion. Now you're glossing it over – smarming it down with your returning vanity, soon you won't be unhappy any more – just vindictive.

Nicky and Bunty imagine that their generation is more realistic (one notes again the clarion call to the young which Coward had already made in *The Young Idea*):

Nicky: It's funny how mother's generation always longed to be old when they were young, and we strain every nerve to keep young.

Bunty: That's because we see what's coming so much more clearly.

Nicky: Wouldn't it be terrible to know *exactly* – I feel frightened sometimes.

Bunty: Why?

Nicky: We're all so hectic and nervy ...

Bunty: It doesn't matter – it probably only means we shan't live so long ...

Drugs were a way of coping with this weightless and futile existence, where the pursuit of transient pleasure was everything, and where families seemed to offer misunderstanding at best, internecine conflict at worst. (Coward is good at writing the arguments; the scenes of affection between Nicky and his father stick with lack of conviction.) *The Vortex* was not, as Kenneth Tynan memorably described it in the Fifties, 'a jeremiad against narcotics with dialogue which today sounds not so much stilted as high-heeled'.[14] It was a play which dramatized the way in which narcotics might offer a release, though a perilous one, from isolation.

The peace was only five years old when Coward wrote this play, but already, as far as he was concerned, disillusion was rampant. And the values of the smart world to which he had aspired were not only far removed from his own suburban values of hard work, respectability and thrift; they also seemed warped. Even Bunty, more level-headed and intelligent than anyone else in the play apart from Helen, admits: 'One gets carried away by glamour, and personality, and magnetism – they're beastly treacherous things.' But if the play expressed Coward's concern at the lack of moral spine he detected in the early Twenties, it also articulated his own ambivalence. Like Bunty, he was impressed by glamour and personality; in fact, he aimed to impress by them. He was critical of a society, moreover, to which he wanted to belong: no one had forced him to forsake the suburbs for the cocktails and badinage of Mayfair.

The Vortex is an unbelievable play, however, for all the truth of the times that Coward managed to record. The ending, with both Nicky and Florence promising to be true to themselves and each other, to renounce drugs and young men, is quite implausible, and shows Coward sacrificing realism, in deference either to the Lord Chamberlain's sensibilities, or to a melodramatically happy ending. There has been much speculation that the drug addiction is a front, and that Nicky's real problem, which he shared with his creator, was his homosexuality. (Like drug-taking, it was illegal and dangerous.) Coward always refused to comment on this possibility. But if that was his design, he was out of step with contemporary psychological belief, and with typical patterns. Nicky's principal complaint to Florence was 'you've given me nothing all my life'. This was in marked distinction to Freud's belief that it was over-protective mothers who produced homosexual sons, a pattern which Violet Coward and her famous son corroborated.

Chapter Two

The production transferred to the West End, and Coward agreed to write another revue, this time for Charles Cochran, who was to present all of his work until 1934. If Charlot pioneered the revue, Cochran brought the form to highly-polished perfection. He commanded considerable respect in the theatrical world – even his chorus girls were known as 'Mr Cochran's Young Ladies'. His revues were famously daring, and famously topical; and his eye for fresh talent (he 'discovered' Oliver Messel) was as acute as his business sense. The revue which Coward wrote for him, *On With the Dance*, was a success, though nothing now survives of it except its best song, 'Poor Little Rich Girl'. Like *The Vortex*, it was an attack on the listlessness and frantic pursuit of pleasure which Coward saw in contemporary society:

> Though you're a child, dear,
> Your life's a wild typhoon,
> In lives of leisure
> The craze for pleasure
> Steadily grows,
> Cocktails and laughter,
> But what comes after?
> Nobody knows,
> You're weaving love into mad jazz pattern,
> Ruled by pantaloon,
> Poor little rich girl, don't drop a stitch too soon.

Meanwhile, acting as producer, Basil Dean took Coward, and *The Vortex*, to America. The play failed in Washington, but was a great success in New York, where it ran for five months. (It went subsequently to Chicago, where it was interpreted as a comedy, and its author wrote 'Noël Coward died here' on the wall of his dressing-room.) Dean was impressed by the way in which Coward knew what he wanted from Manhattan, and marvelled at 'the manner in which this dauntless young artist of the theatre stood up to the pressure of overnight success. In the ensuing weeks it was fascinating to watch him grasping it by the throat to make it sing his tune.' Coward insisted on a first-night party:

He seemed to know by instinct the right people to invite, although the Social Register was a book not yet opened to him. He provided us with the list of guests, which included most of the younger set who mattered in the theatrical and artistic life of New York. The published list of those present was a striking indication of the impression Noël had so quickly made.[1]

Whether or not New York's theatre-going public formed the impression from *The Vortex* that London society was riddled with degeneracy and self-destruction is not recounted. And whether or not they interpreted the guilty secret of drug-taking as a coded reference to the guilty secret of its author's homosexuality is also difficult to establish. It would have been a topical discovery, because by 1925, Noël Coward was in love.

His love life was necessarily shrouded in secrecy. In the more broadminded world of the theatre, he could afford to be relatively unguarded about his affairs, but homosexuality was illegal, and indiscretions could have terrible consequences. Coward's first biographer, Patrick Braybrooke, wrote in 1933 that 'the literary world at the time of Noël's birth had recovered from the Oscar Wilde sensation and poor Oscar had ten more months in which to look back upon his ruined and shattered life.'[2] This remark was as inaccurate as it was complacent, and overlooks entirely the distorted accounts of love affairs which characterize such roughly contemporary homosexual writers as E. M. Forster, Ronald Firbank or Marcel Proust. Discretion was all-important, and Coward knew it. Today we accept his homosexuality as being as integral to his personality as his cigarette-holders and dressing-gowns were to his persona; and of course, friends, and friends of friends, always knew: as Peter Quennell remarked, 'In my raffish world, it was never assumed that he was anything else'.[3] But most of Coward's public confused him with the figure they saw on the stage – that of the womanizer and heterosexual cad. Looking back on 1930, the writer Alan Jenkins remembered:

I have at last seen *Bitter-Sweet*, whose tunes I have been playing on the piano for months. I am also trying to write songs, and I realize that they are all imitation Noël Coward. In my private fantasy, I *am* Noël Coward:

brilliant, witty, adored by women. I do not yet know that he is homosexual: when I find out, the shock lasts for two days.[4]

As late as 1969, Coward was still doing everything in his power to ensure that his general public knew nothing, or could pretend it knew nothing: when Sheridan Morley wrote his biography, Coward insisted that his private life remain unmentioned.

He never had any bisexual inclinations, a fact which he admitted, half-publicly, in 1969.[5] And from what Esme Wynne (who strongly disapproved of homosexuality) remembered, it can be assumed that he was aware that he was attracted exclusively to men at an early stage of adolescence – at any rate, long before 1923, when he met Prince George. The Duke of Kent, as he later became, was the youngest son of George V, whose belief that 'men like that shot themselves' was as strong as it was inaccurate. Prince George was doubtless aware of his father's opinions, but appears not to have minded them unduly, and seems to have practised bisexuality with as little constraint as his rank allowed. Royal officials were regularly confronted by difficult situations, and on at least one occasion, large sums had to be raised to retrieve letters sent to a young man in Paris. The Prince also liked black women and drugs: his marriage to his Greek cousin Marina in 1934 must have seemed a deliverance throughout Saint James's. Long before then, however, during or soon after the run of *London Calling*, he had an affair with Noël Coward.

Strangely, if Coward was the most famous of Kent's lovers, he was also the most likely to prove reliable and discreet. There was no likelihood here of bribery, though news of the relationship probably reached the Prince's family. The Prince of Wales was 'beastly' to Coward from the start, and the latter's affair with his younger brother may have been the reason.[6] And the same explanation perhaps lay behind Queen Mary's opposition to the friendship which developed between Coward and Princess Marina, after Kent's death in 1942. The 'little dalliance', as Coward called the affair with Kent, demonstrated his determination to get to the top in all endeavours, and he was to go on boasting about it to friends for years afterwards. It was soon over, however, because in 1925, the Prince was supplanted.

John 'Jack' Wilson, born in the same year as Coward, in Trenton, New Jersey, was very handsome. He was a stockbroker when he saw *The Vortex* on a visit to London, and his close attention to the action (and, no doubt, his beauty) attracted the notice of the actors. A few days later, the two men met. John Gielgud, who was understudying as Nicky Lancaster (and who assumed the part when Coward took the original production to New York) remembered being introduced to Wilson in London. 'He was strikingly good-looking, in a beautifully-cut dinner jacket with a carnation in his buttonhole.'[7] Esme Wynne-Tyson, inevitably, also met him: Jack 'was a very nice person ... very nice to talk to; a charming young man'.[8]

Present Indicative, veiled though its account necessarily is, gives the impression that the affair did not begin until Coward was in New York with *The Vortex*. Wilson apparently arrived at the stage door of the Henry Miller theatre, having 'drunk enough' to be able to make the move in the first place, to discover that at first Coward could not remember his name.[9] In later life, Wilson needed a drink before doing anything at all; but in 1925, his handsomeness blinded most people to his flaws, and their consequences. Coward, who at the best of times was an impetuous and often inaccurate judge of character, was dazzled completely, and soon persuaded Wilson to abandon stockbroking and become his personal manager. Only the naïve would fail to see that business managers and lovers are best kept separate, but Coward, outwardly so polished, was naïve. And if he was an innocent concerning emotional relations, the small print of life and its binding agreements bored him. As late as 1936, and the writing of *Present Indicative*, he was still trying to convince himself that the partnership on which he and this inexperienced young stockbroker had embarked was financially fail-safe, and that their original assessments of each other's characters were 'fairly shrewd'. But events did not bear out this claim.

The nature of homosexual love and affairs was much on Coward's mind while he was touring with *The Vortex* – the run was so long and taxing that he vowed later never to appear for more than three months in London, and three on Broadway – and led him to write the experimental *Semi-Monde*. While far from being a good play (the critical consensus at its world première in Glasgow in 1977 suggested that this was not a neglected masterpiece), it contains several details of significance and interest. It is set in the Paris Ritz in 1925, and its huge cast is deployed in a succession of quick scenes. At a time when Coward was writing his way to stardom, it contains no large part for its author – its subject matter was too compromising. Most of the characters seem to be either homo-sexuals or lesbians, and the 'action' of the play is no more than the carousel of their amorous couplings. But the characters are prototypes of Coward's finest comic figures: bored, spoilt and heartless, they would be repellent if their frantic pursuit of love and stability did not also make them vulnerable and pathetic. 'Good-looking people are always difficult to manage,' we are told, and the comment recalls Bunty's remark in *The Vortex*.[10] It is all very Noël Coward, clipped and Twenties.

Underneath its frivolity, however, there is the pessimism which informs much of his comedy: 'We're all silly animals, gratifying our own beastly desires, covering them with a veneer of decency and good behaviour.' The play was denied a licence, inevitably, by the Lord Chamberlain, and pretty much forgotten by Coward himself. But its coincidence in his life with the arrival of Jack Wilson is interesting: perhaps he was subconsciously uneasy about the way in which the glamorous and beautiful used their assets on the credulous and merely presentable; perhaps, Coward, too, was desperately in search of stability and permanence.

This first decade of fame was very frenzied, and the combination of hard work, relentless socializing and keeping up of appearances began to tell on his neurotic disposition. Appearing in London in 1926, in *The Constant Nymph* (a play which, for once, he had not also written), Coward collapsed. Basil Dean, the director, said that the strain resulted from his playing a part that was not an extension of his personality, but it was probably simple nervous strain. He went to America, and joined Wilson on holiday in Virginia, but by the end of 1926 he was totally exhausted, and decided that solitary travel was the only solution (an expedient that he was to adopt regularly from now on). He left San Francisco for Hong Kong, and several weeks in the Far East. In Honolulu, he analysed his condition: 'People were greedy and predatory, and if you gave them the chance, they would .steal unscrupulously the heart and soul out of you without really wanting to or even meaning to.'[11]

It took him some time to act on this realization, however. Cecil Beaton encountered him in New York in 1928, and there is some-thing pathetic in the fraught but friendly young man he remem-bered: 'He was very charming and gracious to me which was touching and I liked him for it, but although he talked hard the entire time he didn't succeed in saying anything amusing or clever. He was extremely badly dressed in trousers too short and his face was sweating at every pore.'[12] The fact was that although his professional life was progressing well, Coward still had no idea what he wanted when he was not on public display. He knew that he could never be entirely alone,[13] and also that he would never have a family. He was very much in love with Wilson, but was separated from him for professional reasons a lot of the time. What is more, the entire business was illegal. And it was that, the keeping up of appearances, which was most crucial and most exacting, because those who did not bother made themselves vulnerable to an uncomprehending and potentially vindictive society. When he and Beaton encountered each other again, on an Atlantic crossing in 1930, the tables were turned, and Coward was critical of Beaton's appearance, but for good reasons:

'It is important not to let the public have a loophole to lampoon you.' That, he explained, was why he studied his own 'façade'. Now take his voice: it was definite, harsh, rugged. He moved firmly and solidly, dressed quietly ... 'You should appraise yourself,' he went on. 'Your sleeves are too tight, your voice is too high and too precise. You mustn't do it. It closes so many doors. It limits you unnecessarily, and young men with half your intelligence will laugh at you.' He shook his head, wrinkled his forehead and added disarmingly, 'It's hard I know. One would like to indulge one's own tastes. I myself dearly love a good match, yet I know it is overdoing it to wear tie, socks and handkerchief of the same colour. I take ruthless stock of myself in the mirror before going out. A polo jumper or unfortunate tie exposes one to danger.' He cocked an eye at me in mockery.[14]

Coward's mental equilibrium may have been subject to turbulence, but his public position during the Twenties soon became established. He seemed synonymous with youth. Donald Neville-Willing first encountered him in *On With The Dance*, and later became the impresario who presented Coward in cabaret after the war. But his first impressions were the most vivid:

One realized that there was something different about Noël; he knew precisely what he wanted, and was ruthless about getting it ... He was a tremendous leader, in that we all tried to follow the way he dressed and talked because we knew it was fashionable. He was a very old young man: important and powerful but fantastically kind in private ... His approval was all that mattered. Though he was our age, he knew it all; he was the first of the bright young things.[15]

He became known as the scourge of contemporary evils, and as the playwright whose concern with truth forced him to shock his audience. A Noël Coward play guaranteed daring dialogue; and daring dialogue happily guaranteed, or at least helped ensure, healthy ticket sales. He was in this respect fortunate in having to contend with the Lord Chamberlain: there is nothing like censorship to foster scandal, and nothing like prohibition to stimulate thirst. His modernism and mockery combined on occasions very successfully. Anna Neagle remembered that when *This Year of Grace*, Coward's revue of 1928, was being rehearsed, the cast had to take lessons from the composer himself in how to dance to the production's best song, the rhythm of which seemed so innovative, and the words so characteristic and true for their time:

> Dance, dance, dance little lady,
> Youth is fleeting – to the rhythm beating
> In your mind.
> Dance, dance, dance little lady,
> So obsessed with second best,
> No rest you'll ever find,
> Time and tide and trouble
> Never, never wait,
> Let the cauldron bubble
> Justify your fate.

Chapter Three

Before *The Vortex*, Coward had found it extremely difficult to persuade any management that his work was worth producing, but now that his name was in lights and his music known in restaurants, he faced no such problems. Producers rushed to put his other plays into rehearsal, and theatre-goers in the mid-Twenties were amazed by his prolific achievement. Some productions were more successful than others. *Sirocco* had been written during Coward's first stay in New York in 1921, but audiences had to wait six years to benefit from its questionable wisdom. A turgid melodrama about an English girl's disastrous affair with a cruel and unscrupulous Italian, it was booed off the stage at its première, despite the starring presence of Ivor Novello.

The first of Coward's plays to demonstrate most convincingly the brevity of expression typical of his maturity is *Fallen Angels*, written in 1923, but produced in 1925. Like *This Was a Man* and *Easy Virtue*, and later, better plays like *Private Lives* and *Design for Living*, it braves one of the taboos of its time: adultery. The script was received at Saint James's Palace with predictable consternation. The reader for the Lord Chamberlain decided that the play should not be performed as it 'would cause too great a scandal. Adultery and unchastity are made light-hearted jokes and even though the whole thing is unreal farcical comedy that will not do.' Unsurprisingly, Lord Cromer himself hated *Fallen Angels* – 'like most of that author's plays, it is unpleasant' – but reluctantly granted a licence for its performance on the grounds that it was 'so much unreal farcical comedy'.[1] When he finally saw it, however, he approached the Bishop of London with a view to assessing the extent of impropriety in the West End.

Lord Cromer's reservations seem to have been more than shared by reviewers: Coward was able to remark with satisfaction that the notices were 'vituperative'. Mícheál MacLiammóir said pertinently that the pains Coward took to describe the *haute cuisine* dinner at the end of the second act betrayed the freshness of his sophistication, but the reaction of other friends and acquaintances was more immoderate. When Esme Wynne-Tyson saw the play, she began to realize quite how far her old friend had come since his early days of pacifism, non-smoking and suburban virtue: 'A specimen of Noël's BAD influence on the thought of our generation ... Before that production, most decent people considered drunkenness in women disgraceful. Afterwards (having been shown by the play as amusing), it became something to snigger at, and/or indulge.'[2] Cecil Beaton quite simply hated it. 'I do think the play will help ruin old Coward. It is quite definite that he won't live long – people will get so tired of him.'[3]

Today *Fallen Angels* appears very self-conscious in its desire to shock: 'It's always the same when sex comes up and wrecks everything. It's a beastly rotten thing.' And its author's awareness of belonging to a generation divorced from the smug proprieties of Victorianism was becoming familiar: 'If you think women didn't discuss everything minutely in the Victorian days just as much as they do now you're very much mistaken.' But vindication of the implication of Beaton's criticism – that vices take hold, and shock wears off, very quickly – came as early as a revival of the play in 1949: Hermiones Gingold and Baddeley found that they had to exaggerate their performances wildly in order to hold the attention of already jaded audiences.

Easy Virtue was written in 1924, produced in America in 1925 and brought to England in 1926. It is a play which it is almost impossible to judge from the page (and with good reason, it is seldom revived). It seems so hackneyed, banal and predictable that one finds oneself thinking that there must be more to it than meets the eye. It found immediate favour with Lord Cromer, who considered it 'a very intelligently written play in the most modern style'[4] and granted it a licence without hesitation. Despite this approval, when the production arrived in Manchester on its way to the West End, the management of the theatre took exception to a title it considered provocative and insisted on the anodyne amendment, 'A New Play In Three Acts by Noël Coward'. When it finally reached London, most of the reviewers found the play outdated, though James Agate in the *Sunday Times* managed to suggest that the young and salacious dramatic iconoclast was at it again. 'The higher the brow the narrower the mind. That is if one is a fashionable young playwright familiar with the tawdry round of the Riviera and unable to conceive a world elsewhere. Give your aesthete a horse he can't ride – and farewell Leicestershire ... there are no moments, apparently, in which Mr Coward, the playwright, refrains from thinking in terms of sex.' Helped no doubt by this rather cryptic and misleading notice, the play ran as well in London as it had done in New York, but the critical consensus that *Easy Virtue* was old-fashioned was correct. The reason is not hard to find. Coward had written one early play, *The Young Idea*, in homage to one of his mentors, Shaw. Now he decided to write another in homage not only to a specific playwright, Sir Arthur Wing Pinero, but also to the tradition of drawing-room drama exemplified by Pinero's best-known work, *The Second Mrs Tanqueray*, of 1893.

But a lot had happened, to the world, to England and to its theatre-goers, between the Boer and the Great Wars, and the moral conventions which the tradition of drawing-room drama had assumed were fading rapidly. (The favourite situation of this tradition, and its leading exponents, Pinero, Galsworthy and later Maugham, was that of the woman with a past – usually involving divorce, or love with a younger man – which was disclosed by compromising letters.) Coward knew that the morality of these plays was antiquated:

It is easy nowadays to laugh at these vanished moral attitudes but they were poignant enough in their time because they were true. Those high-toned drawing-room histrionics are over and done with. Women with pasts today receive far more enthusiastic social recognition than women without pasts. The narrow-mindedness, the moral righteousness and the over-rigid social codes have disappeared but with them has gone much that was graceful, well-behaved and endearing. It was in mood of nostalgic regret at the decline of such conventions that I wrote *Easy Virtue*.

For once, he was not writing in modernity, and certainly not to provide himself with an important part, but out of nostalgia. But he must also have found the idea of a woman with a past intriguing. After all (as John Lahr pointed out in his study of Coward's plays), it was another way of looking at the predicament of the outsider with a guilty secret, a predicament Coward knew all too well. Later, when he came to adapt Oscar Wilde, he chose *Lady Windermere's Fan*, which covers the same ground. It seems plausible that Coward also wanted to express views on the snobbish and narrow-minded exclusivity of English society, a society which he could not yet be said to have penetrated.

The woman with a past of *Easy Virtue* (which the *New York Times* reviewed as '*The Second Mrs Tanqueray* brought down to date') is taken home by her husband to meet his family. Larita is older than John, but is effortlessly charming and attractive. With the exception of John's father, Colonel Whittacker, the family has convinced itself that she is a woman of easy virtue, and the conflict between Larita's bohemian, urban tolerance, and the narrow-minded snobbishness of the shires as embodied by the Whittackers, lours like a thundercloud within five minutes of the opening.

Colonel: He had to marry somebody – she's probably a very interesting woman.

Mrs Whittacker: I've no doubt you'll find her so.

Hilda: She may be frightfully sweet.

Mrs Whittacker: When you've reached my age, Hilda, you'll probably realize that the sort of women who infest French watering-places are generally far from being 'frightfully sweet'.

Hilda: Cannes isn't exactly a French watering-place – I mean it's better than that – I mean everyone goes there.

Colonel: Everything's changing nowadays, anyhow.

Mrs Whittacker: I fail to see that that makes the slightest difference.

Coward makes Larita read Proust, to indicate to the Whittackers that she is dubious and Continental, and to indicate to his audience that he is familiar with the most fashionable novelists of the day. He invests her also with complete charm. But that is the play's problem: its imbalance of loyalties and sympathies is overwhelming. At the climactic confrontation, we know that Larita is going to tell the Whittackers, and provincial England generally, what she, and Coward, think of them. And we approve, but the battle has been too easily won, because Coward has made all the family apart from Colonel Whittacker so odious. (Of Mrs Whittacker, for instance, the stage directions say, 'the stern repression of any sex emotions all her life has brought her to middle age with a faulty digestion which doesn't so much sour her temper as spread it.')

Coward was to return to the class-conscious drawing-rooms of middle-class drama many years later, but by then his views were entirely different. Meanwhile, in 1926, during the first weeks of the affair with Wilson, he wrote *This Was a Man* (and dedicated the published text to his lover). It contains occasional remarks on contemporary society which were all to the good, partly true and partly what was expected of Coward, but they occurred too infrequently. Of infidelity, for instance, we hear:

It's the obvious result of this 'barriers down' phase through which we seem to be passing. Everyone is at close quarters with everyone else. There's no more glamour. Everything's indefinite and blurred except sex, so people are instinctively turning to that with a rather jaded vigour. It's pathetic when you analyse it.

The play's hero, passive, unmemorable and unheroic, is a cuckolded society portraitist (perhaps he owed something to Philip Streatfield), who can only laugh when he discovers that his wife is having an affair with his best friend. This scripted reaction scandalized Lord Cromer, who withheld the licence, and the play has never been performed in England. It was presented in New York though, and at its opening Coward announced that in future he would scribble bland trifles for censored London, and offer only liberated Manhattan the fruits of his serious thought. (Liberated Manhattan was not interested: the first night ended with a near-empty theatre.) Lord Cromer was probably rather tired of Noël Coward by now, but the feeling was reciprocated. Of course the latter invited official rebuke every time he wrote explicitly about promiscuity or drugs, or implicitly about homosexuality, and of course that very disapproval often excited profitable public curiosity. But Coward must have resented the constraints nevertheless, and his occasional outbursts against them are entirely understandable. Shortly after the difficulties with *Easy Virtue*, he voiced his irritation with the double standards of British censorship in the *Sunday Chronicle*:

Almost any day the law courts and police courts reveal the details of some unorthodox human alliance or intrigue. Yet no one makes a shout about it. But let a variation of these same circumstances be translated to a stage play that even sets out to show the wickedness of the thing, and see what an uproar they evoke. See how the Censor will arise in his wrath to smite with his blue pencil ... what I am calling for is a freer stage ... If we must have a Censor, at least let us have one that is able to discriminate between vulgarity and wit.[5]

Inevitably, someone as successful and controversial as Coward intrigued the public, which in turn hoped for information from its journalists. If Coward was keen to ensure that his plays and songs were the talk of the town, however, he jealously guarded his privacy, and reporters often had to content themselves with the usual platitudes: 'Unlike the other successful moderns, Noël has not taken a luxurious flat in Mayfair ... he still lives at home with his people, of whom he is very fond ... he will tell you with pride that whatever success he may have gained he owes entirely to his little mother, his greatest pal, who goes everywhere with him. When he was a small boy, she was the only one to recognize the spark of genius in Noël.'[6] If he was cautious with journalists, Coward was also cautious about putting too much of himself into his writing. Despite occasionally using fragments of his own experience as the basis of his plays – genteel poverty in *I'll Leave It To You*; recollections of Mrs Cooper amongst the hunting shires in *The Young Idea* – he was not an autobiographical playwright, and his autobiography and even the diary he later kept suggest that he was instinctively shy of self-analysis and very circumspect indeed about committing its findings to paper. One's past, except what one chose to show of it, was a private place.

Hay Fever, the first of his major comedies, shows Coward's carefully selective memory at work. Written in 1924 and produced in 1925, it appeared unannounced between the laboured and second-rate dramas which he wrote in his first years of fame. In the presentation copy he gave to Esme Wynne-Tyson, he affected to dismiss it coyly as being 'just a winsome fragment' and in his autobiography he declared that he was unimpressed with it when he wrote it. However, *Hay Fever* is a work of pure delight and originality – the first to emerge from its twenty-four-year-old author's imagination. Furthermore, one can see in retrospect that it marked the point where the fashionable young commentator signalled his potential as a comic writer of enduring worth – but this transformation was not to be achieved by means of autobiographical revelation.

The play was inspired by the evenings at Laurette Taylor's in New York when the young and hungry unknown had watched the actress hold court in her West Side apartment and supervise obligatory parlour games which terrified her guests. Coward was presumably forced into participation in these games and was surely in awe of the famous actress who was his hostess, yet when he came to dramatizing the situation, he created an impersonal comedy, in that none of the male characters in the play bears any resemblance to the author. His preoccupations dominate his characters, however, because his first great comedy – which he wrote in three days – addresses matters on which the precocious and ambitious twenty-four-year-old was already something of an expert: charm, performance and pretence. *Hay Fever* established also the other hallmarks of vintage Coward comedy: rejection of plot; the celebration of frivolity and irresponsibility; and the use of dialogue which is not only brilliantly concise, but relies for its comic significance on the disparity between the spoken words and their real meaning.

Originally and inexplicably called *Oranges and Lemons*, and equally inexplicably renamed (though it is set in June, the month of hay fever), the play takes place over a weekend at the country home of the Bliss family. Judith is a retired but formerly successful actress. Her husband, David, is a novelist. Their son, Simon, is an artist. Their daughter, Sorel, does nothing, but is pretty and charming. They are a talented family. (Noël Coward, an actor, a writer, a painter *and* a charmer, was even more talented, though he never dreamed of doing nothing.) It is made immediately clear that not everyone can join the ranks of the talented. Simon, the most outspoken of the family, insists that 'it's so silly of people to try and cultivate the artistic temperament.' The Blisses' talent is established at the outset, and is seen to be the inevitable partner of selfishness:

Simon: Clara's looking tired. We ought to have more servants and not depend on her so much.

Sorel: You know we can never keep them. You're right about us being slapdash, Simon. I wish we weren't.

Simon: Does it matter?

Sorel: It must, I think – to other people.

Simon: It's not our fault – it's the way we've been brought up.

Meanwhile, their mother is in the garden. This otherwise unremarkable condition attracts suspicion in a family as remarkably urban as the Blisses.

Sorel: Where's mother?

Simon: In the garden, practising.

Sorel: Practising?

Simon: She's learning the names of the flowers by heart.

Judith belongs in the West End, and is as improbable in Cookham as Noël Coward later was in Kent. But Cole Lesley remembered that he liked zinnias, so he must have known more about flowers than Judith:

Judith: Delphiniums are those stubby red flowers, aren't they?

Simon: No, darling; they're tall and blue.

Judith: Yes, of course. The red ones are somebody's name – Asters, that's it. I knew it was something opulent.

Every member of the family has invited a guest down for the weekend, but because they are all so selfish, they are all ignorant of the others' plans. Sorel expects Richard Greatham, a diplomat; Judith, Sandy Tyrell, a young hearty; Simon, Myra Arundel; and David, Jackie Coryton, a young flapper he wants to use as raw material for his novel, *The Sinful Woman*. When this discovery is made, irritation stems not from anxieties about insufficient food, or a shortage of bedrooms, or whether the guests will all get on, but from the fact that each member of the family will be less able to adopt the role chosen to impress the guest. With their conviction that their talent exempts them from society's rules about consideration and tact, the Blisses have no real anxieties about their guests, except in so far as they themselves will be inconvenienced.

Some of the themes and convictions apparent in *The Vortex* are revived. That dreaded Twenties disease, boredom, continually threatens, because the theatrical need attention, and attention can always wander:

Richard: I wanted to come – I've thought about you a lot.

Sorel: Have you really? That's thrilling!

Richard: I mean it. You're so alive and vital and different from other people.

Sorel: I'm so frightened that you'll be bored here.

Richard: Bored! Why should I be?

Sorel: Oh, I don't know. But you won't be, will you? – or if you are, tell me at once, and we'll do something quite different.

In a rare moment of sanity and clarity, Sorel screams, 'we're a beastly family, and I hate us', reminding us that *The Vortex* had established the family as an arena for battle and misunderstanding. Sandy Tyrell is another brainless but good-looking young man, like Florence Lancaster's Tom Veryan. Judith's reluctant farewell to youth and glamour is similar – though comic rather than tragic – to Florence's, while David shares Bunty Mainwaring's doubts about attractiveness: 'You're very attractive, and I'm always suspicious of attractive people, on principle.' But youth, glamour and attractiveness hold a special appeal for the Blisses, because they can combine to charm and seduce.

The Blisses may be ill-mannered; they are not, however, hypocrites. Selfishness is seen as a kind of honesty; 'bad manners', to Simon, indicate a 'lack of social tricks and small talk'. In no time, the guests all find themselves disoriented by the rudeness of their hosts, and subjected to play-acting, flirtation and charm of the most blatant and outrageous variety:

Sandy: It seems too good to be true – sitting here and talking as though we were old friends.

Judith: We *are* old friends – we probably met in another life. Reincarnation, you know – fascinating!

Sandy: You do say ripping things.

Judith effects a similar conquest later with Richard. He then kisses her on the neck, and provokes a noisy, but meaningless display of outrage. Similarly, when Judith catches her husband kissing Myra, she plays the part of the brave heroine defeated by a stronger love than her own. All the guests take these displays, not only on Judith's part, but on the part of her children and husband, seriously. But, as Sorel points out to Sandy Tyrell, it is all a game, and a way of seeing how far role-playing can go in impressing and winning over ordinary people:

Sorel: Don't protest; you know you don't [love me] – any more than I love you.

Sandy: But you told Judith –

Sorel (nonchalantly): I was only playing up – one always plays up to Mother in this house; it's a sort of unwritten law.

Sandy: Didn't she mean all she said?

Sorel: No, not really; we none of us ever mean *anything*.

As Sorel says, it is the unwritten law that Judith's fantasies are always accommodated by the others. She instigates, they follow. But the family's need to show off and to play-act is such that when there is no audience there, they will perform simply among themselves (the favourite escape being a scene from Judith's old stage success, *Love's Whirlwind*: Coward indulges in a brief but brilliant parody of the Victorian melodrama of his youth). There is nowhere, not even home, it seems, where charm and flamboyance can be forgotten. And when the guests are forced to participate in a more formal game of play-acting, the mime game 'In The Manner of The Word' in Act Two, it all ends in tears, with Judith's staggeringly rude, but revealing, remark: 'I think, for the future, we'd better confine our efforts to social conversation and not attempt anything in the least intelligent.' Polite behaviour, and social conversation, have no place in the Bliss household, and are certainly much less important than the ability to charm, and to transform oneself, while entertaining others. *Hay Fever* shows charm and theatricality triumphant: Coward may indicate that the Blisses are tiresome and selfish, but on the whole we laugh with, rather than at, them. What is more, although their current lot of guests, Myra, Richard, Jackie and Sandy, will never return, many others will, because charm can always find its victims.

The play established the sort of comedy that Coward at his best was going to write, and it was not going to be Wildean and epigrammatic. Many years later, as the Grand Old Man of British theatre, he remarked:

It was noted ... that the play had no plot and that there were few if any witty lines, by which I presume is meant that the dialogue is non-epigrammatic. This I think and hope is quite true ... To me, the essence of good comedy-writing is that perfectly ordinary phrases such as 'Just fancy!' should, by virtue of their context, achieve greater laughs than the most literate epigrams. Some of the biggest laughs in *Hay Fever* occur on such lines as 'Go on', 'No there isn't, is there?' and 'This haddock's disgusting'. There are many other glittering examples of my sophistication in the same vein.[7]

It might be added that the work shows another aspect of Coward's astute theatrical sense. His dialogue is so spare that he must be confident that every word of it will work. On the page, *Hay Fever* appears flat, but it has been a success in the theatre now for sixty-five years because Coward knew that his words needed only the additions of intonation and gesture for them to become real and funny.

The play was an immediate success in London, but failed completely in New York. Coward's first biographer, Patrick Braybrooke, writing in 1933, developed a theory that Coward was 'born to a shocked world', and it was therefore only to be expected that war-damaged Europe would understand him better than America. But Braybrooke was not terribly impressed by *Hay Fever* anyway: 'It was an amusing light comedy but was not particularly important in any way. Perhaps it brought out rather necessarily that Coward could still write an ordinary comedy, that if 'depravity' was in part of his mind, it was not by any means in all of it.'[8]

By the late Twenties, critics were trying to define the nature of Coward's work. His relentless self-promotion, the endless photographs that appeared of him in illustrated magazines and his hard work and success made him a difficult figure to ignore. As early as 1925, he had had three productions running concurrently in the West End: *Fallen Angels, Hay Fever*, and the revue *On With the Dance*. He was the influence in accent, appearance, and fashion – he set a trend in polo-necks in his early twenties – which the young respected. And as the writer of comedy, songs and serious drama, he seemed a phenomenon of variety.

Two attitudes prevailed. There were those who saw him as the representative of his age, the commentator best equipped to chastise the follies of the Jazz Age; and there were those who were anxious already about the depth of his thought, and the aim and seriousness of his attacks. Braybrooke himself belonged in the first category.

By 1923 Coward had thought a lot about English society and he was quite evidently not impressed. It amused itself while the rest of the world worked. It was full of nasty old women who loved pasty-faced youths whose main amusement was becoming entangled with other men's wives. It was crammed with tragic people who would not grow old gracefully. He was more cruel than Oscar Wilde and he was more cruel than Oscar would have been had he lived in 1923.[9]

Beverley Nichols saw Coward in the same light. 'Consider his dialogue, smooth, hard, swift pebbles of thought thrown disdainfully against the glass windows of the houses in which we have ensconced ourselves.'[10] But others were reluctant to see him as the nemesis of his age, because they found no substance in his writing. James Agate, of the *Sunday Times*, had given some of Coward's earliest work good reviews, but with the exception of *Cavalcade*, of 1931, he disliked Coward's drama, claiming that he found it as mean with feeling as a moneylender was with money. And St John Ervine said in 1927, writing at the time that *Sirocco* was booed off the stage, 'We must not allow ourselves to be dazzled by his youth.' A couple of years later, he returned to the attack with more determination:

Coward's entire existence has been spent in a corner of the theatre, remote from the general contacts of everyday life. I am amazed and disturbed at the slenderness of his intellectual resources ... we might well wonder whether he has ever read a great book, seen a fine picture or a notable play, listened to music of worth, observed a piece of sculpture or taken any interest in even the commonplaces of a cultured man's life ... his political, social and religious interests are negligible or non-existent.[11]

Throughout his life, Coward loudly proclaimed his indifference to critics and their theories. Towards the end of the decade, for instance, journalists began to elect him the spokesman for the disillusioned post-war generation. Thus Ivor Brown, assessing the Twenties in the *Observer*:

Ten years ago we were all looking for that 'new world after the war'. We had grand hopes of peace and plenty, of democracy fired by a common sympathy, of a new and kindly social order. People trumpeted the word 'Reconstruction' as if it were magic. We had had our disillusions. Reconstruction withered where it grew ... Bravery of thought was replaced by bitterness of mood. It was easy to doubt everything, hard to find acceptable faiths. The younger generation may have been dismayed; but at least it could dance. It turned its back on solemn creeds. It was light of toe, light of touch. Of that period and temper, Mr Coward is the dramatist.[12]

But Coward would have none of this glib association. He had avoided involvement in the war as much as possible, and he was far too politically indifferent to nurture hopes for higher social orders at its conclusion. When he wrote *Present Indicative*, he took the opportunity to press the point: the war, he insisted, 'was little more to me at the time than a dully oppressive background ... the reasons for my disenchantment with life must be sought elsewhere.' He knew what the real causes of his disillusion were – his cynicism about families and his scepticism about the possibility of lasting love in a heterosexual world – although he could not say so. Regarding the other comments critics made, he found it less easy to be dismissive, and usually contented himself with saying that he was only interested in commercial success:

Personally I was a playwright of great promise from 1920 until well into the '30s, but after that the mirage faded and all hope died ... The critical laurels so confidently prophesied for me never graced my brow and I was forced to console myself with the bitter palliative of commercial success, which I enjoyed very much indeed.

But this airy disregard for critical opinion, like so much else of Coward's, was a show. He wrote a short story, 'Penny Dreadful', about a popular writer who was critically denounced, and feeling sometimes flickers in its prose:

He had long ago faced without undue chagrin, that his writing would never be accepted by the literati; in fact he was frequently known to make wry little jokes about this to his more intimate friends. He was aware, however, in his heart of hearts, of a small pang of disappointment. It would be so gratifying, just once in a way, to be praised for his style, to be taken seriously as the eminent writer he knew himself to be ...[13]

If Coward's frequent protestations to the contrary suggest anything, it is that he cared acutely for what critics thought. Never having been taught to respect learning as a schoolboy, he was ill at ease with intellectual minds, and approached them, he admitted, with 'deep-dyed prejudice'. His instincts did not mislead him: intellectuals tended to ask awkward questions, and were not so easily blinded by outward display. Later, in middle age, and especially in his diaries, he began to attack them, since they seemed to condemn not only his work, but everything about England that he admired:

> I wish the intellectuals,
> The clever ones,
> Would go to Russia.
> Those who have University Degrees,
> Those 'Leftist' boys and girls
> Who argue so well
> About the 'Workers' Rights'
> And 'Man's True Destiny' and the delights
> Of equal independence, State controlled.

Let them leave England please
If our traditions hold
No magic for them; if new Gods compel
Their very new allegiance, let them go.[14]

In the late Twenties, that hardening of attitude was still a long way off. But now, while critics were asking how long Coward's work would last, he moved one step further from the social criticism which had informed much of his most memorable early writing, and began to court wider acceptance. As the Twenties drew to a close and the Thirties began, and life gradually but perceptibly became more gloomy, he turned to costumed escapism, and the comforting shadows of the past, to entertain. He first toyed with period romance in *The Marquise*, a romantic comedy set in eighteenth-century France, which he had written for Marie Tempest, the actress who had played Judith Bliss. A great success at the time, it is no longer revived, being riddled with sentimentality, cliché and pat coincidence.

Most of his comedies, or rather those set in his own time, tend to be pessimistic about the motives of love and the possibility of its survival. They also refuse to contemplate a love affair between people of different classes. His period plays are the opposite: the lovers usually struggle across the great social divide between rich and poor and, as often as not, they will live happily ever after. *The Marquise*, of 1926, fulfils both these schemes. *Conversation Piece*, of 1934, contains a young English lord in love with a penniless French girl. In *Operette*, of 1937, the young English lord is in love with an actress. Whether they end happily or not, the costumed plays diverge interestingly from, say, *Private Lives*, *Design for Living* or *Blithe Spirit*. Those plays dramatize the condition of lovers who are not only social equals, but who have lived together before, and have failed. Love, for them, is not the great and glorious thing that it is for the deluded creatures of Coward's period romances. No violins throb, no sunsets blaze for Elyot and Amanda; for Leo, Otto and Gilda; for Charles and Elvira Condomine. For them, love is painful, difficult, complicated; but it is also the lesser of two evils, since solitude is unthinkable. For Coward, the unreality of period romance allowed him to envisage dramatic and emotional situations that his instincts told him were improbable.

The most successful of all his retreats into the past was *Bitter-*

Sweet, which he began in 1928, and which opened to scenes of almost unprecedented excitement in London and New York in 1929. The story of doomed love between a rich young lady and her music teacher, it was blatant nostalgia, and the biggest success of Coward's career to date. Its most famous song, 'I'll See You Again', confirmed his gift for poignant and romantic lyrics. More than that, the great success of the project confirmed not only what uncanny luck Coward had, but his gift for anticipating popular mood. Just as his coming of age had coincided (to quote John Lahr) 'with the arrival of youth as a new and demanding force in English society',[15] so now it was as though he sensed the longing for romance and escapism, as the frenzy of the Twenties died down. If his auto-biography is to be believed, the idea fell into his head after hearing a recording of *Die Fledermaus* and his shrewd commercial sense told him that 'there had been little or no sentiment on the London musical stage for a long while ... It seemed high time for a little romantic renaissance.'[16]

Whether it was simply an urge to write romantic operetta, or whether it was a carefully calculated attempt to dispel as lucratively as possible the gloom which followed the General Strike, *Bitter-Sweet* could not have come at a more appropriate moment. It is built around the familiar structure of an opening and an ending set in contemporary time, with the central episode a flashback. It begins at a dance in London given by the elderly Lady Shayne. As her young guests begin to Charleston, she interrupts them: 'Stop – stop – it's hideous – you none of you know anything or want anything beyond noise and speed – your dreams of romance are nightmares. Your conception of life is grotesque. Come with me a little – I'll show you ...' She sings and we are transported back to the London and then the Vienna of the 1870s, and her doomed love affair with Carl Linden.

Had it been attempted ten years before, or ten years later, *Bitter-Sweet* would have failed. In 1919 it would have jarred with the intense, if short-lived, relief that followed the ending of the war. In 1939 it would have seemed an idle distraction. With unerring precision, or luck, Coward chose the one time in the dark corner of the inter-war years when his project would prosper. The noise and speed which Lady Shayne mentioned ended with a Crash: Coward's indictment of the feverish Twenties came at the exact moment when Wall Street fell and the pavements of Manhattan were thought to be littered with skyscraper suicides. (Coward, incidentally, was lucky: Jack Wilson – whether from shrewd judgement, or simply a belief in unadventurous investment – had only put his lover's money in gilt-edged securities, rather than speculating. Several members of the cast of *Bitter-Sweet* were less fortunate and lost large sums of money.) Despite that, tickets changed hands at the opening in New York for $150 each ('thirty pounds!', Coward translated gleefully for his mother). A police cordon had to be arranged to restrain the first-night crowds and traffic, and the show was soon grossing $55,000 a week. In London, the first night had been equally rapturous: 'Tiara'd women clapped till the seams of their gloves burst; the older generation could say with more complacency than truth that this was the way they had fallen in love, and the younger generation were wondering if in rejecting romantic love they might not have missed something.'[17] The operetta had an immediate effect on fashions: nostalgia prevailed, and hemlines dropped that autumn.[18] Altogether, the production was seen by nearly one million people in England alone.[19]

Chapter Four

'Too much urbanity is limiting,' Coward remarked in his auto-biography. Although he was incurably urban, he had already discovered in 1926, during his nervous collapse in Honolulu, that it was imperative that he escape the tensions of city life from time to time. With fame came wealth, and he was able to travel more often, and to secure a retreat in the country in England. He rented Goldenhurst Farm, in Kent, in 1926, and bought it, along with its surrounding one hundred and fifty acres of land, in 1927.

He greatly enlarged it, and dutifully installed Violet and Arthur Coward there, along with his two aunts, Ida and Vida. There were terrible rows, but it seems to have been a generally happy home, and Coward was to remember it nostalgically from the tropical exile of his middle and old age. Weekend invitations were amongst the most highly coveted accolades in British showbusiness; but although press supposition had it that these house parties were orgies of theatrical abandon, they were in fact sober affairs, with cocoa and early nights a regular feature. The ownership of Goldenhurst instilled in Coward a lifelong passion for Kent, and many of the characters in his plays live there. (Characteristically, however, he shows absolutely no interest in the dramatic evocation of Kent life.) In 1930, he also acquired a new home in London, a large artist's studio in Gerald Road, near Eaton Square, which he was also to keep until he left England.

To maintain equilibrium however, retreating to the country was not enough: like Amanda, he felt that 'foreign travel's the thing'. In 1929, having seen *Bitter-Sweet* settle down to steady success, Coward decided to return to the Far East, this time with Lord Amherst, who had been his companion on his first trip to New York in 1921. They went to Honolulu, Yokohama, Tokyo, Shanghai, Hong Kong, Haiphong, Saigon, Angkor, Thailand, Bangkok, Singapore, Kuala Lumpur, Penang, Ceylon (where they stayed with Eric Coward), and thence home via Marseilles. Some aspects of exotic travel never change, and Amherst fell prey to dysentery.

Other aspects do, and Coward was able to report that they were very impressed by the 'admirable' French administration, which seemed to ensure 'excellent coffee and rolls in the remotest villages'.[1] Bored by sightseeing, he was free for quite a lot of the time to indulge in his favourite relaxation: working. He wrote well during this holiday, producing *Private Lives*, *Post-Mortem* and 'Mad Dogs and Englishmen'; and although he was never an acute observer, he still absorbed details of a vanished tropical and colonial life which he was later able to use in songs and poems:

> These little men who travel far
> Drinking forlornly at the bar
> 'This is my round' and then 'One more'
> 'Stop me if you've heard this before'
> Each one endeavouring to cap
> The story of the other chap.
> From Trinidad to Panama,
> From Brindisi to Zanzibar,
> From Alexandria to Crete,
> These lethal raconteurs compete.
> The loudest laugh, the coarsest joke,
> Each shouting down the last who spoke,
> Each straining more and more
> Insensately to hold the floor.[2]

If Coward relied on travel to restore his balance and energies, rather than to broaden the mind, he eventually came to realize also that it had fixed his attitude towards his own countrymen abroad. He had his generation's unswerving faith in England's uniqueness and importance. When, after the Second World War, he saw the collapse, not only of the British economy, but also of British imperialism, he reacted by closing his eyes and writing plays that continued to insist on England's colonial and financial might. He drew the material for these later plays from his extensive travels around the world in the Thirties, because they had taught him all about the daily existence – in its remotest corners – of the servants of Empire: of the incestuous cocktail parties and tennis matches; of the clubs with chintz armchairs and yellowing back numbers of *Country Life*; and of the homesickness in remote hill stations.

Coward seemed to be able to write almost anywhere: perhaps it was something to do with his boundless self-confidence (or his

devotion to hard work and its facilitating gift for concentration).
Later in life, he claimed that Jamaica offered him the most pro-
pitious creative environment, but that assertion is contradicted by
the catalogue of his achievement. There was no particular chair, or
typewriter, or room with a view, which proved magically con-
ducive to fine work: Coward was peripatetic, but his muse was
never homesick. *The Vortex* was written in London, while *Hay Fever*
was completed in a rented cottage in Kent. *Present Laughter* was
also written in Kent, but in a different house, and one which Coward
owned, while *Blithe Spirit* was the business, strangely, of a holiday
in Wales. *Design for Living* was begun and completed while its
author was sailing up the Pacific coast from Panama to Los Angeles;
but it was in a hotel room in Shanghai (which used to bear a
plaque commemorating the occupancy – perhaps it still does), that
immortality beckoned, and Coward wrote *Private Lives*. He was
recuperating from influenza brought on by the unremitting pressures of his public life, and his new play concerned two couples
recovering from divorce and marriage, and the pressures of their
private lives.

Once he had thought of a subject, Coward wrote the play with
his customary speed and effortlessness. Inspiration, however, had
not come easily. The Orient did not capture his imagination: there
had been blizzards in Yokohama, heavy rain on the road to Tokyo,
and Tokyo itself had seemed very dismal. Glamour, and warmth,
were very important to Coward, so it is not surprising that in these
uncongenial surroundings he found his mind wandering to the
south of France, then glamorous beyond question. One evening,
according to *Present Indicative*, the longing was particularly insistent, and he lay in bed unable to think of anything other than
Gertrude Lawrence, dressed by Molyneux, and unhappy in the
south of France.

He had promised to write a part for her when she had been a
partner in his revue days, but, apart from seeing her in other
people's plays, he can have had no measure of her dramatic abilities.
She was determined to prove herself as a serious theatre actress
(which is partly why she later resisted the overtures of Hollywood),
but at this stage she was still relatively untried in comedy and
drama. Besides, if contemporary accounts are to be believed, the
most glib and determined of playwrights could be forgiven for
finding her charm and her style as daunting to his ambitions as it

was inspiring. To Binkie Beaumont (who first met her during the run of *Private Lives*), she was bewitching:

She had a radiance which lit up like a lighthouse whenever she appeared. Your couldn't take your eyes off her, she glittered and sparkled like a Christmas tree. She never gave the same performance twice and sometimes she could be very naughty and irresponsible, but at her best she was sheer magic and there was nobody who could give you the same thrill.[3]

Cecil Beaton, however, detected more disconcerting ambiguities:

She was the distaff personification of this new charm. Though not a great beauty, she used her gifts to heighten her attractiveness and possessed the flavour and personality of the age to a high degree. She was a combination of remarkable contrasts. Her mellifluous voice was yet rather curdled. Her somewhat simian features were sunburnt. The long, loose-fitting dresses she wore suggested more than an indication of the vital, well-shaped figure beneath them: she could look remarkably provocative in a dress that covered her body almost completely. She smoked cigarettes with a nuance that implied having just come out of bed and wanting to get back into it.[4]

If such an amalgam represented a challenge to most playwrights, Lawrence's fellow performers – unless brilliantly protean – must also have found her intimidating. Coward was not a versatile actor; and it is an indication once again of his extraordinary self-confidence, helped by the fact that he too 'possessed the flavour and personality of the age to a high degree', that he was able to write the part of Amanda for Lawrence – the part for which she is remembered – and play opposite her without suffering eclipse.[5]

The play (set eventually in Deauville, rather than on the Riviera) takes its title from Amanda's – and possibly Coward's – forlorn realization that 'very few people are completely normal really, deep down in their private lives'. Having wondered what sort of dramatic mood or convention would best suit Lawrence, he opted for comedy, for the good reason that he preferred watching it and performing it (and was very much better at writing it). After *Hay Fever*, however, the comedy here is much more ambiguous. (The Lord Chamberlain, in granting *Private Lives* a licence, was wearily suspicious of its exact nature, and felt that it 'can hardly be regarded as a moral play ... at the same time it is not in any way indecent.')[6] At first, the situation Coward outlines – that of a divorced couple,

Elyot and Amanda, who coincide while on honeymoon with their new partners, Victor and Sybil – looks distinctly farcical. But farce, with all its frantic concealments under beds and in wardrobes, is preoccupied with respectability, and its comedy is generated by the *semblance* of bad behaviour, not by bad behaviour itself. But Elyot and Amanda behave wickedly. When they meet, five years after their divorce, they know that they do not love Sybil and Victor. 'That old black magic', as Coward later called it, overcomes them, they realize that they are in love and elope to Paris, where Amanda conveniently has a flat.

For 1930, this was outrageously dangerous behaviour. They may hope occasionally to contain the damage:

Elyot: What shall we do if they suddenly walk in on us?

Amanda: Behave exquisitely.

But such respectable behaviour is beyond their natures and their understanding. This is most emphatically not a farce (a dramatic form with which, anyway, Coward had little sympathy, as he later showed when he came to adapt Feydeau).

Instead, it marks an important stage in its author's development as a dramatist. It continues the indulgent depiction, begun in *Hay Fever*, of characters who, by virtue of their wit, glamour, beauty or charm, consider themselves exempt from conventional manners and from the morality of the majority. The Blisses were Coward's first experiment with egotism. Amanda and Elyot are more incorrigibly selfish; and while they are equally funny, they are less comic, because they confront a less accommodating world than that which the Blisses occasionally encounter. Selfishness interested Coward, perhaps because he understood it. With *Hay Fever* he discovered that he could capture it well in dialogue. From now on until after the Second World War (when all his plays preach something or other), whenever Coward wrote pure and undidactic comedy, he found laughter in selfishness and egotism. The claim on our sympathy of figures like Elyot and Amanda is that there is something pathetic and childlike in their search for self-gratification. The claim on our interest is that they are reflections, albeit distorted, of their creator. Elyot and Amanda are typical of Coward's comic figures in another way: they are incapable of living together or apart – a predicament which would receive further examination in *Design for Living* and *Blithe Spirit*.

95

Coward wrote the part of Elyot Chase ('about thirty, quite slim and pleasant-looking') for himself. It was the first of several parts which he engineered to help him project publicly the role of womanizer, adulterer and heterosexual cad. The arrangement worked well in the theatre, where disbelief is meant to be suspended: he was given a sort of camouflage, while his audiences could consider him *risqué* but not unacceptable. Coward's stage persona was enamelled, flippant and cynical, as well as being irresponsible and very slightly sexually dangerous. Elyot Chase fully conforms to this type. Nevertheless, despite this flippancy, there is an unmodified sadness at the heart of *Private Lives*. More directly and more unequivocally than any of his other plays, it articulates Coward's pessimism about domestic and emotional permanence, a pessimism which the complications of his sexuality compounded.

Amanda: What's so horrible is that one can't stay happy.

Elyot: Darling, don't say that.

Amanda: It's true. The whole business is a very poor joke.

Elyot: Meaning that sacred and beautiful thing, Love?

Amanda: Yes, meaning just that.

Although Coward and Wilson were inseparable at this time, there was no knowing how long it would last, and what infidelities there might be before the affair ended. Pain, and the desire to inflict it, was almost a part of being in love:

Elyot (viciously): I was madly in love with a woman in South Africa.

Amanda: Did she have a ring through her nose?

Elyot: Don't be revolting.

Amanda: We're tormenting one another. Sit down, sweet, I'm scared.

Coward must have known about jealousy, because he wrote well about it: all the couples in his comedies of love suffer it acutely. And like Elyot, who gives full reign to his testiness – his remark to Sybil, 'I should like to cut off your head with a meat axe', is not mere badinage – he could be very nasty. Joyce Grenfell knew him quite well later in his career, although her feelings about him were always ambivalent. She saw his vindictive side on several occasions:

He made a sharp and beastly attack on Dick [Richard Addinsell, her close friend and collaborator] for writing film music. Noël hates movies and radio but even so it was unkind ... Noël ... can't resist hurting where he knows it will make the most sting. It's a form of bullying and power ... one of those strange complex things that have some psychological reason ... it was cruel of Noël and what's more he knew it. You could see him doing it deliberately. I wonder if he has a heart?[7]

Elyot and Amanda are not heartless, but they dread emotional commitment because of the vulnerability it entails. Depth in anything is better avoided, as far as they are concerned, so charm substitutes for engaged feeling, and banter is their preferred manner of speech. In Act Three, the uncomprehending bore, Victor (like Tom Veryan and Sandy Tyrell, another hearty, there to be manipulated and ridiculed), fails to understand why:

Victor: If you don't stop your damned flippancy, I'll knock your head off.

Elyot: Has it ever struck you that flippancy might cover a very real embarrassment?

In one way, *Private Lives* is a tragi-comedy about two irresponsible people determined to live on life's surface with minimum inconvenience and romantic liability, but who – perhaps to their credit – feel deeply for each other. (Noël Coward lived predominantly on life's surface, obsessed as he was with stardom, fame and glamour. His adoration of his mother was absolute; so, at that time, was his adoration of Jack Wilson, but this was a love that could not speak its name.) Concealment of feelings, rejecting the significant for the frivolous, and all with great style – these were the preoccupations of Amanda, and Elyot, and perhaps of Coward too. It is no accident that the famous balcony scene, where mention of love is nervously avoided, is the best thing in the play, perhaps in all Coward's work, because it was written from the heart:

Amanda: Don't: I feel terrible. Don't leave me for a minute, I shall go mad if you do. We won't talk about ourselves any more, we'll talk about outside things, anything you like, only just don't leave me until I've pulled myself together.

Elyot: Very well. (There is a dead silence.)

Amanda: What have you been doing lately? During these last years?

Elyot: Travelling about. I went round the world you know after —

Amanda (hurriedly): Yes, yes, I know. How was it?

Elyot: The world?

Amanda: Yes.

Elyot: Oh, highly enjoyable.

Amanda: China must be very interesting.

Elyot: Very big, China.

Amanda: And Japan –

Elyot: Very small.

Amanda: Did you eat sharks' fins, and take your shoes off, and use chopsticks and everything?

Elyot: Practically everything.

Amanda: And India, the burning Ghars, or Ghats, or whatever they are, and the Taj Mahal? How was the Taj Mahal?

Elyot (looking at her): Unbelievable, a sort of dream.

Amanda: That was the moonlight I expect, you must have seen it in the moonlight.

Elyot (never taking his eyes off her face): Yes, moonlight is cruelly deceptive.

Amanda: And it didn't look like a biscuit box did it? I've always felt that it might.

Elyot (quietly): Darling, darling, I love you so.

Amanda: And I do hope you met a sacred Elephant. They're lint white I believe, and very, very sweet.

Elyot: I've never loved anyone else for an instant.

Amanda (raising her hand feebly in protest): No, no, you mustn't – Elyot – stop.

Elyot: You love me, too, don't you? There's no doubt about it anywhere, is there?

Amanda: No, no doubt anywhere.

David Pryce-Jones, reviewing a revival of *Private Lives* many years later, insisted that the scented and moonlit world which Coward evokes was far more glamorous than the reality ever was, and that the play was escapist even to its author. He may have been right: after all, Coward had not been rich or famous that long, and was still seeing the smart world with eyes of some wonder. But that in no way invalidates the drama, which is preoccupied with surfaces, attractiveness, and a nervous turning away from what lies beneath. Thus Elyot:

... Let's be superficial and pity the poor Philosophers. Let's blow trumpets and squeakers, and enjoy the party as much as we can, like very small, quite idiotic school-children. Let's savour the delight of the moment. Come and kiss me darling, before your body rots, and worms pop in and out of your eye sockets.

Amanda: Elyot, worms don't pop.

Coward considered *Private Lives* 'a shrewd and witty comedy, well constructed on the whole, but psychologically unstable'. The principal psychological instability lay with the portrayal of Victor and Sybil, who are no more than puppets, there to enable the action, such as it is, to progress. But Coward knew that no audience would complain about that, and suspected that, with judicious casting of the wooden secondary couple, the play could be a great success.

The young and struggling Laurence Olivier was summoned to an informal interview. Coward was not always an accurate judge of character, but where quality and ability were concerned, he often showed the exceptional man's ability to distinguish his peers from the crowd. What little he had seen of the young actor's work had impressed him: John Mills talked to Coward backstage during the opening performance of *Private Lives*, and remembered that Coward prophesied Olivier's future greatness. If Coward had got the measure of Olivier, however, Olivier was still far from under-standing Coward. Offered the part of Victor Prynne, he fought instead to play Elyot Chase, underestimating to a charming extent Coward's thirst for the limelight. When he arrived for his interview, he found the youthful prodigy conforming to press report by busying himself at ten o'clock with breakfast in bed. Coward prom-ised Olivier that, after *The Vortex* and *Bitter-Sweet*, he was about to produce his greatest success yet.

Seats for the opening night were an exorbitant £2 4s. 6d., but the three-month season in which Coward and Lawrence appeared, before transferring the production to New York, was a great success. Their ensemble performance vindicated Lawrence's original suggestion that they should appear in one of his plays together, and made all Coward's efforts worthwhile. T. E. Lawrence saw the production and was very impressed: 'I could not always tell when you were acting and when talking to one another,' he wrote.[8]

Arnold Bennett called Coward 'the Congreve of our day' (a double-edged commendation in Coward's eyes, since he was so fond of insisting on his own uniqueness, and disliked Restoration comedy anyway). Others were less hasty to acknowledge the immortality of his endeavours. Ivor Brown, writing in the *Observer*, proved again that clairvoyance is not a required skill in theatre critics:

The brilliance of the business lies in Mr Coward's capacity, as producer and as actor, to persuade us that his lines are witty and that his thin little projections of humanity are the real and triumphant clowns of eternal comedy. He does persuade us. He enormously entertains ... Within a few years the student of drama will be sitting in complete bewilderment before the text of *Private Lives*, wondering what on earth those fellows in 1930 saw in so flimsy a trifle.

Well, they saw Mr Coward as actor and producer and they saw Miss Gertrude Lawrence; in short, they saw a species of magic.

Like *Hay Fever*, *Private Lives* has never been out of production since its première. The staccato dialogue (Mrs Patrick Campbell remarked famously that Coward's characters talked like typewriters), the concision, the ellipsis of his writing, all became famous and much imitated. Introducing an American edition of *Easy Virtue*, *Fallen Angels* and *Bitter-Sweet* in 1929, Somerset Maugham had assessed the playwright's position:

For us English dramatists the young generation has assumed the brisk but determined form of Mr Noël Coward. He knocked at the door with impatient knuckles, and then he rattled the handle, and then he burst in ... since there is no one now writing who has more obviously a gift for the theatre than Mr Noël Coward, nor more influence with young writers, it is probably his inclination and practice that will be responsible for the manner in which plays will be written during the next thirty years.[9]

Chapter Five

He was the embodiment of success now, an arbiter of style, an important playwright, the voice of youth, the man of the moment. With *The Vortex*, he had arrived, and by 1930 it was obvious that he had remained. Harold Acton, remembering that the noise of the gramophone challenged ordinary conversation, observed that a new tendency was abroad in society: 'The talkative devised a special basic English in which to shoot wisecracks at each other in the style of Noël Coward.'[1] His example was pervasive; and even his old adversary, Cecil Beaton, had to concede the wide domain of his popularity:

In the rise of the whole new spirit of affectation and frivolity, the influence of the theatre was far from negligible. By the later '20s young women gave up speaking in mellifluous tones in favour of cigarette-throat voices, rasping and loud. Men enjoyed imitating the exaggerated, clipped manners of certain actors and adapted the confident manners of those who were aware of their charm ... Noël Coward's influence spread even to the outposts of Rickmansworth and Poona ... All sorts of men suddenly wanted to look like Noël Coward – sleek ... clipped and well-groomed, with cigarette, a telephone, or cocktail in hand.[2]

But if, according to Beaton, there was emulation in Poona, in London there was also ill will, for the successful are never without enemies. Coward's determined alienation of the Sitwells – who were well-connected – was reckless, and there were plenty of other people who triumphantly saw through his eager charm. James Lees-Milne thought him 'red in the face, assertive'.[3] To Emerald Cunard, he was 'the artful dodger of society'.[4] To Chips Channon, he was 'flattering (he is an arch-flatterer), insinuating, pathetic and nice. I have never liked him so much, though he talked mostly about himself. At length, after many compliments and vows of eternal friendship, he left.'[5]

Generally, however, Coward's years of strenuous social-climbing had equipped him with a wide circle of wealthy and influential acquaintances and friends. Wilde had learnt that all the wealthy and influential friends in the world count for nothing if one's behaviour and values do not conform. Coward, however, was less of a rebel (or a determined reformist) and had a stronger urge to belong. Even as he was making his name in his revues by mocking the Establishment (a harlot of a word, but somehow irreplaceable), and by glancing, half in amusement, half in disparagement, at the young and fashionable, and enjoying the outraged fame of the provoker, he was also earning a less controversial success as a writer of love lyrics. He continued to goad and taunt for the rest of his life, but the conformist and the conservative in him wanted to be heard too, and eventually Coward came to champion the established order. The process did not happen suddenly, nor was it planned with foresight. In fact, it could well have been something of an accident.

Shortly after writing *Private Lives*, while travelling in the Far East, he had encountered a group of strolling players, The Quaints, in Singapore. Coward never needed much encouragement where showing off was concerned, and he was prevailed upon to appear as Stanhope in the troupe's forthcoming production of R. C. Sherriff's *Journey's End*. It was a work which was sufficiently emotional and direct to appeal to the novice who had written *The Rat Trap*, and to the budding propagandist who would later create *In Which We Serve*. The experience fermented in his mind and while sailing home, between Ceylon and Marseilles, he wrote his own play about life in the trenches of the Somme, *Post-Mortem*.

'To the historian,' Desmond MacCarthy remarked in 1930, 'the year 1930 will be remembered chiefly as that in which men's emotions first began to turn against the war.' In fact, that process was well under way by the late Twenties. The decade may have begun with a frantic pursuit of pleasure, certainly amongst the more moneyed strata of society, but it ended with an inevitable chorus of reminiscences, laments, exequies and excoriations of the First World War. 1927 saw T. E. Lawrence's *Revolt in the Desert*; 1928, Cummings's *The Enormous Room* and Blunden's *Undertones of War*; 1929, Aldington's *Death of a Hero*, Remarque's *All Quiet on the Western Front*, Graves's *Goodbye To All That*, and Hemingway's *A Farewell to Arms*. Coward read a lot of this war literature after acting in Sherriff's play, which also appeared in 1929. One could speculate cynically that with *Post-Mortem* he was not only making use of a strong dramatic idea which *Journey's End* had given him, but was also making a bid to join the ranks of a new and fashionable literary school. Yet Coward had purported to be a pacifist during World War One; the vehemently anti-war play which he wrote in 1930 was not inconsistent with the views of the young man who, a dozen years earlier, had so admired Shaw's pacifism, and who had urged friends facing conscription to claim conscientious objection.

Revolving around the temporary return to the living of the ghost of a soldier killed in the trenches, *Post-Mortem* contains Coward's first use of the supernatural as a dramatic device. The ghost wants to assess the nature of the peace, and the effectiveness of the sacrifice he was called on to make:

Now I must know something about Peace, I must know whether by losing so much we have gained anything at all, or whether it was just blind futility like Perry said it was, I must know whether the ones who came home slipped back into the old illusions and are rotting there, smug in false security, blotting out memory with the flimsy mysticism of their threadbare Christian legend, or whether they've had the courage to remember clearly and strike out for something new.

Of course, the world to which the ghost returns, that of 1929, is already one of rampant disillusion, with the idea of a war to end war already becoming a poor joke. His former fiancée, now consorting with worthless socialites, resents his criticism of her apparently empty life and friends: 'You died young, who are you to judge, you hadn't yet found out about everything being a bore.' And Perry, the radical hothead he had known in the trenches, delivers the play's most memorable philippic:

They'll all start itching for another war, egged on by dear old gentlemen in clubs who wish they were twenty years younger, and newspaper owners and oily financiers and the splendid women of England, happy and proud to give their sons and husbands and lovers, even their photographs. You see, there'll be an outbreak of war literature in so many years, everyone will write war books and war plays and everyone will read them and see them and be vicariously thrilled by them, until one day someone will go too far and say something that's really true and be flung in prison.

Coward's former mentor, Esme Wynne-Tyson, a lifelong pacifist, considered *Post-Mortem* his finest achievement. Eager for other opinions, he sent a copy of the script to T. E. Lawrence, who was also impressed:

It's a fine effort, a really fine effort. I fancied it hadn't the roots of a great success. You had something far more important to say than usual, and I fancy that in saying it you let the box-office and the stalls go hang. As argument it is first rate. As imagination magnificent: and it does you great honour as a human being.[6]

Whatever others thought, however, its author was not content, and *Present Indicative* is ready with urbane apologies. Coward declared that his intentions in writing the play were the 'purest', but despite that, it contains some of his 'worst' writing. His explanation is that although he wrote with conviction, a 'lack of detachment' and of 'real experience of my subject' clouded his dramatic sense. All that may have been true, but lack of thematic clarity or reasoned argument had not stopped him before, as *Easy Virtue* and *The Vortex* had demonstrated. 'Lack of real experience of my subject' has afflicted many writers, but they have usually endeavoured to overcome the problem by exercising their imaginations. *Post-Mortem* is certainly not a good play, but it is not a work of which its author need have felt deeply ashamed. It is written with great fluency, and what it lacks in subtlety, it gains in dramatic impetus. Yet it was not presented, despite being superior to some of Coward's more anodyne productions of the Thirties. It is difficult to know why. Perhaps Lawrence's feeling, that he had 'let the box-office and the stalls go hang', occurred to Coward too, and disturbed him. Perhaps he wanted to be seen to be as good as the young writers who had just addressed the same theme. Many of them, however, had written from experience, and therefore had greater licence to write seditiously. Perhaps Coward felt that *Post-Mortem* would offend popular taste. Perhaps, like *Semi-Monde* before it, he suspected that it could prove too great a threat to his career. It was risky enough being homosexual, but even more dangerous to be a homosexual writer who dramatized life in the trenches, but whose only battle during the First World War had been to get out of it as soon as possible.

In a sense, *Post-Mortem* – as a provocative work – was true to the young Noël Coward. The innuendo of *Fallen Angels* and the sexual preoccupation of *Easy Virtue* had shocked the older generation; the pacifism of his war play, had it been produced, would have done the same. Yet suddenly, within a year of writing it, he had completed *Cavalcade*. He had confided to the impresario Charles Cochran, whose faith in him was 'absolute', that he wanted to embark on something more lavish, and the result, more ambitious by far than anything he had attempted before, and probably more successful, was this patriotic epic. The starting-point for the play had eluded him at first, as it had done with *Private Lives*; but he was eventually inspired by some photographs of soldiers departing for the Boer War. When *Cavalcade* finally came to the stage in 1931, amazing Londoners with its scale, it had become a patriotic 'highlights from history' play, which exactly encompassed Coward's own life, from New Year's Eve, 1899, until New Year's Eve, 1929.

He makes his audience relive the events of these traumatic years through the fluctuating fortunes of two families, the affluent Marryots and the below-stairs Bridges. (The device was one he returned to when he presented another national chronicle, *This Happy Breed*, nine years later. The use of a family as the focus of an audience's sympathies was not in Coward's time the hackneyed trick it is today. Cinema and television have made us wearily familiar with the sight of ordinary families tossed on history's turbulent tide. It is not Noël Coward's fault that *Cavalcade* at times seems uncannily like *Upstairs, Downstairs* without Hudson.) Suddenly, his protagonists are respectable and hard-working. They would not gallivant around Europe, like Elyot and Amanda, nor would they discuss adultery, like Jane and Julia in *Fallen Angels*. They were not the 'Children of the Ritz' or the 'Poor Little Rich Girls' of the songs. The people on whom they were based knew nothing of the frenzied urge to enjoy and forget which had swept Park Lane in the Twenties. They did not belong to the entourage which swirled around the Prince of Wales, nor to any of the other higher echelons of society which, to a greater or lesser degree, turned a blind eye to Coward's unglamorous origins, his proscribed sexuality, his blatant currying of aristocratic and royal favour, because he wrote clever dialogue and melancholy lyrics. (The Prince of Wales's favourite song was 'A Room With A View'.) They were ordinary. *Cavalcade* is important, not because of its artistic merits or influence, but because it marks its author's decision to court a new audience: the Backbone of England.

He liked to say that the remarkable success of this epic was entirely fortuitous, and that instead of stumbling across pictures of the Boer War in the *Illustrated London News*, he could have found photographs of any of the other apocalyptic events that had made the history of his own times so turbulent. But he chose pictures of British soldiers, and they inevitably led to a story of British heroism. *Cavalcade* opened just before a general election returned the strongly Conservative national government to power in 1931, and the coincidence not surprisingly led many to suppose that Coward had hoped to influence electoral sympathies. *Present Indicative* denies the charge. How closely he did follow political developments at this stage it is impossible to say. If he was aware of the implications of the approaching general election, it is improbable that he would have had any radical thoughts on the matter. But he had an acute instinct for sensing, even anticipating, popular mood. He had proved it once as the spokesman of disillusioned youth, and would prove it now with his endorsement of patriotism and populism. One should remember also that whatever changes he had wrought in his exterior, he shared intuitively the responses of respectable south London (and was to do so increasingly as he aged) towards a spectrum of symbols, problems and institutions: capital punishment, the royal family, intellectuals, socialists. He could look at events like the Great War, the General Strike, the first Labour government, the ensuing abandonment of the gold standard – all of which would have been unthinkable forty years before – and gauge, emotionally if not intellectually, the impact of such changes on ordinary opinion. *Present Indicative* reveals that his original scheme had entailed moving the young and privileged of the Nineties against the history of the time, and culminating with their children's reaction to the events of the Twenties. But the bright young things were discarded suddenly: 'My vehemence against them had cooled.' Possibly: but Coward was also a shrewd populist, and he knew that Florence Lancaster or Elyot Chase would be inadequate dramatic cyphers for his purpose.[7]

Cavalcade is unique amongst Coward's plays in its dependence on visual, rather than verbal, seduction. He used many popular songs to evoke the different periods of the play – vindicating Amanda's remark about the potency of cheap music – but relied principally on dramatic staging of huge crowds: troops departing for the Boer War, or Armistice night in Trafalgar Square. He showed great stage flair, however, in realizing that small numbers could be as eloquent as large ones. The scene of Queen Victoria's funeral was justly celebrated: the cortège was placed off-stage, and a handful of on-stage spectators were left to express the gravity and dignity of the occasion. The statistics of the production generated much press excitement: the enterprise cost an unprecedented thirty thousand pre-war pounds. It kept nearly four thousand people employed in the dark days of 1931, and over a year took £300,000 at the box-office.

Coward did not waste his time, and tried not to waste his audience's, so the play opens with an immediate affirmation of the importance of patriotism. Robert Marryot and his butler are both going to fight. The womenfolk have no interest in the principles that lie behind the war, and are fearful only for their husbands' lives. Marryot reminds his wife, half in jest, that 'Britons never, never shall be slaves'. Bridges, cavalier with consonants and vowels like all Coward's below-stairs characters, recapitulates John Bull's views about the balance of imperial power and the duties of global sovereignty:

Ellen: What's the war for, anyhow? Nobody wanted to 'ave a war.

Bridges: We've got to 'ave war every now and then to prove we're top-dog –

Ellen: This one don't seem to be proving much.

Bridges: 'Ow can you tell sitting at 'ome 'ere safe and sound? 'Ow can you tell what our brave boys are suffering out there in darkest Africa, giving their life's blood for their Queen and country?

In Scene Four, Mafeking is relieved, and the large on-stage crowd sings 'Auld Lang Syne'. But as the new century progresses, we see the changes it brings about in the fortunes of its two families and come to understand that the Victorian age was a time of golden stability. The Bridges decide to leave domestic service and set up a pub in the East End. In no time, Bridges himself is an incorrigible drunk, and soon dies in a road accident. The Marryots' elder son, Edward, gets married. Unfortunately, he and Edith go on their honeymoon in the *Titanic*. Before the ship weighs anchor, the couple wonder how happy they will be together, and draw comparisons with Edward's parents. But Edith, like several of Coward's characters before her, is aware that her generation seems different: 'They had a better chance at the beginning. Things weren't changing so swiftly; life wasn't so restless.' World War One breaks out, and

Coward's stage directions again show a highly-developed theatrical sense:

Above the proscenium 1914 glows in lights. It changes to 1915, 1916, 1917 and 1918. Meanwhile, soldiers march uphill endlessly. Out of darkness into darkness. Sometimes they sing gay songs, sometimes they whistle, sometimes they march silently, but the sound of their tramping feet is unceasing.

The Marryots' younger son, Joe, has been having an affair with Fanny Bridges who, like Coward himself, has escaped her background by going into showbusiness. Ellen Bridges thinks that they should get married. Jane Marryot is not so sure; but as her former parlourmaid points out, times have changed:

Ellen: I suppose you imagine my daughter isn't good enough to marry your son; if that's the case I can assure you you're very much mistaken. Fanny's received everywhere; she knows all the best people.

Jane: How nice for her; I wish I did.

Ellen: Things aren't what they used to be, you know – it's all changing.

Joe dies shortly before the war ends, so the problem is left unresolved. *Cavalcade* ignores the Twenties altogether: the action jumps from 1918 to 1929, and the last scene occurs in a nightclub. Fanny Bridges is singing:

> Blues, Twentieth Century Blues, are getting me down.
> Who's escaped those weary Twentieth Century Blues?
> Why, if there's a God in the sky, why shouldn't he grin?
> High above this weary Twentieth Century din,
> In this strange illusion,
> Chaos and confusion,
> People seem to lose their way.
> What is there to strive for,
> Love or keep alive for?

Stage directions indicate: 'Noise grows louder and louder. Steam rivets, loud speakers, jazz bands, aeroplane propellers, etc., until the general effect is complete chaos.' Darkness falls and a Union Jack appears above the stage: the evening ends with the entire cast singing 'God Save The King'.

Cavalcade reads tritely, but amidst its jumble and ambiguity, one thing was clear – its author was holding up the Victorian age as a time of unexampled prosperity and harmony; modern times, by comparison, seemed mean and unsettled. He was celebrating that very age which the dancing Twenties had so proudly and so self-consciously superseded. The play had nothing new to say; indeed it was its very rejection of novelty that made it remarkable. As the Thirties progressed, an increasing number of English intellectuals, and certainly some of the most prominent young writers of the time, saw socialism as a remedy for contemporary ills. Not all of them went as far as Cecil Day Lewis, who joined the Communist Party, but Oxford and Cambridge developed a reputation, in the press at least, as centres of political extremism, and the Oxford Union passed its famous resolution, only two years after *Cavalcade* opened, that: 'This House will in no circumstances fight for its King and country.' (The young Terence Rattigan voted in the motion's favour.) But at the beginning of the decade, Coward seemed to be espousing patriotism and conservatism.

Let's couple the Future of England with the Past of England. The glories and victories and triumphs that are over, and the sorrows that are over, too. Let's drink to our sons who made part of the pattern and to our hearts that died with them. Let's drink to the spirit of gallantry and courage that made a strange Heaven out of unbelievable Hell, and let's drink to the hope that one day this country of ours, which we love so much, will find dignity and greatness and peace again.

That famous last speech, which toasts England's glorious past, and her glorious future, without establishing how the two might be connected, is remarkably woolly. But it sounded right: at thirty-one, Coward was showing a nervous middle class that not all the young men of England were radical. On the opening night, leaving no room for ambiguity, his curtain speech ended with the ringing invocation: 'I hope this play has made you feel that, in spite of the troublous times we are living in, it is still a pretty exciting thing to be English.' Shortly after *Cavalcade* opened, the entire royal family attended a performance, and in so doing appeared to sanction the play's conservatism. The *Daily Telegraph* reported their attendance:

Not since Armistice night, perhaps not since Mafeking night, has there been such a tumultuous demonstration of loyalty. Thousands of people surged around the theatre, and the appearance of the King, followed by the Queen and other members of the Royal Family, was the signal for a demonstration that will be historic.

There was talk that Coward would be knighted that evening.

Not for the last time, such speculations were premature. But there were consolations. It now seemed that he could do no wrong commercially; and he was very proud of his promotion from fashionable writer to spokesman of patriots. The *Daily Mail*'s response to the pageant was not untypical: 'It is a magnificent play in which the note of national pride pervading every scene and every sentence must make each of us face the future with courage and high hopes ... Drury Lane has come into its own again – our national theatre has a theme worthy of itself.'

Shortly before he died, Coward insisted in a radio interview that the thought of mocking England 'would shock me to the core'. 'I'd never dream of doing so,' he added.[8] He may genuinely have felt that in 1972; but opinions change and harden with time, and many of the friends he had known before fame were convinced that he had written *Cavalcade* as a joke, to mock British patriotism and the Empire spirit.[9] The fact that the play is virtually contemporary with *Post-Mortem* lends weight to their suspicion, since it is quite plausible that he wrote a serious advocation of pacifism, and an ironic tribute to patriotism, in the same frame of mind. Perhaps both were experiments designed to test popular mood (Coward's pen was nothing if not swift and slick), and when *Cavalcade* proved such a success, he embraced patriotism rather than pacifism. At any rate, he could not have believed in both plays in 1930. One of them must have been dishonest, unless his opinions at that time were exceptionally volatile. Whatever, *Post-Mortem* was never professionally produced, while *Cavalcade* became one of his proudest achievements. The new telegram address for the studio in Gerald Road was 'Cavalcade, Knights, London', and he often used to parry criticism or irritation from friends by saying, 'Don't shout at me, I wrote *Cavalcade*.'

Chapter Six

Coward's conviction that he was more a writer than an actor allowed him to step aside from the world of the theatre for the occasional appraisal. 'Theatrical people are notoriously facile of emotion, and frequently victimized by their own foolish sentimentality,' he once observed. His success, coupled with his sublime self-confidence, may have encouraged him to suspect that he was unique; but that suspicion apart, he also had a considerable sense of *esprit de corps* where actors were concerned. During the casting of *Cavalcade*, he tried to ensure that those actors who had been most severely affected by the aftermath of the Crash were given work before others, and there are numerous stories of his kindness to less prosperous colleagues. Implicit in his many pronouncements on the obligations of stardom was a belief that actors should not let their profession down – a belief that Irving would certainly have approved. When Sir Gerald du Maurier died in 1934, Coward happily succeeded him as President of the Actors' Orphanage, a position he held with distinction and success until 1956. He found its finances in a parlous condition, but with energy and hard work, restored them.[1] During the war, he was responsible for evacuating the orphans to America. It also fell to him to organize numerous fundraising midnight matinées, and to continue the Orphanage's famous garden parties.

This commitment to the theatre did not extend, however, to writing parts for a wide variety of actors. Apart from Marie Tempest, for whom he wrote *The Marquise* following her success in *Hay Fever*, and Gertrude Lawrence, his most famous inspiration, he only wrote for one other dramatic talent, that represented by the combined skills of Alfred Lunt and Lynn Fontanne. Since his first encounter with them in New York in 1921, they had gone on to become one of the biggest successes of Broadway. In 1932, they reminded Coward of the plan they had all made of appearing together in one of his plays, and *Design for Living* – 'pure Coward' to the Lord Chamberlain's office – was the result.

111

Whereas Gertrude Lawrence was an intuitively brilliant interpreter of Coward's comedy, the Lunts were meticulous and highly-respected professionals whose perfectionism was celebrated. Their talents demanded very different writing, and one notices at once that *Design for Living*, for all the brilliance and slickness of its dialogue, appears almost verbose by the side of *Hay Fever* or *Private Lives*. In other respects, it recapitulates the themes which those plays have already made familiar: the bohemian life, the impulses of selfishness in conflict with the manners of the outside world and the destructive obsessiveness of lovers. It also attempts to dramatize two issues very close to its author's heart – the pressures of fame, and unorthodox sexuality.

It has the small cast which Coward could best deploy in comedy: there is one secondary character, Ernest, an art-dealer, and what he calls the 'three-sided erotic hotch-potch' of Leo, a playwright, Otto, a painter, and Gilda, with whom they are both in love. Otto, Leo and Gilda, like the Blisses, are gifted and selfish – Ernest complains of 'a ruthless egotism, an utter disregard for anyone's feelings but your own'. They are also bored by conformity. Otto remarks: 'We are different. Our lives are diametrically opposed to ordinary social conventions; and it's no use grabbing at those conventions to hold us up when we find we're in deep water. We've jilted them and eliminated them, and we've got to find our own solutions for our own peculiar moral problems.' Unlike Elyot and Amanda, they declare their love for one another, and their selfishness, by their loquacity and their insatiable appetite for self-analysis.

Otto: So many words! That's what's wrong with us! So many words – too many words, masses and masses of words, spewed about until we're choked with them ... I'm sick of this endless game of three-handed, spiritual ping-pong – this battling of our little egos in one another's faces!

And like Elyot and Amanda, or the Blisses, or Garry Essendine or Elvira Condomine (or, perhaps, Noël Coward himself), their flippancy is defiant, and their refusal to be serious about anything is determined:

Gilda: It doesn't matter enough about the small social situations, those don't concern me much, anyway. They never have and they never will. I shouldn't feel cosy, married! It would upset my moral principles.

Leo: Doesn't the eye of Heaven mean anything to you?

Gilda: Only when it winks!

They have the inconstancy and impatience of children. In Coward's words, they are 'unable to share the lonely outer darkness, and equally unable to share the light without colliding constantly and bruising one another's wings'. Like Elyot and Amanda, they have never developed emotional self-sufficiency, and at the same time know nothing of the give-and-take, or the mutual trust, of maturity. They dread isolation, but dread also emotional commitment. Thus Gilda: 'The only reasons for me to marry would be these: to have children; to have a home; to have a background for social activities, and to be provided for. Well, I don't like children; I don't wish for a home; and I can't bear social activities, and I have a small but adequate income of my own.'

If these characters are not mirror images of their creator, they are certainly the types he wrote about best and most happily. At the same time, they represent a degree of wishful thinking on his part. However much he was conspicuous through his wealth, flamboyance and stardom, Coward behaved with propriety. He may have wanted to flout convention, like Elyot, Amanda, Judith Bliss, Otto, Leo, or Gilda, but he knew better than to try.

If *Design for Living* looked again at the comic clowns Coward knew best, it contained a stronger element of autobiography than his earlier comedies. The Thirties saw him putting more of his own experience into his drama: *Cavalcade*, history measured by Coward's own lifespan, began the process in 1931; *This Happy Breed* and *Present Laughter*, which looked at what Coward had been born, and what he had become, were the culmination. When Leo's play finally strikes success, for instance, Coward had only to remember his own exhilaration when *The Vortex* made him the talk of the town. By 1933, however, having endured the strain of publicity, and the nervous collapse of 1926, he knew as much about the penalties of fame as he did of fame itself. He gives Leo a wisdom which he himself acquired only through experience:

Leo: ... It's inevitable that the more successful I become, the more people will run after me. I don't believe in their friendship, and I don't take them seriously, but I enjoy them. Probably a damn sight more than they enjoy me! I enjoy the whole thing. I've worked hard for it all my life. Let them all come! They'll drop me, all right, when they're tired of me; but maybe I shall get tired first.

Design for Living anticipates *Present Laughter* in its analysis of fame, but it is a much more serious, almost pessimistic play. Fame, says Coward's alter ego, Leo, is wonderful:

Let's make the most of the whole business, shall we? Let's be photographed and interviewed and pointed at in restaurants! Let's play the game for what it's worth, secretaries and fur coats and de luxe suites on transatlantic liners at minimum rates! Don't let's allow one shabby perquisite to slip through our fingers! It's what we dreamed many years ago and now it's within our reach.

It is wonderful for talent and energy to be acclaimed, but success means acceptance by society, and Gilda knows that that usually compromises individuality: 'I laughed too loudly just now at the thought of Leo being rich and rare. Too loudly because I was uneasy, not jealous. I don't want him to be any different, that's all.' Success attracts enemies and imposes conditions of behaviour; it is 'far more perilous than failure, isn't it? You've got to be doubly strong and watchful and wary.' And Leo eventually concedes: 'It's all a question of masks, really; brittle, painted masks. We all wear them as a form of protection; modern life forces us to ...'

Fame means that one has no privacy, that sexual nonconformity is more fraught with risk. *Design for Living* is typical of Coward's comedies in its lightness of plot. But what does not happen in it is as revealing as what does. He can just get away with making Gilda have an affair with Leo and with Otto, but he knew that the final, and obvious, permutation, an affair between Leo and Otto, was out of the question. The most he could hope for was that the possibility would flutter, unformulated, in the minds of his audience:

Otto: Thank God for each other, anyhow!

Leo: That's true. We'll get along, somehow – (his voice breaks) – together –

Otto (struggling with his tears): Together –

Leo (giving way to his, and breaking down completely): But we're going to be awfully – awfully lonely –

Design for Living is a melancholy play, for all its comic cleverness. Coward said that the title was 'ironic rather than dogmatic': certainly he – with his insistence on discretion and order – would never have lived in such a bohemian fashion, careless of public opinion and cavalier with the spoils of success. In a sense, the play disappoints, because it provides no answer to its central question, of how to live and love without being conventionally domesticated or creatively emasculated. It also sees Coward too dependent on his brilliance with dialogue (which, *The Times* said, 'dips and swings and glitters'): there is a feeling that there is less here than meets the eye.[2] Nevertheless, with its impressive and popular cast, the play beguiled Manhattan in 1933; and in 1939 in London (where the production marked the photographic début of Angus McBean), despite having a different cast, it ran comfortably for over two hundred performances.

In contrast to the muddled bohemianism of Otto, Leo and Gilda, Coward's life, for all the Atlantic crossings, the star-studded parties at Gerald Road and the weekends at Goldenhurst, was as ordered and routine as he could contrive. He rose early every morning and worked hard until lunchtime. The afternoons he would spend in reading the morning's achievements to his guests or the household he had gathered round himself, or else in self-education, making good with Dickens and the Brontës the deficiencies of his earlier schooling. If he was appearing on stage in the evening, he would rest every afternoon. While he was in England, or in America, a second place of home and work, this discipline was inflexible. Holidays were for relaxation, but even then Coward often reports that a song, or a play, or an idea for a sketch, has slipped onto paper.

He had the enduring conviction of his background and his time that only hard work brought enduring contentment. Fame was more important to him than money (which he prized more for the security it seemed to promise than for the baubles it could buy) but the two seemed inseparable. In 1932, under a headline 'The World's Richest Writers', the *Daily Express*, putting Coward's earnings at £50,000 per annum since 1929, declared that his income was greater than Shaw's or A. A. Milne's, and that he was the richest writer in the English-speaking world. Fleet Street's claims were always audacious, but there is no doubt that Coward had been immensely successful. (Sheridan Morley estimates that his earnings from *Bitter-Sweet* alone amounted to £250,000.) If he had been born a happy miser, he could have supervised the management of these earnings himself, but the particulars of prosperity bored him and he was happy to leave investment to Jack Wilson. This arrangement (which, after all, had shielded him from loss during the Wall Street Crash) worked so well that in 1933 he decided, or allowed himself to be persuaded, to venture into management. In later life, Coward talked of having been cheated by Charles Cochran, the impresario who had presented his work since 1928; and it was perhaps that conviction, reasonable or not, which precipitated the departure from Cochran's management. If the latter had been guilty of any malpractice, however, Coward was to discover that he had also been extremely professional: theatrical management, he soon learned, was less easy than it looked, and his next two decades were to pass under the shadow of financial difficulty.

He ended his partnership with Cochran with *Conversation Piece*, a romantic musical set in Regency Brighton. It was a success in 1934, though any hopes that Coward had of repeating the lucrative triumph of *Bitter-Sweet* went unrealized. Now, like all of his costumed escapism, it seems unrevivable. The dialogue suggests Hollywood period drama at its worst, and it takes little to imagine George Sanders or Basil Rathbone mouthing the part that Coward himself played: 'No, I have merely transformed myself, owing to hard circumstances, from an effete aristocrat, into a cunning and unscrupulous adventurer.' However, the play contained one good song, a coded declaration of authorial intent, 'I'll Follow My Secret Heart'.

In his letter of severance to Cochran, Coward stated that he considered management an inevitable development in his career. But, from the first, John C. Wilson Ltd was beset with problems, and Coward's Midas touch seemed to have forsaken him. *Design for Living* was successfully sold as *Sérénade à Trois* in France[3] and in that same year, 1934, Laurence Olivier appeared under Coward's direction in *Theatre Royal*, an American comedy loosely based on the Barrymores. That, too, made money, but *Biography*, by S. N. Behrman, in which Coward again directed Olivier, failed to repeat its Broadway success. Olivier was inclined to blame the director:

Towards the end of rehearsals, I found myself wondering what Noël ... was up to; Ina [St Clair, the principal actress] never lacked for speed or sharpness of performance, and here he was hastening her and hastening the play which was a reasonably tranquil thing ... Noëlie had always been a termagant about speed, but now he seemed to be getting a bit paranoiac with his tempo ... The play went for nothing, or very little.[4]

Costly failures, Coward learnt, sometimes came in pairs. *Point Valaine*, his second play tailor-made for the Lunts, was an abject

Arthur Sabin Coward.

Violet Agnes Veitch.

The Young Noël Coward. His sailor suit proclaims his naval ancestry.

Noël Coward with his younger brother Eric.

Coward, incomplete but unmistakable, photographed by Esme Wynne in 1917.

Noël Coward photographed with Philip Streatfield in Cornwall on the eve of the First World War.

Coward's dressing-gowns became more opulent with fame. On the back of this early picture, taken in about 1925, and sent to Esme Wynne-Tyson, Coward wrote: 'Oh I *am* a naughty girl!'

Coward and Esme Wynne at the height of their collaboration in 1917.

Like a film star: the young Jack Wilson.

Coward with Wilson and Gertrude
Lawrence at Goldenhurst in about 1936.

The embodiment of youthful style and success. Coward in about 1927.

The most famous theatrical partnership of its day: Coward and Lawrence as Elyot and Amanda in *Private Lives*.

Coward was an incessant and glamorous traveller.

OPPOSITE ABOVE The closing tableau of *Design for Living*: Coward with Alfred Lunt and Lynn Fontanne.

OPPOSITE BELOW The pressures of fame were relentless. Coward with Princess Marina at the annual Actors' Orphanage garden party in 1937.

Coward inspecting the costumes for *Operette*. With him is Gladys Calthrop.

For victory: Coward auctions gifts from the Duke and Duchess of Kent in 1941.

Coward and Graham Payn relaxing in Bermuda.

A tropical paradise: Graham Payn, Cecil Beaton, Coward, Mrs Jack Wilson and Mrs Ian Fleming in Jamaica.

OPPOSITE ABOVE Coward never doubted that stars are different. He is photographed here with Gina Lollobrigida, Margot Fonteyn and Roberto Arias in 1959.

OPPOSITE BELOW February 1970, and Coward – accompanied by Gladys Calthrop and Joyce Carey – receives a knighthood.

Coward as he will be remembered: to an entire generation the paragon of style and effortless sophistication, here in Las Vegas in 1955.

failure. Critics had made much of the variousness of his work: when he was not writing polished dialogue, it seemed, he was contriving the score to a musical, acting or writing amusing songs. One of the dangers of fame is that one begins to believe the endless praise, and with *Point Valaine* Coward decided to test his reputation for versatility by trying to write a play in the manner of Somerset Maugham (to whom it is dedicated). Set in the British West Indies, it is the turgid and improbable tale of a doomed love between a young man and an older woman. The theme, Coward later saw, was 'neither big enough for tragedy nor light enough for comedy'. One of the characters, Mortimer Quinn, is a writer who could have said interesting things about the creative process, but does not:

Linda: ... You see something, perhaps, because you are a writer, and it's your job to make little dramas out of people.

Quinn (meekly): I sometimes make little comedies.

Linda (ignoring his interruption): But what you see needn't be anywhere near the truth.

Quinn: It needn't be, but it occasionally is.

No one wanted to know. Coward nearly quarrelled with the Lunts over the affair, and the play, surviving less than eight weeks in New York (it did not come to London until after the war), lost a great deal of money. He had gone into partnership with a man whose principal credential lay with his handsome looks, but as a result of that partnership Coward now found himself, for the first time in ten years, badly in debt. It was an extraordinary situation, not least because he had shown in his management of the Actors' Orphanage that he understood good husbandry. He lived well, but was not profligate; but now, despite being one of the highest earners of his time, he was forced into retrenchment. His secretary, Lorn Loraine, informed Violet Coward of the position in April 1935:

We have got to go very, very easy on money and economize rigidly wherever it is possible. Mind you, I am pretty sure the shortage is only temporary and would never have arisen if it were not for the fact that all Noël's personal earnings have to go into a special tax account as soon as they are received. Still, the fact remains that money is definitely tight and has been for some months. Both the bank accounts have overdrafts and there is very little coming in just now – a good deal less than has to go out.

Unfortunately, these reversals in prosperity coincided with a lean period creatively. There was no drop in the quantity of work Coward produced in the middle and late Thirties, but there is a fall in its level of invention.

One way of making money which was open to Coward was in films. He would have been a box-office attraction in many British films of the period, and he was certainly well-known enough in California to have been welcomed by the major studios. Unfortunately, Coward disliked films. Even though he had only acted in one, *Hearts of the World*, nearly two decades before, he had a conviction that the process of cinematography annoyed him and that only a theatre audience could elicit his theatrical best. But, in 1935, he had second thoughts. If his agreement to appear in *The Scoundrel* was a concession to his financial problems, it was an ineffectual one, as he was only paid $5,000, a fraction of the sum he could have commanded in Hollywood. Coward said he was excited by the prospect of acting opposite Helen Hayes, who was originally to have been the female lead – in the event, her part was taken by Julie Haydon. But it is more likely that he was attracted by the excellent part of Anthony Mallare, which could have been written with Coward in mind, and which served well the persona of the heartless womanizer he found it expedient to project.

The working title of the film, which was the work of Ben Hecht and Charles MacArthur, was *Miracle on 49th Street*. In 1933, Hecht, whom Coward had met through the New York critic Alexander Woollcott, filmed *Design for Living*, after that project had been rejected by Ernst Lubitsch, who considered Coward a 'cheap vaudevillian' and *Design for Living* a play of derivative wit. Coward hated Hecht's adaptation (which contained only one line from his original script), but was impressed by its successor, *Crime Without Passion*. The films which Hecht and MacArthur completed in the Astoria Studios on Long Island, despite being made for Paramount Studios, were self-consciously removed from the more formulaic entertainments of Hollywood, and *The Scoundrel* particularly was a film for New Yorkers.

It was based on an unpublished play by Hecht and his wife called *All He Ever Loved*, and was the story of a Don Juan moving in Manhattan's literary and publishing worlds. Anthony Mallare, based partly on the publisher Horace Liveright, a friend of Hecht's, is vindictive to lovers and clients alike. Abandoning his current passion for an innocent poetess, Cora Moore (Julie Haydon), who had been engaged to an aviator, he then jilts her for a pianist who is his match in invulnerability and indifference. He pursues her to Bermuda, but the plane crashes and he dies. Miraculously, he returns. As an unmourned spirit he cannot hope for eternal rest and must therefore find someone to weep for him. He has only a month, and on the last day he finds Cora and her fiancé, who shoots Mallare and then himself. Mallare invokes divine intervention to restore the aviator, Cora cries for Mallare, and he then dies a happy soul.

The film was notable for its excellent depiction of the literary world of Manhattan, a world 'bonded together by a mutual interest in literate insult, drinking, and very bored seduction',[5] and for the appearance of Alexander Woollcott who, thinly disguised as himself, played Vanderveer Veyden. Above all, however, it offered Coward a flamboyant role which, if not professionally challenging, was well written, and which he could interpret with panache. And the portrayal which emerged offers what is now the most telling documentation of his persona, for Mallare shared his cynicism, his bored philandering, his enamelled ego and the charm with which he could conquer with the best of Coward's own comic heroes. Basil Dean, directing Coward in *The Second Man* as far back as 1928, had marvelled at the finish of the young actor's manner: 'There were no accidentals. Every effect was sharp and clear as a diamond. By way of minor example he had already learned – no one more effectively – how to use the cigarette as an instrument of mood, punctuating witticisms with a snap of his lighter, and ill-temper with a vicious stubbing-out in a nearby ashtray.'[6]

With *The Scoundrel*, Coward's mastery of that mannerism, with all its wickedly destructive connotations, was crystallized. Long afterwards Laurence Olivier said that all actors of his generation had learned that manner from Sir Gerald du Maurier who, after Charles Hawtrey, was the biggest influence on Coward's stage style. And it has been suggested that Coward's famous cigarette and holder were admissions of his debt to the great actor-manager.[7] If so, by 1935 the assimilation was elegantly and plausibly complete, and Coward gave a superb performance: 'the quintessence of bored nastiness, a drink in one hand and smoke wafting out of his mouth, each line well turned but not overplayed'.[8]

Mallare: Do you think it's easy for me to stand here watching you sob your heart out? You like our present relations. The victim and the criminal. The victim howling. The criminal cringing. All the typical aftermath of love known as married bliss. Oh, no thank you, no.

Cora: Don't you want my love?

Mallare: Not when it's handed to me on a platter, like the head of John the Baptist; not when it's lying in the middle of the road, run over.

Critically, the film was well received in New York. Commercially, however, it was not a success because all the characters bar one were repellent to Middle America, and because Coward was considered effete. Nevertheless, it gained a following (Penelope Gilliatt said that from the age of twelve she had recited lines of it by heart), and turned out to be a useful preparation for the film work which was to occupy Coward later.

There was little here though to console Coward as he returned to England and to John C. Wilson Ltd's financial problems. He knew, after the fiasco of *Point Valaine*, that experimental writing was fraught with risk and that he must try instead to produce something which was likely to restore solvency. *Tonight at 8.30* was his solution. It was a blatant attempt to capitalize on the success which he and Gertrude Lawrence had enjoyed together in *Private Lives* six years earlier, a group of nine one-act plays to be performed three an evening, and designed specifically as vehicles for their acting partnership. The season accordingly opened at the Phoenix, where they had found instant success in 1930, but *Tonight at 8.30* was a less happy collaboration. Coward's financial anxieties were eclipsed by Lawrence's. Owing to simple profligacy, she was, as Coward put it, 'busy being bankrupt'. During the day, in a desperate attempt to clear debts, she was working very hard on the set of Alexander Korda's biographical venture, *Rembrandt*, with Charles Laughton (improbably, she was cast as a maid) and then appeared in the theatre every evening. The strain of it eventually overwhelmed her, and when she collapsed from nervous exhaustion, Coward closed the production rather than appear with another actress. (Fortunately, he was able to transfer with her to New York later in 1936.)

There were other worries besides. Only three years after Eric's untimely death, Arthur Coward was growing increasingly infirm and Noël knew that his mother must take another death badly. He himself, as the diplomatic Cole Lesley remarked, 'found nothing in his father to admire or respect' and must have been more sanguine at the prospect of this next loss. Sometimes visitations of regret and recrimination mean that it is more difficult to bury an estranged parent than a close one. This did not prove to be the case with Coward; and when his father eventually died, in 1937, he was working abroad, and left funeral arrangements to Lorn Loraine. In the meantime, Alfred Lunt declined Coward's invitation to become a partner in John C. Wilson Ltd, which would have found his directing and casting skills invaluable, opting instead to become a director on the board of New York's Theatre Guild. And the beloved Wilson himself was neither help nor support in any of these problems. He had been spending increasing periods away not only from Coward – since the affair had been cooling – but from London, and suddenly, in 1936, he announced his engagement. However much of a shock to Coward the news was, he left no comment about it. The partnership survived several more years, and the affair may have continued fitfully. Coward liked the great beauty his lover married, an exiled Russian princess called Natasha Paley, and was always good to her. But the Wilsons' marriage was far from blissfully happy.

The combination of these unhappy circumstances would prompt some reflexion in all but the most callous and shallow minds. But if Coward had any opinions, he kept them to himself and his public behaviour remained that of the imperturbable professional. The rehearsals and eventual opening in London of *Tonight at 8.30* cannot have been auspicious or relaxed, and the plays themselves seemed to some reviewers to be slight and dull (although Coward and Lawrence were praised for their theatrical harmony). In New York in 1937 the production encountered a similar response, and Coward suffered his second nervous collapse in ten years.

The plays had no binding theme. *Hands Across the Sea* is about the confusion of a socialite, Lady Maureen 'Piggie' Gilpin, and the mistaken identities of two colonial guests. The playlet was specifically a vehicle for Gertrude Lawrence, and according to Coward, it elicited a bravura performance:

Without remembering the infinite variety of her inflexions, her absurd, scatterbrained conversations on the telephone, her frantic desire to be hospitable and charming, and her expression of blank dismay when she suddenly realized that her visitors were not who she thought they were at all. It was a superb performance in the finest traditions of high comedy, already over now and done with forever but as far as I am concerned never to be forgotten.

The play was also an indictment of the manners of its class, and a parody of the cocktail parties of the Mountbattens.

Shadow Play, a characteristically 'Coward' piece about divorce in Mayfair, was acclaimed for its use of disconnected scenes played in pools of light, and for its exquisite song, 'Here in the light of this unkind familiar now', one of the loveliest he wrote. *Red Peppers*, a comic sketch about failing vaudevillians, was also famous for its songs, particularly 'Has Anybody Seen Our Ship?'. *We Were Dancing* introduced the tropical island of Samolo, where Coward was to set much of his post-war writing. *Still Life*, which was later turned into the film *Brief Encounter*, showed Coward's awareness that the sacrifice of passion to propriety, a sacrifice with which he had some familiarity, was always commercially attractive. But he most enjoyed performing Henry Gow, the henpecked husband of *Fumed Oak*.

This vignette of south London was not exactly a tribute to the class which bore him – that was still three years away, in *This Happy Breed* – but a distorted glimpse of the childhood Coward might have had, and a reminder of the way in which he had escaped the suburbs. Henry Gow is surrounded by a nagging mother-in-law, a shrewish wife and a plain and petulant daughter. Mother and grandmother argue incessantly, as Violet and Vida did, and the claustrophobia of suburban existence is evoked by the daughter's practising the piano 'with the loud pedal firmly down all the time'. It was a picture of the relentless and grinding respectability which Coward could have endured had it not been for his far-sighted mother and his own determination to transcend his background. Henry Gow escapes Clapham because he has saved money and has decided to travel with it, thus exercising the sort of initiative Coward approved. Before leaving, he delivers a homily on behalf of his creator: 'As for you, Elsie, you've got a chance, it's a slim one, I grant you, but still it's a chance. If you learn to work and be independent and, when the time comes, give what you have to give freely and without demanding lifelong payment for it, there's just a bit of a hope that you'll turn into a decent human being.'

Coward had worked and learnt independence automatically, and had got away. But the more his wealth, fame and experience distanced him from the background he had escaped, the more he came to applaud its values and conduct. Once he was no longer lower-middle-class himself, once he had arrived, Coward extolled the class structure, preached acceptance of one's lot, and trumpeted the common decency of the multitude.

In 1937, also in a bid to raise money, he published *Present Indicative*, the first volume of his autobiography, in London and New York. It described his life until his departure for South America after *Cavalcade*. A second volume, *Future Indefinite*, which described the war years, came out in 1954. In 1965, he decided to make good the hiatus which the two books left, and began an account of the Thirties. Unfortunately, *Past Conditional* is only an abandoned fragment.

Coward was by nature no precisian: his instinct was for style rather than detail. In any case, he had spent his first thirty-six years consciously and vigilantly shaping the way in which he was seen by others, so it was inevitable that the discipline of honest and accurate autobiography would prove exacting. Although he could incorporate details from his life into his plays and short stories, presenting a coherent, comprehensive picture was more difficult for him. The story of a born attention-seeker, *Present Indicative* begins as it means to go on, with details of his earliest photographs, and his tone as he regales his readers with accounts of some of his first misdemeanours is jaunty. We are given a desultory account of his family's moves around south London, scraps of information about his relations, but the early pages are taken up primarily with anecdotes about his own naughty or amusing antics.

Esme Wynne-Tyson, who remembered the times he described, felt that he had consistently sacrificed the truth to the urge to amuse and that, whenever his always unreliable memory let him down, he simply invented. Her family was so annoyed by some of Coward's inaccuracies that she faced pressure to sue him. The relationship with Wilson is naturally left undescribed, beyond being referred to as a business partnership, and recent events of importance, like the deaths of Eric and Arthur Coward, are almost entirely ignored. According to Esme Wynne-Tyson, Coward thought his mother's intense grief over Eric Coward's death unreasonable. 'After all, she has *me*!' she remembered him complaining.[9]

Coward's earliest idol, George Bernard Shaw, once complained to Mrs Patrick Campbell about careers that could be traced 'in stale press notices'. 'You remember what I said ... about autobiographies being unreadable when childhood and apprenticeship is over and the career set and started.' *Present Indicative* canters through Coward's achievements, but when he is not appearing in a play, not indulging in self-display, he has nothing to say. He has no wisdom to offer about the creative process, and no speculations about where his genius for entertainment came from. He is, at least, honest about his snobbery, mentioning, for instance, that he was 'a bad celebrity snob' at the time when he sailed from New York to London on the same liner as the Fairbankses, and 'my mind busied itself with secret plans to get to know them well'. That is fair enough, but it never seems to occur to him to wonder why he felt like that. Nor does it occur to him that, if the Fairbankses, or the Prince of Wales, whom he met through them, were so interesting, then his readers might appreciate details of their conversation.

'My object in this book,' he declares on page 90, 'is to be as truthful as possible.' By then, however, one has taken the measure of his prose and reached different conclusions. Chattily uninformative, briskly genial, nervous of intimacy and determined above all not to take offence – 'I considered, without rancour, that my real feelings were nobody's business but my own' – *Present Indicative* is frustrating and evasive. (*Future Indefinite* was even worse: its pomposity suggests a combination of Movietone News and the stiff-upper-lipped control of *In Which We Serve*.)

The book was in general well received, but there was one important dissident voice, that of Cyril Connolly, in the *New Statesman*. Connolly, despite being a great admirer of Coward's songs (he had also felt that Sherlock Holmes should have been included in *Cavalcade*), was not the most appropriate reviewer for *Present Indicative*. A brilliant Classicist, who from an early age had been steeped in august literature, he was a literary perfectionist who looked upon writing almost as the practice of a morality. He was unlikely to prove sympathetic to theatrical reminiscence. Some of his remarks, not least his contention that Coward's plays 'are written in the most topical and perishable way imaginable, the cream in them turns sour overnight', are inaccurate and unfair. But he advanced good reasons for his pronouncement that the book is 'the picture, carefully incomplete, of a success', and reserved his finest fury for what he considered its author's deliberate omission of important details:

I think Noël Coward is deliberately dull, dull because he knows his minute details of minor performances will satisfy the fans, and above all dull because he has so much to conceal behind the smoke screen ... First his childhood ... I suggest it was really a kind of agony for the stage-struck little boy, clever as a mongoose, who tasted success as a page in the comedies of Charles Hawtrey, and that it generated in him a passionate hatred of failure, an intense craving for luxury and fame. Poverty and dinginess were the stick of the rocket, to be dropped only when his talent was well away and exploding into its shower of stars.

Connolly's attack resolved itself into irritation with Coward's 'volubility about trivialities' and his refusal, as he saw it, to contemplate privately, let alone disclose publicly, what spurred him to achieve. 'Beneath [the trivialities] I believe were real privations and humiliations, things that would have made a great writer, in him only to be buried guiltily by the subconscious, ignored in the fierce struggle for success.' Connolly was doing his subject an injustice: he knew very well that Coward could never be honest about such a profound influence upon his life and attitudes as his sexuality. But his main point, that there is more to any life, particularly a successful one, than success, remained valid:

It is the absence of all aesthetic criticism that I find so appalling – not one word about schools of acting, styles of writing, creative methods, ideas of any kind whatsoever ... There is only success, more and more of it, till from his pinnacle he can look down to where Ivor Novello and Beverley Nichols gather samphire on a ledge, and to where, a pinpoint on the sands below, Mr Godfrey Winn is counting pebbles.

Coward was apparently very upset by this attack. In his diaries he complains that Oscar Wilde had a brilliant wit but entirely lacked a sense of humour. If a sense of humour means being able to take jokes and criticism (and it often does), Coward was similarly witty but humourless: he hated all criticism, so Connolly's was noted and reprisals considered. The *New Statesman* seemed to have little effect on public opinion, at least; and *Present Indicative* sold well in England and the United States.

PART THREE
THE WAR

Chapter One

In all the writing Coward accomplished between *Design for Living* and the beginning of 1939, there is only one indication, in *Hands Across The Sea*, that the maelstrom was fast approaching and irresistible: 'Everything was going beautifully when Vera arrived unasked, my dear, and more determined than Hitler.' He had begun his dramatic career with the belief that the theatre should provoke and educate. But the *enfant terrible* had tired of provocation and, excepting the patriotic 'politics' of *Cavalcade*, he had increasingly offered pure escapism: through the successive crises of the Thirties, those who could afford it went to Noël Coward's plays to forget, and he proudly offered them oblivion. But not even he could remain so blithely indifferent. 1937, the year of *Present Indicative* (and the second year of the Spanish Civil War), saw Neville Chamberlain's arrival as Prime Minister, and Coward's conversion to anti-appeasement. He had been friendly since the Twenties with Duff Cooper and Anthony Eden – both of whom eventually resigned from office in protest at Chamberlain's policies – but if their friendship influenced him politically, there was no sign of it until a couple of years before the war when, at a party given by Binkie Beaumont, he records that 'everyone flew at me for my hatred of Chamberlain'.[1]

Hugh 'Binkie' Beaumont had first met Coward during the run of *Private Lives*, and by the late Thirties his career as a theatrical manager, which eventually led to his virtual control, through H. M. Tennent, of the entire West End theatre district, was already established.[2] In 1938, Coward and Beaumont joined professional forces with *Operette*. Only two things need be noted about this dreadful musical of backstage romance in the Edwardian theatre: that it was another attempt, after *Conversation Piece*, to repeat the success of *Bitter-Sweet*; and that, despite containing the song 'The Stately Homes Of England', it deserved to fail. Ivor Brown, in the *Daily Sketch*, marvelled at the change in Coward which the Thirties had seen: 'It is odd to think nowadays that Mr Noël Coward was once regarded as the spirit of flaming and audacious youth. His new piece is modishly nostalgic, gently romantic, and shows a definite dislike ... for smartness and brilliance.'[3]

In 1939, Beaumont – then supervising the London opening of *Design for Living* – was offered much more substantial writing: a brace of plays, to be produced and performed together: *This Happy Breed* and *Present Laughter*. (The Shakespearean allusions of their titles bore witness to Coward's self-education of the late 1930s.) They were an extraordinary coupling: one, effectively the beginning of Coward's war work, was a celebration of ordinary, suburban England and the resilience of its people, the other was an effervescent study of triumphant stardom. *This Happy Breed* was a sentimental, but deeply serious, lecture. *Present Laughter* was high and unrepentant comedy.

While loving the comedy, Beaumont had doubts about the other play: its characterization and theatrical sense impressed him, but he did not want to take it. Coward, however, now that he was secure in the affluent and classless estate of stardom, was intent on celebrating the world he had escaped, and insisted that Beaumont took both or neither: 'You must never, never forget your roots,' he told Beaumont.[4] *This Happy Breed* and *Present Laughter* were Coward's stylized versions of what he had been, and what he had become.

When the plays were eventually presented – the turmoils of war delayed their arrival in the West End until 1943 – there were complaints that *This Happy Breed* patronized the subjects it purported to celebrate. Coward always had an answer, even if it was not an honest one, and he patiently put his detractors right:

Many of the critics detected in this play an attitude on my part of amused patronage and condescension towards the habits and manners of suburban London. They implied that in setting the play in a *milieu* so far removed from the cocktail and caviare stratum to which I so obviously belonged, I was over-reaching myself and writing about people far removed from my superficial comprehension. In this as usual they were quite wrong. Having been born in Teddington, having lived respectively at Sutton, Battersea Park and Clapham Common during all my formative years, I can confidently assert that I know a great deal more about the hearts and minds of South Londoners than they give me credit for. My metamorphosis into a 'Mayfair Playboy' many years later was entirely a journalistic conception. Since I achieved my first theatrical success, with

The Vortex, in 1924, I have moved observantly and eagerly through the many different cliques and classes of society.[5]

This Olympian denial was somewhat disingenuous. Coward's dialogue owed more to mimicry than to observation; he had encountered some cliques and classes of society more eagerly than others; and the 'journalistic conception' of the 'Mayfair Playboy' was one to which he had always given active encouragement.

Cavalcade had shown Coward that audiences liked remembering recent history. He had ended that play in 1930, although its action effectively finishes with the end of war in 1918. About the Twenties, it had nothing to say. *This Happy Breed* takes over where the earlier play finished, beginning in 1919 and ending in 1939. *Cavalcade* offered the responses of two different classes to the momentous events of the times. The later play, however, with its eye on the importance of national unity, celebrates only one class: its author's own, the lower-middle, embodied by the Gibbons family of Sycamore Road, Clapham. Through their eyes, audiences saw all their yesterdays – the General Strike, the Abdication, the rise of appeasement – collapsed into two hours of didactic entertainment.

If Coward did know the lower middle class, he could not resist treating it with a patronage which jars today. This attitude had been apparent, though to a lesser degree, in *Cavalcade* and *Fumed Oak*, but it is one's abiding impression of *This Happy Breed*, where Coward conforms to certain stage traditions which help to give lower-middle-class life a comic aspect. For instance, the menfolk are generally law-abiding and 'respectable', but every so often they defy respectability, go out together and get drunk, and return to face the wife, irate in hair curlers and cold cream. Another tradition dictated that at least one female in the household portrayed should be a hypochondriac, and thus prone to palpitations, the vapours, headaches or whatever. In Sycamore Road, Frank's mother-in-law, Mrs Flint, has a bad back and a weak bladder, and these conditions encourage a carping pessimism. His sister, Sylvia, has endless complaints and is too ill to work, much to Mrs Flint's contemptuous amusement. There are many exchanges on the subject:

Sylvia: ... Oo, my poor back!

Mrs Flint: It was your feet this afternoon.

Sylvia: Well, it's me back now, so there.

It is a fact of life that much conversation is banal. But banality can be put to striking dramatic effect; more than anything else, *This Happy Breed* reveals Coward's apparently unshakeable conviction that suburban workers express themselves exclusively in empty proverbs. Thus, Mrs Flint: 'Thank 'eaven for small mercies'; Sylvia: 'No peace for the wicked'; and Frank: "E'll have to take the will for the deed.' In *Cavalcade*, Flo Bridges had wondered, "Ow was Hoxford when you left it?', and the Gibbonses talk also in the same stylized Cockney used by all low-life that strayed onto the stage, no matter where it came from, before the 1960s. (While putting it to a different use, Kipling had been familiar with the same dialect: 'Where the silence 'ung that 'eavy you was 'arf afraid to speak!/On the road to Mandalay ...')

Frank and Ethel Gibbons have many crosses to bear, apart from the perpetual squabbling of Sylvia and Mrs Flint. Their son, Reg, becomes friendly with a young communist, Sam Leadbitter, who starts filling his head with nonsense about the injustices of inequality, and so on, and then encourages him to become involved in the General Strike. Sam is eventually tamed by Reg's sister, Vi. They get married and have children and live happily ever after. Reg marries, but he and his wife die in an accident at the end of Act 2. Frank's younger daughter, Queenie, is the biggest worry. Like Henry Gow in *Fumed Oak*, she longs to escape the stifling and stagnant life of suburban Clapham:

I'll tell you something awful. I hate living here, I hate living in a house that's exactly like hundreds of other houses. I hate coming home from work in the Tube. I hate washing up and helping Mum darn Dad's socks and listening to Auntie Sylvia keeping on about how ill she is all the time, and what's more I know why I hate it too, it's because it's all so common!

Who can blame her? Coward, for a start. Henry Gow was allowed to escape, but Queenie, like Sam Leadbitter, is tamed. 'You don't believe in people trying to better themselves, do you?' she angrily asks her father. Frank does not: 'You'll find out that there are worse things than being ordinary and respectable and living the way you've been brought up to live,' he tells her. Coward was here hardly preaching what he had practised but, having established himself, he had become a keen supporter of the established order. Accordingly, his mouthpiece, Frank, damns any institution – such as the Labour Party or the Communist Party – designed to promote the well-being of the workers. Queenie, incidentally, absconds only to return and marry the boy next door.

In 'The Quest', Saki had mocked Christian Science; and as so many of Coward's friends and acquaintances defected to that faith – Esme Wynne-Tyson, of course, but also Moya Nugent, Clemence Dane and Norah Howard – he decided to follow Saki's example, and Sylvia is suddenly made to see the light, in order to provide her author with the opportunity to tease and annoy Esme Wynne-Tyson and her spiritual compatriots. And one opportunity was as good as the next when it came to ridiculing Chamberlain, whose return from Munich Sylvia and Vi are discussing:

Sylvia: Your very life has been saved at this moment by the triumph of right thinking over wrong thinking.

Vi: Well, that's nice, isn't it?

Sylvia: I've often thought Mr Chamberlain must be a Christian Scientist at heart.

Vi: Well, let's hope that Hitler and Mussolini are too, and then we shall all be on velvet.

Sylvia was played on stage by Joyce Carey, but when plans were afoot to film *This Happy Breed* in 1943, it was suggested that Joyce Grenfell should do a screen test for the same part. As Carey and Coward knew Joyce Grenfell quite well, they must both have been aware that she was also a Christian Scientist. Innumerable actors would have been delighted at the prospect of appearing in a new Coward film, but Grenfell, writing to her mother, was rather less enthusiastic: the part was that of 'the silly woman who is what Noël thinks a C.S. is like! Isn't it magic? To be offered a very big part in Noël's picture and not to be able to take it from conscience *is* tough!' She continued to waver – 'My latest line on it is that it is perhaps better for me, who knows a little about it, to make the part as inoffensive as possible, rather than let someone else ridicule and make it awful'[6] – before deciding that the money and the prestige connected with the project could not outweigh Coward's dubious pulpitry.

Whatever their transgressions and follies, however much they snivel with hypochondria and drop their aitches, the Gibbonses and their like are, Coward insists, the salt of the earth. Frank refers to his family, at one stage, only half in jest, as 'the backbone of the

Empire', and regularly delivers himself of rather laborious homilies which insist that, provided he keeps his head and, more importantly, his place, the working man is equal to anything that might happen in England or abroad. Coward is so determined to make this point that he loses sight of plausibility and stagecraft, and closes the play with Frank leaning over a pram and lecturing his invisible grandson: '... the people themselves, the ordinary people like you and me ... We know what we belong to, where we come from, and where we're going ... We 'aven't lived and died and struggled all these hundreds of years to get decency and justice and freedom for ourselves without being prepared to fight fifty wars if need be – to keep 'em.' As John Lahr remarked, Frank Gibbons is 'the mouthpiece of a static society'.[7]

The officially sanctioned belief was that all classes should work together in fighting the war. Coward implied in *This Happy Breed* that the suburban worker could best serve the struggle for victory by not entertaining any ideas above his station. Secretly, he was more specific. His diary records an entry made early in the war which is explicit about his real attitude to the happy breed: 'I have no real support with the "workers", in fact I actively detest them en masse.' The play is now a curiosity, a relic of the wartime spirit, and of Coward's class sense; and if it is ever performed, it would be in the interests of historical study rather than entertainment. But its companion piece, *Present Laughter*, 'written with the sensible object of providing me with a bravura part', is vital and brilliant theatre, a summary of Coward's preoccupations with vanity, charm, selfishness and the triumphant ego. It is a more perfectly realized piece than *Private Lives* and a less verbose one than *Design for Living* – those plays having been his most recent excursions into that territory – and, with the exception of *Hay Fever*, written fifteen years before, it is the sunniest of the major comedies.

That buoyancy of mood stems from the fact that its central figure, Garry Essendine, has been able to resolve his vanity, charm and selfishness into professional assets – he is a successful actor – rather than being a prey to them. In this respect, he is luckier than Coward's other principal comic figures, and is the only one among them whose references to work are credible. Elyot and Amanda would not, of course, have known what work was. Otto and Leo claim to paint and write, but such claims never really convince us, any more than we are convinced by Charles Condomine's and

David Bliss's writers' talk. But Essendine is triumphantly and plausibly a professional attention-seeker, an actor. *Present Laughter* derives its energy from its unrepentant narcissism: Coward, pointing to the many parallels, was always eager to stress that Garry Essendine was a self-portrait, and it is clearly one he enjoyed completing. He was pleased with the results of his self-creation and could now immortalize them in drama. Even his psychological warts could be turned to comic account.

Like his creator, Garry is surrounded by a surrogate family: his ex-wife, Liz; his secretary, Monica; his valet, Fred; his manager, Morris; and his business partner, Henry. But no nexus of friends and associates can be sustained simply by financial interest. There is the matter of loyalty. Coward never deserted his dependants, and Garry – despite being a prima donna, selfish and irresponsible by turns – reveals his author's respect for friendship and the allegiances forged over years of mutual service: 'Here we are, five people closely woven together by affection and work and intimate knowledge of each other. It's too important a "set up" to risk breaking for any outside reason whatsoever.'

Charm is a crucial factor in the matter of attracting potential friends. Although as an eager and aspiring young actor Coward had failed to beguile everyone, he had by now polished his charm famously. Kenneth Tynan, never at a loss for the *mot juste*, found him 'gracious, socially, as a royal bastard; tart, vocally, as a hollowed lemon', and William Marchant, who later wrote a memoir of Coward, was won over entirely:

His offstage personality differed radically from what I judged the man underneath to be like: the clipped, rapid speech was the same and the silken voice identical, but the words were different. The flippancy and archness were replaced by a manner that was entirely sober, and his concentration on what others were saying gave him a look of intensity, unlike that of anyone I have ever known. When he smiled it was like a benediction, and his laughter was an announcement of approval.[8]

Garry has the same effortless charm:

Daphne: I think he's even more charming off the stage than on, don't you?

Monica: I can never quite make up my mind.

In his analysis of *Present Laughter*, John Lahr said that it presents a situation which 'epitomizes the predicament of charm which lets people escape the responsibility of their actions'. As always, this was well said, and within the confines of the play, it is more or less true. Garry's charm seems never to annoy; it merely attracts more admirers:

Monica: You'd better hurry, Mr Maule will be here in a minute.

Garry: Who's he?

Monica: You know perfectly well, he's the young man who wrote that mad play half in verse and caught you on the telephone and you were so busy being attractive and unspoiled by your great success that you promised him an appointment.

Garry: I can't see him – you ought to protect me from things like that.

In life itself, however, the same did not apply. Coward doubtless thought that his charm worked as infallibly with his close friends and intimates as it did with onlookers like Kenneth Tynan, but he deluded himself. The loyal and gentle Cole Lesley conceded that behind the irresistible display there was a selfishness which was 'total', while Ann Fleming (writing to Cecil Beaton, an eager audience) often found the enchantment rather leaden: 'Noël ... should be used as a cabaret and not as a guest, he does not understand the give and take of talk and the deserts of pomposity between the oases of wit are too vast.'[9] This performing for attention only disguised a craving for affection, and Peter Quennell, who never knew Coward well but had the chance to observe him at close range, asked himself: 'When did Noël act, and when was his private behaviour totally spontaneous?' He found that Coward's charm was inherent in his undisguised theatricality, and recounted a significant story:

Given an audience, he seldom entered a room; he almost always made an entry; and I remember ... at a house in France ... a number of English guests were assembled. Among them was the singer Olga Lynn – 'Oggie' to her large and affectionate circle ... she was then recovering from a slight stroke, but of this Noël happened to be unaware. He arrived late and, a suitable entry having been made, moved genially around the room, distributing kisses and smiles and bows, until at last he came to Oggie. 'Darling Oggie; and how are *you*?' he demanded. 'Thank you, Noël; I've been ill you see,' she replied in muffled accents and patted her poor flaccid cheek. Noël dramatically threw up his hands. 'Not – a – tiny – *strokey* – Oggie – darling?' he enquired in tones of heart-felt consternation, carefully spacing out the words and lending each a poignant emphasis. We were all tempted to laugh, and quickly resisted the impulse; but although the enquiry may perhaps sound brutal, it had the right effect upon the sufferer, since it implied that a stroke was the kind of harmless minor mishap ... that might come anyone's way.[10]

Garry freely admits that his constant attempts to secure adoration and enchantment motivate his behaviour: 'I'm always acting – watching myself go by – that's what's so horrible – I see myself all the time eating, drinking, loving, suffering – sometimes I think I'm going mad.' But that very admission is a way of pre-empting criticism, and part of his seducing charm, which is just as well, as Garry, like all actors, wants to be loved:

Monica: You could never get rid of Miss Erikson, she worships you.

Garry: Everybody worships me, it's nauseating.

Monica: There's hell to pay if they don't.

Coward's performing, like Garry's (and like Judith Bliss's), was incessant; but whether the audience was charmed or annoyed, it was not allowed to ask for information which was not volunteered. Essendine is equally guarded, as Joanna, Henry's wife, discovers:

Joanna: ... It would be nice to know what you were really like, under all the trappings.

Garry: Just a simple boy, stinking with idealism.

Joanna: Sentimental too, almost Victorian at moments.

Garry: I spend hours at my sampler.

Joanna: Are you happy on the whole?

Garry: Ecstatically.

One important particular in which Coward diverges from his alter ego is, inevitably, in his sexuality. Garry is a compulsive womanizer; and Coward's writing (aided perhaps by his experience) rises effortlessly to the challenge of giving Garry the pat replies of the romantic matinée idol.

Coward was at the peak of his mature fame when he wrote *Present Laughter*, and he used the opportunity to deliver an exuberant defence of his conviction of the primacy of entertainment over instruction in the theatre. Essendine is pursued throughout the play by a young and earnest playwright called Roland Maule, who hopes for help and advice (just as the apprentice Coward hoped for help and advice when he despatched *The Young Idea* to Shaw). Unfortunately, however, Essendine and Maule disagree completely about the purpose of the theatre, as they discover when Garry delivers his verdict on the young man's first play:

Roland: I just took a chance. I mean I know you only play rather trashy stuff as a rule, but I thought you just might like to have a shot at something deeper.

Garry: What is there in your play, Mr Maule, that you consider so deep? Apart from the plot, which is completely submerged after the first four pages.

Roland: Plots aren't important, it's ideas that matter. Look at Chekhov.

Life rarely imitated art, at least where Coward's plays were concerned, and when *Present Laughter* was produced, and played to the grateful applause of audiences at war, its author could not know that in the very different cultural climate of the late Fifties and early Sixties, younger playwrights would frequently damn him for writing plays which aspired simply to entertain rather than to instruct.

Chapter Two

The exuberant froth of *Present Laughter* was extraordinary for its time. As the Thirties drew to a close, most writers could think of nothing except the impending conflagration (Auden spoke of 'waves of anger and fear ... obsessing our private lives'), but Coward could make comedy out of his self-invention, the seductiveness of his persona and the shamelessness of his charm. It was either an act of remarkable disengagement from darkening reality, or an affirmative action. In any case, the greater the crisis, the more urgent the need for laughter. Following the Munich Crisis the year before, England had begun to assume the aspect of a nation at war: London's parks were entrenched; gas masks were distributed amongst civilians; the evacuation of children began, as did the recruitment for air-raid wardens; and blackout precautions were issued. 'For me,' Coward wrote in *Future Indefinite*, 'the pre-war past died on the day when Mr Neville Chamberlain returned with such gay insouciance from Munich in 1938.' The plays were put into rehearsal in 1939, but it was sadly apparent that events would overtake their production. In the summer of that year, as though aware that it was all about to slide into history, Coward decided to inspect Eastern Europe. In Poland, he discovered a feudal and fatalistic aristocracy. After Sweden, Norway, Denmark and Finland he continued to Russia, but was not impressed: 'I have always believed more in quality than quantity, and nothing will convince me that the levelling of class and rank distinctions, and the contemptuous dismissal of breeding as an important factor of life, can lead to anything but a dismal mediocrity.'[1]

During the Great War, patriotism had been the least of Coward's concerns. But now, on friendly terms with Earl Mountbatten, and on intimate terms with the Duke of Kent, he could feel himself brushed by the panoply of royalty and Empire, and it was an exquisite sensation. Furthermore, with *Cavalcade*, he had become the spokesman for the national pride of the multitude, and anti-appeasers were guests at Goldenhurst. With the Second World War, he had to prove the sincerity of his position, and his fame would guarantee coverage of his endeavours. In fact, if he had not acquitted himself well in 1918, Coward's time in the Second World War was very full. It was productive and exacting in equal measure, a period marked by neither laziness nor cowardice, and the reason was that he genuinely believed in it all. He had created his own voice, appearance, position, circle of friends: the addition of patriotism to his accomplishments was the matter of a moment. It is often said of Coward that – even more than most – he only saw what he wanted to see; and this trumpet voluntary from *Future Indefinite* betrays no embarrassment for the inconsistencies of his military career, nor for the fact that his 'code of morals', for most of his life until then, had resided largely in self-promotion:

Now was the moment ... to face facts honestly. If I bungled this moment, and by doing so betrayed my own code of morals, I should never be comfortable with myself again and ... whatever books or plays I lived to write ... [would be] tainted by the fact that I had allowed to slip through my fingers the opportunity to prove my own integrity to myself.

For all these fine words, and fine intentions, his war began slowly, and the finest monument of those years (since patriotism seldom sponsors art) is *Blithe Spirit*, his great comedy of 1941. He eventually realized that his duty at this time lay with his ability: in entertaining others. But to begin with, in 1939, he was determined to be put to use in a more supposedly serious way: 'I knew in my innermost heart that if I were intelligently used by the government, preferably in the field of propaganda, where my creative ability, experience of broadcasting and knowledge of people could be employed, I could probably do something really constructive.'[2] This was all very well, but tailor-made jobs were difficult to find in the war, particularly when it began, and the full extent of the nation's confusion and lack of preparation became apparent. What is more, fame, which during the peace had only regulated the discretions of his private life, during war imposed many restrictions. He was first made aware of this when he asked the advice of Winston Churchill, then still a backbencher, about what he should do, and discovered that the reputation for frivolity and cynicism which he had so assiduously polished in the distant Twenties continued to cling: '"Go and sing to them when the guns are firing – that's your job" ... I saw Mr Churchill's point clearly. In his view I was primarily an entertainer, a singer of gay songs.'[3] Happily for Coward, Sir Campbell Stuart – who was no friend of Churchill's – did not agree.

He was Canadian, and a director of *The Times*. During World War One, he had worked with Lord Northcliffe in the department of enemy propaganda. In 1938, he had been approached by the government to plan covert propaganda in the event of another war. He authorized Coward to go to Paris when hostilities commenced and establish a bureau of propaganda which would cooperate with the French Ministry of Information, under the aegis of Jean Giraudoux, in broadcasting misinformation to Germany. One may wonder about Coward's credentials for the job, other than his relative proficiency in French. (He took extra lessons in Paris; when covering the subjunctive, he remembered being made to learn '*il faut que vous ne me guillotinassiez pas*'.) Stuart may have felt that Coward would get on with his fellow playwright Giraudoux, but his avowed reasoning behind the appointment, for which, he admitted, he was 'much criticized', was that Coward was 'a man of great ability who wanted to serve his country in her time of trouble quite properly in some other way than as an actor'.[4]

When war broke out, the theatres were closed (only to be reopened quickly when their importance to national morale was realized), and Coward left for Paris, installing himself in an office in the Place de la Madeleine and a flat in the Place Vendôme. He quickly realized that for all the feverish secrecy of the Phoney War there was little for him to do in Paris, and no one, certainly among the French, seemed to care anyway. As a corrective to the charge of the German propaganda machine that the RAF never flew over German cities, he made the inspired suggestion that it drop thousands of confetti-sized sticky flags, bearing the Union Jack and the Tricolor, over Berlin. There was another idea, that the RAF should drop leaflets containing speeches by Lord Halifax and Neville Chamberlain over German cities, but Coward's memorandum archly declared that there was not time to bore the enemy to death.

To add to his difficulties, he was muzzled by officialdom, and could do nothing to defend himself against the snide inventions of the British press. The *Daily Telegraph* reported that he had been seen 'sauntering along the Rue Royale in naval uniform' and the *Sunday Pictorial* printed a list of bogus servicemen, 'The Civilians in Uniform', which was headed by Coward. Indeed, his spell in Paris was frustrating, and would have been entirely unproductive had it not been for the affair of Radio Fécamp. The British and French authorities had agreed that, in the event of war, all radio stations would only be allowed to operate on controlled wavelengths, in order to prevent them from giving radio cross-bearings to German aircraft heading for the Channel. Coward discovered that Radio Fécamp was continuing to broadcast in defiance of that agreement and, by overcoming vested interests and bureaucratic inertia, had it silenced.

In April 1940, he left Paris in disillusionment and Stuart sent him to America to reconnoitre impressions of the war. While he was away, Churchill's new administration replaced Stuart with Duff Cooper. With a friend in a high place, Coward must have felt that he would finally be given a more taxing and responsible job. But it was not to be: and on Duff Cooper's advice he returned to the United States as an unaccredited representative of the British government to canvass influential opinion and assess the extent of isolationism. As the 'posting', which lasted until his departure for Australia in October, was unofficial, he had to bear the cost of it – about £11,000 – himself. Nor was that the only problem. Reaction to his departure was scandalized. Joyce Grenfell, who knew him, though not yet well, wrote to her mother: 'I think it is a great mistake. Everyone knows his past history and altho' those things don't matter if one is merely writing stuff for the theatre, it is definitely a pity, to say the least of it, that the man who represents this country at a time like this should be famous as a queer.'[5]

Having seen Coward in the indulgent world of the theatre, Grenfell probably had an exaggerated opinion of the 'fame' of his 'queerness'. But there is no doubt that his glamorous and frivolous reputation disqualified him in the eyes of many from any government business. The *Sunday Express* was blunt:

The despatch of Mr Noël Coward to the States can do nothing but harm. In any event, Mr Coward is not the man for the job. His flippant England – cocktails, countesses, caviare – has gone. A man of the people, more in tune with the new mood of Britain, would be a better proposition for America.[6]

There were also hostile reactions, from both sides, in the House of Commons. Some speakers considered him unsuitable for the job; others felt that his main motivation for going was cowardice.[7] Harold Nicolson, the Parliamentary Private Secretary to the Min-

istry of Information, defended Coward's mission: 'His qualifications are that he possesses a contact with certain sources of
opinion which are very difficult to reach through ordinary sources.'[8]

He certainly did have a 'contact with certain sources of opinion',
and even found himself in May 1940 a guest of the Roosevelts at
the White House. He travelled extensively in America, visiting
California among other places. There was a large community of
expatriates living in Hollywood, amongst whom were many British
actors, including Claude Rains, Charles Laughton, Sir Cedric Hardwicke, Leslie Howard, Ray Milland and Cary Grant. Alfred Hitch-
cock had left England for California simply because there was
more work in Hollywood, in 1939. Alexander Korda followed him
in 1940, and was attacked in England for desertion, even though
he was only British by naturalization. By no means all of the
Englishmen resident in Hollywood were avoiding the war. And
although expatriate stars were vilified in England for having 'gone
with the wind up', British officialdom realized that having British
actors in Hollywood tended to promote a British tone to American
films. Coward, an increasingly zealous patriot, did not agree. 'If I
ran away,' he wrote to his mother, by then sheltering from the air-
raids in New York, 'and refused to have anything to do with the
war and lived comfortably in Hollywood as so many of my actor
friends have done, I should be ashamed to the end of my days.' He
expressed his disapproval at the highest possible level, to the British
Ambassador to Washington, Lord Lothian, who cabled the Minister
of War in London in 1940:

Noël Coward, who has just been to Hollywood, is strongly of the opinion
that the continued presence of young British actors in this country at a
time when heroic and tragic events are taking place in Europe, and some
American actors are joining up for ambulance and other services, is
creating a bad impression ... I agree with Coward in thinking that it is a
mistake for young men of military age with all the limelight on them ...
not to go home to help in the present emergency. Even if they are not of
great military value, they could probably be used for recreation and
entertainment of the troops and civilians in these difficult days.[9]

It was all to no avail. The Foreign Office replied:

National Service Act does not apply to British residents in foreign coun-
tries and no official steps can be taken to recall these young men. If you

think it desirable please take such unofficial steps as you can to persuade young British actors in the USA to return home and offer their services.[10]

There was nothing more that could be done. In disgust, Coward wrote a short story, 'A Richer Dust', about a young British actor who spends his war on Hollywood's film sets and whose family excuses his failure to return home to fight by claiming that he suffers from a tubercular lung. (The tubercular lung which had exempted Coward from active service in the Great War had been genuine.) And when he eventually returned to England, he wrote a poem about all those, including actors, who slept safely while others defended them:

> Lie in the dark and listen
> City magnates and steel contractors,
> Factory workers and politicians
> Soft, hysterical little actors
> Ballet dancers, 'Reserved' musicians,
> Safe in your warm civilian beds.
> Count your profits and count your sheep
> Life is flying above your heads.[11]

Coward's stay in America had other purposes. Along with Alexander Korda and his brother Zoltan, Ian Fleming, Leslie Howard and others, Coward was one of 'Little Bill's Boys': he was involved in intelligence work for Sir William Stephenson, whose British Security Co-ordination represented British intelligence in America. As Coward was not a scrupulously accurate autobiographer concerning even mundane facts, it is not surprising that he is imprecise about his activities for Stephenson. In *Future Indefinite*, he says that they met on his second trip to America, in New York in July 1940. Shortly before his death, he claimed instead that they met in London in a hotel in Caxton Street 'very appropriately positioned between the House of Lords and Victoria Railway Station'.[12] Churchill was also somehow aware of Stephenson's interest in Coward, but was against his involvement in security work on the grounds that he was too well known. That, however, was Coward's camouflage: 'My celebrity value was wonderful cover. So many career intelligence officers went around looking terribly mysterious – long black boots and sinister smiles. Nobody ever issued me with a false beard … My disguise was my own reputation as a bit of an idiot.'[13]

Stephenson hoped to give him a major assignment in 1941, so

again his hopes of firm responsibility in the war were raised. 'Everything okay,' he wrote, 'very very excited. Feel at last I can be really utilized properly. I am to pick my own staff in London. All blissfully efficient. Very thrilled about everything.'[14] Returning to England via Bermuda, however, he was cabled by Stephenson and told the plan had been cancelled. Anxieties that Coward's activities inevitably generated publicity had prevailed. He was very disappointed, and was sure that he detected the intervention of Churchill and Lord Beaverbrook, another influential enemy. Nevertheless, he was apparently able to send reports to Stephenson while travelling through Latin America later in the war.

As a footnote to Coward's espionage activities, such as they were, one should note that he made them sound like schoolboy games when in fact they were perilous. Ian Fleming, who worked for Stephenson in 1941, remembered the story of two 'justified killings' and, bound forever by British secrecy laws, wrote in fictional terms about the double-O classification which carried a licence to kill. And Leslie Howard, then most famous as Ashley Wilkes in *Gone With The Wind*, was travelling on a mission for Stephenson when his plane was shot down by the Germans. The German Air Force orders had been monitored by British intelligence, but the plane was still allowed to take off in order to prevent German intelligence from discovering that its codes had been broken by the British.

Chapter Three

In 1941, Coward began a diary, the better to record the inconstancies of life in the embattled capital. Its earliest entries record two preoccupations: financial problems, and the random deaths of war. Although Jack Wilson was far away in America, the consequences of his financial negligence were inescapable. Thus, in August 1941, the diary records a discussion about money with Lorn Loraine which left Coward with the unsettling suspicion that, however hard he worked, he would never be able to accumulate any wealth. And, a month later, another entry refers to a long letter to Wilson, in which he apparently hoped that the financial confusion of those years could be resolved after the war. However, if fiscal salvation seemed a distant though certain prospect, other considerations and anxieties were more immediate, and by the third year of the fighting, great danger and violent death were facts of life. It was only a matter of time, therefore, before someone known to Coward perished; but he could never have supposed that it would be the Duke of Kent, a former lover as well as a friend of nineteen years, and someone whose rank might have protected him from harm in other wars. Kent died in an air crash, and in the brisk obituary he wrote in his diary, Coward expresses annoyance as well as regret, annoyance that someone 'young' and 'charming' should die by 'accident', while the Duke of Windsor remained alive.

Coward himself had already escaped death when his studio in Gerald Road was bombed in 1941. Luckily, he was not at home when the bomb fell. Returning from the West End in a taxi, he remembered:

I was interested to note, this being my first experience of a blitz, that I was not frightened at all. This surprised me, because physical courage has never been one of my strong points ... To me the feeling of inevitability, the knowledge that there was nothing I could possibly do about it, numbed any fears ...[1]

This was the period of the most intense bombing, and the former capital of the world, while suffering less than some other cities, sustained terrible damage. Coward, a convert to patriotism perhaps, but a born Londoner, wrote one of his most haunting and evocative songs, 'London Pride', that summer:

> London Pride has been handed down to us.
> London Pride is a flower that's free.
> London Pride means our own dear town to us,
> And our pride it forever will be.
> Grey city
> Stubbornly implanted,
> Taken so for granted
> For a thousand years.
> Stay, city,
> Smokily enchanted,
> Cradle of our memories and hopes and fears.

For once, he had written a song about a love that dared to speak its name, for the city of his birth, and the scene of his first triumphs. But 'London Pride' also extolled the only great European city to retain its freedom, and paid tribute to the determination of its besieged population.

It was specifically the spirit of the Blitz which engaged not only Coward's new-found patriotism, but also his sense of humour, which had always owed a lot to understatement and incongruity. *Future Indefinite* records that when he returned to Gerald Road and discovered that it had been bombed, he rushed out to see if there were any wounded in the street:

The spectacle at the corner of Ebury Street was horrifying. Houses were blazing, the road was a mass of rubble: some fire-fighters were standing quite silently with a hose directing streams of water on to the flames. There was a momentary lull in the raid and the sudden cessation of noise was eerie. I asked an A.R.P. warden if I could be of any help with the injured and he said all who could be got out had been taken away an hour ago. At this moment I noticed, coming towards me rather mincingly across the rubble, two smartly-dressed young girls in high-heeled shoes. As they passed close by me I heard one say to the other: 'You know, dear, the trouble with all this is you could rick your ankle.' This example of British understatement so enchanted me that I laughed out loud.

In reality, however, the damage to the studio was another financial problem to add to the ones which were already plaguing him and should have been plaguing Jack Wilson, and underlined the need for some sort of interim solution pending the more radical financial reorganization which Coward envisaged after the war. Diary entries in April reveal his suspicions that only a new play offered hope of salvation, and imply that he hinted at his designs to Binkie Beaumont. The scheme was fomenting in his mind when he decided to go on holiday with his old friend Joyce Carey, who at that time was herself involved in writing a play about Keats. With foreign travel out of the question, they settled on Port Meirion in Wales, and packed their typewriters. If she hoped to discuss her work, Joyce Carey was naïve, because *Future Indefinite* reports that only Coward's play was discussed and that Keats was forgotten. Shelley, however, was not. Coward had admired that poet when writing *Present Laughter* (Garry Essendine had remarked that there was nothing that Shelley did not know about love), and now he invoked him again with the title of his new play, *Blithe Spirit*.[2]

The war must have seemed blissfully remote in the tranquillity of north Wales; but having had a narrow escape when Gerald Road was bombed, even Coward, so often blind to the distressing, knew that sudden extinction, especially for young men, was now a fact of life. (This fact was brought home again later in the war when his close friend Gladys Calthrop lost her only son Hugo in Burma.) His shrewd commercial sense quickly rejected the idea of writing seriously about death, however: it was not easily done, as *Post-Mortem* had shown, and would hardly draw the crowds while the Blitz raged. His preference was always for comedy – which makes light of all embarrassments and problems – and now the need for laughter was acute. So it was rather clever of him to conceive of a comedy about ghosts.

Coward himself was sceptical about religion and about the supernatural. When his mother died after the war, he regretted in his diary that he could not believe in any reunion on some distant Elysian shore, and on another occasion he related his conviction that 'our minds are concentrated upon an unproven afterlife'. Accordingly, he was probably no more than amused by the legend that Goldenhurst was haunted, a legend which Cole Lesley later described: 'It was well known in the village that a ghost had walked the path over which the new room had been built; a local lad of long ago going nightly to keep a tryst with his lass until he discovered that she was unfaithful and had drowned himself.' But if he was a sceptic, Coward certainly found the idea of ghosts intriguing, because he incorporated them in *Cavalcade*, *Post-Mortem* and *Shadow Play*, and in 1941 – when life expectancy, even for civilians, was so drastically reduced – they became agents of reassurance as well as of disturbance. They offered the possibility that there was not only life, but laughter, after death.

He felt inspired. It was two years since he had written *Present Laughter*, and his autobiography insists that he had anxieties that his gift for comic dialogue might have rusted with disuse; but those anxieties proved groundless, because *Blithe Spirit* materialized effortlessly on the paper, and seemed to need neither modification nor correction. He knew at once that the play was good, and later he would imply that more than his habitual brilliance had enabled him to complete it when he did: 'I shall ever be grateful for the almost psychic gift that enabled me to write *Blithe Spirit* in five days during one of the darkest years of the war.'[3]

It is set in the home of a writer, Charles Condomine, and his second wife, Ruth. Coward subtitled the play 'An Improbable Farce in Three Acts', but *Blithe Spirit*, with a beginning, a middle and an end, is less a farce than a drawing-room comedy, so it is appropriate that at a later moment of calm Ruth, like Wilde's Algernon Moncrieff before her, serves cucumber sandwiches. (Whether they were available during the war, even for ready money, is beside the point.) Elyot and Amanda, Otto, Leo and Gilda, knew nothing of the Depression; and the Condomines are blithely unaware that beyond the footlights, a war rages. Their preoccupations, established in early bickering exchanges, revolve entirely around themselves: they inhabit a period when selfishness was permitted, and when the collective hopes and disappointments of war were unknown, a period of timeless stability suggested by Coward's first stage direction: 'When the curtain rises it is about eight o'clock on a summer evening. There is a wood fire burning because it is an English summer evening.' Charles turns out to be a widower, but it seems that his first wife, Elvira, died of nothing more disagreeable than an uncontrollable fit of laughter induced by a BBC broadcast.

Ruth: Does it still hurt – when you think of her?

Charles: No, not really – sometimes I almost wish it did – I feel rather guilty about it.

Guilt is often pointless – Coward certainly wasted no time wishing that he missed his dead brother and father more keenly.

But it rapidly becomes apparent that Condomine, for all his polish, is not a particularly sympathetic figure. Like David Bliss, he feels no compunction in treating other people as specimens for observation, and *Blithe Spirit* is about the punishment he brings on himself in treating people so arrogantly.[4] To prepare for his projected novel, *The Unseen,* he has organized a séance to be conducted with some neighbours, the Bradmans, and a local medium, Madame Arcati. However, over cocktails before the latter's arrival, he frankly announces that he has no faith in her skills: 'I suspect the worst. A real professional charlatan. That's what I am hoping for anyhow – the character I am planning for my book must be a complete impostor, that's one of the most important factors of the whole story.'

However, when Madame Arcati arrives, she immediately confounds expectations. Her dress has 'a decided bias towards the barbaric' yet she asks for a dry martini rather than a 'concoction'. She announces that she has had a delightful journey cycling through the woods, but she is not all innocence. She used to practise in London, but tired of 'that horrid little flat with the dim lights – they had to be dim, you know, the clients expect it'. She is also a writer; and like Coward himself, works 'every morning regular as clockwork, seven till one'. Based on Coward's friend, the writer Clemence Dane (who had become a Christian Scientist), Madame Arcati is his finest and best-known comic creation – a fact which he recognized when he told Binkie Beaumont that he too wanted to play her. She is realized not only with affection, but also with some respect. Ever since his own brilliant destiny had been foretold by Anna Eva Fay, Coward had been intrigued by clairvoyance and necromancy. He had addressed the subject in one of his earliest dramatic sketches, 'Weatherwise', and in his professional maturity he continued to write characters who consult mediums: the 'refained' Myrtle of *Still Life*, or Miss Erikson of *Present Laughter*. And although he was never slow to sneer, as regular targets of his contempt, like Socialists or Christian Scientists, knew, he never ridiculed those who claimed to divine the future. Furthermore, he showed a surprising degree of impatience with those who did:

Dr Bradman: Who's Daphne?

Ruth: Daphne is Madame Arcati's control – she's a little girl.

Dr Bradman: Oh, I see – yes, of course.

Charles: How old is she?

Madame Arcati: Rising seven when she died.

Mrs Bradman: And when was that?

Madame Arcati: February the sixth, 1884.

Mrs Bradman: Poor little thing.

Dr Bradman: She must be a bit long in the tooth by now, I should think.

Madame Arcati: You should think, Dr Bradman, but I fear you don't – at least, not profoundly enough.

The séance summons Elvira, the first Mrs Condomine, back from the dead. (Coward, incidentally, liked the extraordinary name: he used it in a very early sketch, and in a short story, 'The Wooden Madonna'; Binkie Beaumont's housekeeper was also called Elvira.) She can observe the entire party, but is invisible and inaudible to all but Charles. She first speaks in a 'very charming' voice; but in no time, after Madame Arcati and the Bradmans have left, ignorant of the forces they have helped to conjure, mayhem threatens. Coward brilliantly exploits the cruel comedy of these scenes of displacement, in which Ruth, smug as she is, is isolated by her selfish and irresponsible predecessor:

Ruth: Would you like some more brandy?

Charles: Yes, please.

Elvira: Very unwise – you always had a weak head.

Charles: I could drink you under the table.

Ruth: There's no need to be aggressive, Charles – I'm doing my best to help you.

Elvira is another of Coward's arch creations whose pleasures are self-indulgence and malicious banter, and whose dislikes are children and everything associated with the happy family hearth. She brings chaos to the Condomines' house, and inevitably threatens their marriage. Ruth consults Madame Arcati again, hoping that another séance will put matters right; but the medium proves powerless to remit Elvira to the shadows, not least because the 'old Bell and Book method' no longer works: 'It was quite effective in the old days of genuine religious belief but that's all changed now, I believe the decline of faith in the Spirit world has been causing grave concern ...'

Meanwhile, Elvira is plotting to kill Charles so that she can have him to herself. Edith, the maid, falls on the stairs, after they have been 'covered with axle grease'; and Charles falls, pruning a pear, after the ladder has been discreetly sawn. But as well as having murder on her mind, Elvira is restless: 'I can't stand another of these dreary evenings at home, Charles – it'll drive me dotty – and I haven't seen a movie for seven years ...' Eventually, she engineers a car crash which succeeds in killing off Ruth, rather than Charles. By then, it has become apparent that Charles and Elvira are that familiar Coward couple, the lovers who adore and torment each other by turns, and have always done so:

Elvira: You never suspected it but I laughed at you steadily from the altar to the grave – all your ridiculous petty jealousies and your fussings and fumings –

Charles: You were feckless and irresponsible and morally unstable – I realized that before we left Budleigh Salterton.

Elvira: Nobody but a monumental bore would have thought of having a honeymoon at Budleigh Salterton.

Charles: What's the matter with Budleigh Salterton?

Elvira: I was an eager young bride, Charles – I wanted glamour and music and romance – all I got was potted palms, seven hours a day on a damp golf course and a three-piece orchestra playing 'Merrie England'.[5]

By the time it has been discovered that the maid, Edith, has unwittingly been attracting spiritual attentions, and Madame Arcati has found a way to get rid of both Elvira and Ruth, relations between Condomine and his first wife have deteriorated very badly:

Charles: I'm sick of these insults – please go away.

Elvira: There's nothing I should like better – I've always believed in cutting my losses. That's why I died.

On his return to London, Coward presented his latest offering to Binkie Beaumont, and was not bashful in his assessment of its qualities or its deserts: 'It's my best, it has "smash-hit", "long run" written on every page. Shakespeare never wrote anything so quickly. Not even *Twelfth Night* or *Macbeth*.'[6] Kay Hammond, who had been a highly popular actress since making her name in *French Without Tears* in 1936, was cast as Elvira; and playwright and producer both hoped to interest Margaret Rutherford, then playing

Mrs Danvers in *Rebecca*, in the part of Madame Arcati. At first, however, they were disappointed: she took mediums very seriously, and questioned Coward's intentions. Happily, she relented, and the production transformed her from a well-known supporting and character actress into a star.[7] She annoyed some of the other actors (Dennis Price, Fay Compton and Joyce Carey) because her lack of stage technique caused her to 'tread' on the retorts and laughs of the others, but the *Tatler* was delighted by her performance: 'To see her Madame Arcati get up from an armchair is a lesson in eccentric observation. To hear her tra-la-la-ing in the hour of victory is to assist at a comic inspiration of the first order.'

Indeed, happiness smiled on the enterprise. Winston Churchill adored the play, which became one of the biggest successes in the history of the West End, running for over four and a half years for nearly two thousand performances. It was another example – as it turned out, the last – of Coward's genius for the moment. When youth stirred, he was youthful. When Britain abandoned the gold standard, he wrote *Cavalcade*. Now, when death had become bitterly monotonous, he wrote a classically-tailored comedy which treated death as a joke and enchanted the British at war. (No modern interpretation can quite recapture the bizarre note which underlay the first production, a note stressed by the solemn but absurd notice contained in the programme: 'If an air-raid warning be received during the performance the audience will be informed from the stage ... those desiring to leave the theatre may do so but the performance will continue.')[8] Never one for false modesty, Coward alluded to the ingenuity of his achievement as he recalled the opening night in *Future Indefinite*: 'The audience, socially impeccable from the journalistic point of view and mostly in uniform, had to walk across planks laid over rubble caused by a recent air-raid to see a light comedy about death.'

Sadly, triumphs are rarely total, and the *Spectator* raised a voice of discontent. Its reviewer, Graham Greene, had many criticisms. He said the play was derivative. The idea of ghosts as the stuff of comedy was not new, but then Coward had never laid claim to its novelty. Greene applauded the 'admirable and witty' first act, but took exception to the increasingly farcical flavour of the remainder of the play. He remarked, justly, that the characters spoke more than in Coward's earlier plays, though to insist that 'with one eye on the laggard clock they talked in long paragraphs' was silly.

Above all, however, Greene quite simply missed the point: 'Apart from the first act it has been a weary exhibition of bad taste, a bad taste all the more evident now when sudden death is common and dissolves more marriages than the divorce courts.' The causes of Coward's distasteful display sprang, it was clear to Greene, 'from an ability to produce the appearances of ordinary human relationships – of man and wife – and an inability to feel them.' The implications of this pompous, obtuse and self-righteous conclusion were presumably that everyone in London should wear deep mourning throughout the war, as taste, if not morale, dictated it; and that Greene knew nothing about 'ordinary human relationships' (a fact his fiction sometimes suggested anyway) if he thought that they were faithfully captured in Coward's portrayal of the Condomines.[9]

Coward read Greene's review and was annoyed, as he always was by criticism. He was a believer in settling scores, especially with those who had publicly attacked him, and vented his anger in a poem, 'The Ballad of Graham Greene':

> Oh there's many a Catholic Priest, my boys,
> And many a Rural Dean
> Who, ages later – long ages later
> When all has been, has been,
> Will secretly read an old Spectator
> And pray for Graham Greene.
> (Let's hope its sales have decreased my boys
> Because of Graham Greene.)[10]

Chapter Four

While *Blithe Spirit* was in rehearsal, Coward received a further reminder that death was ever present, and that friendships might suddenly be extinguished: news came that HMS *Kelly* had been sunk off the coast of Crete, and there were fears for the lives of her captain and crew. Coward, his diary reports, immediately contacted the Ministry of Information, and was relieved to learn that although the *Kelly* had indeed been lost, her crew, and her captain, Earl Mountbatten, the principal object of his anxiety, were safe. The sailor's friendship with the *arriviste* actor and writer (which began at the time of the latter's first fame, and probably led to his liaison with Kent) struck many as surprising. Although Mountbatten was known to be amused by flamboyant homo-sexuals[1] (and Coward was notoriously amused by royalty, even of the merely collateral variety), it seemed remarkable that apparently strong affection should endure; and Coward himself later conceded the strangeness of the alliance:

Temperamentally we were diametrically opposed; practically all our inter-ests and pleasures and ambitions were so divergent that it was difficult to imagine how ... we could have found one another such good company. We had, I knew, a mutual respect for one another, admiration too for our respective achievements, but although respect and admiration may form a basis for affection they do not explain it.[2]

The friendship was cemented when, in 1938, Captain Mountbat-ten decided that there was too little method and coherence in the way in which the Royal Navy screened films for the entertainment of its sailors. He called for the installation on all ships of 16mm equipment and conceived of an organization, the Royal Naval Film Corporation, which would supply new films for diversion at sea, films moreover which the men wanted to watch. Mountbatten had enough experience of the bureaucracies of Whitehall and the Admiralty to know that committees would have to be called into being, and paperwork generated, before anything could be done.

155

He approached Coward for help, and the latter, without needing much persuasion, departed on a tour of the Mediterranean Fleet 'to discover the film tastes of the lower deck' and duly write a report to the Chairman of the Admiralty Film Committee. His researches established the popularity of James Cagney, Edward G. Robinson, Spencer Tracy, Charles Laughton ('in practically anything'), and a variety of other actors ranging from Gary Cooper and Ronald Colman through to George Formby. He discovered also that the men liked the partnerships of Fred Astaire and Ginger Rogers, William Powell and Myrna Loy, and Nelson Eddy and Jeanette MacDonald. Popular actresses included Hollywood stars like Dorothy Lamour, Loretta Young and Bette Davis; Mae West ('in moderation, if such a thing is possible'); homegrown girls like Gracie Fields and Jessie Matthews; and more exotic creatures like Simone Simon. He found that 'the five stars who are quite unmistakably *not* liked by the sailors are: Greta Garbo, Marlene Dietrich, Robert Taylor, Douglas Fairbanks Jr, Dick Powell (who was ill-advised enough to do a picture called *The Singing Marine*).'

Western films are extremely unpopular, but not as wholeheartedly detested as ... any films dealing with the English Navy or the United States Navy. This, I think, is quite natural, as in the former they are quick to observe the manifold technical inaccuracies which so far have distinguished any English film dealing with the Services, and in the latter, that is films dealing with the United States Navy, I think they are oppressed by the obvious luxuriousness of the life depicted in that delightfully free-and-easy organization.

He added that he had been 'received with the utmost courtesy and kindness by everyone concerned'. The report was filed and the project executed, but only just in time, in September 1939.[3]

In the light of this collaboration, it was only natural that Coward should follow Mountbatten's career, as the war continued, with interest, and that he should be relieved to hear of his surviving the wreck of the *Kelly*. About a week after the hero's return, on the night following the opening of *Blithe Spirit*, he heard a fuller account over dinner at the Mountbattens', an account which, despite being told without 'frills', Coward found 'heart-breaking' and 'magnificent'.[4] As *Blithe Spirit* drew the crowds, fortune continued well-disposed to its author. Within a few days of hearing the moving story of the shipwreck, Coward was approached by an unforeseen deputation: the director of Two Cities Films, Filippo del Giudice, the producer Anthony Havelock-Allan, and a representative of Columbia Pictures, Charles Thorpe. They hoped to persuade a leading dramatist to write a film for them, but Coward still nurtured a strong prejudice against the cinema, and it seemed that they were wasting their time. He later admitted that the prejudice was founded on nothing more substantial than 'intellectual snobbery', but the resulting conviction, that actors of 'mediocre talent' were 'idolized beyond their deserts', while authors, 'talented or otherwise, were automatically massacred',[5] was nevertheless characteristically staunch – for the time being, at least.

However, work on *Blithe Spirit* was finished, and Coward – though still determined to be seen to be contributing to the war effort – was once again idle. (He did not appear as Charles Condomine until 1942.) Mountbatten's story was the stuff of heroic cinema, and del Giudice's terms had been temptingly generous: provided he wrote the film and acted in it, Coward would be given control of the cast, director, subject and cameraman. The deputation's offer, and Mountbatten's close collision with oblivion, seemed to combine with the neatness of fiction, and he relented: here was the opportunity to capture 'the true sentiment, the comedy, the tragedy, the casual valiance, the unvaunted heroism, the sadness without tears and the pride without end', not only of the last hours of the *Kelly*, but of the Royal Navy as a whole.

The road ahead was long and arduous, and one wonders if Coward would have taken it had he been able to predict the obstacles in his course. At first, everything seemed straightforward. Mountbatten gave enthusiastic approval, though with the rider that the film was not to be recognized as a portrait of either his ship, or his career, since that would be seen as naked self-glorification, condemned by the Navy at the best of times but in war considered inexcusable. Coward was an incorrigible snob, however, and Mountbatten remembered that to begin with his stipulation was ignored: 'The very first script he showed me had the captain married to Lady Celia Kinross, living in a large country house with a Rolls-Royce and a driver ... the car was turned into a Ford without a driver and his wife lost her title, and they lived in a small villa.'[6]

Once amendments were made, Mountbatten was all cooperation and *Future Indefinite* duly applauds his 'personal enthusiasm'. He apparently saw the venture as a 'tribute to the Service he loved', and was quite determined to set 'many wheels turning' and to sever 'strings of red tape' on Coward's behalf. The latter meanwhile joined HMS *Nigeria* for a spell in the North Sea in the interests of establishing maritime accuracy, and wrote the script, as ever, quickly – and it was his first screenplay – in under a month. The film was to be called *White Ensign*.

Almost immediately, however, problems began, principal among them the matter of Coward's persona, the cause of so many of his difficulties since 1939. Fleet Street had heard of the project, and the *Daily Express*, which disliked Coward and Mountbatten, ran a headline story in August saying that they were both to be involved in a film about the Navy which was going to cost £150,000. Another article appeared in the same newspaper in September. At best, such coverage was embarrassing and unhelpful; at worst, its consequences could be very serious. Coward summoned what contacts he could to contain the damage, and an entry in his diary in September 1941 reveals that allies in the Admiralty Press Division were trying to persuade the Director General of the Ministry of Information, Walter Monckton, that pressure should be brought to bear on the *Express*.

The publicity was harmful. The Minister of Information Brendan Bracken had doubts about the propriety of Coward's playing not only one of the early heroes of the war, but the King's cousin at that. (His disquiet stemmed, presumably, not from thespian considerations, but from Coward's fame, in London at least, as a homosexual and a socialite.) The Ministry despatched an official, Sidney Bernstein, to try and talk him out of playing the lead in the film.[7] However, Coward knew all about such persuasion from the very beginning of his career, when managements had not wanted him to play in *The Vortex*; and his thirst for the limelight, particularly when he had written the main part with himself in mind, was equal to every pressure. He knew also that the Ministry had to be placated, otherwise an export licence for the film – which was essential if it was to recoup its production costs and fulfil its propagandist purpose – could be withheld. As late as December 1941, there were still problems; and the Ministry decided that any film which depicted the sinking of a British ship would have appalling consequences for national morale. Again strings were pulled: Mountbatten was given a script to take to the Palace, and charged also with mollifying Brendan Bracken. These obstacles were daunting enough, but worse was to come, and it arrived in the form of another unforeseen deputation, this time from the police. Coward was told that shortly before war was declared, emergency currency regulations had been introduced which made it illegal for British citizens to hold money in the United States without declaring it, and also forbade them to spend it in any circumstances whatsoever. Coward, served with three summonses for violating this law, immediately consulted his solicitor, Sir Dingwall 'Dingo' Bateson, who apparently listened sympathetically to the problem. He was unable to offer much comfort, however: it could count for little that his scrupulously respectable client had broken the law while on government business, since it was known that the Treasury was looking for a well-known offender.

This was disastrous. It seemed inevitable that the press would find out (with the Beaverbrook empire being especially unsympathetic), and that sensational stories about his supposed profligacy in Manhattan and Los Angeles would occupy the head-lines. Such publicity would certainly destroy any hopes of making the film. But, more seriously, the sorry affair must have brought home to him the full extent of Jack Wilson's financial mal-administration. He had had a dollar account in America since his first successes (and had depleted it by £11,000 while travelling there in 1940). Wilson, as a close friend and partner, would certainly have known of the existence of the account. Coward said that he knew nothing of the new currency regulations passed on the eve of war. His claim was perfectly plausible, as they had probably been made official in a hurry, while many more momentous things were also happening. And it is very unlikely, given his enthusiasm for respectability, that he would deliberately have violated any law. At some time during the Thirties, Wilson had proposed a business arrangement whereby, in exchange for half of all Coward's earn-ings, he would provide comprehensive financial services. This was fiscal management at an obviously exorbitant price but, Cole Lesley remarked, 'Noël signed, as always trusting others where his money was concerned.' Wilson had let him down, and Coward was now advised by 'Dingo' Bateson, and his counsel, Geoffrey 'Khaki' Roberts, that he could be penalized by as much as £60,000. They urged him to plead guilty and hope for the best.

Press coverage of the affair was surprisingly muted before the court appearances. But George Bernard Shaw must have read of

Coward's predicament somewhere, because he wrote to him, saying that there could be no guilt without intention, and that he must plead not guilty. Perhaps because he had received sound advice from Shaw as an aspiring playwright, or perhaps because Shaw's logic seemed unassailable, Coward followed his advice, and was given token fines. The press, equally miraculously and uncharacteristically, had behaved with forbearance, and he could carry on with the film. But it was more clear now than it had been when Coward wrote to Wilson in 1940, that drastic rearrangement of his finances and financial managers was going to be one of the priorities of the peace.

A production company was established, Coward was appointed director and the tyro David Lean was asked to be assistant director. Coward was at first astonished and irritated by his insistence that they be billed as co-directors, but then acquiesced, and Lean rapidly discovered that Coward's boredom with the mechanics of filming allowed him autonomy on the set:

Noël used to go back to his dressing-room with Gladys Calthrop to play this card game of four-pack bezique, and then we'd call him when we were ready. Finally Noël said, 'Look, my dear, you know what you are doing. I'll just leave it to you, and I'll come down when I'm to be photographed.'[8]

Ronald Neame became the director of photography; Anthony Havelock-Allan was associate producer. (This triumvirate was later responsible for transferring *Blithe Spirit*, *This Happy Breed* and *Still Life* to celluloid, with varying degrees of success.) Scrupulous where accuracy was concerned – presumably because he remembered the complaints about technical infractions he had heard while researching for the RNFC – Coward appointed Commander 'Bushy' Clarke and Lieutenant Charles Compton 'ward-room and bridge advisers'; and Terry Lawlor, who had been Mountbatten's servant on the *Kelly*, was 'lower decks adviser'. Finally, *White Ensign* became *In Which We Serve*, the new title being a quotation from a naval prayer, and filming began, at Denham Studios, in February 1942.

Seven months had already elapsed since the film's inception, and they had been filled, as *Future Indefinite* reported, with casting discussions, budget conferences, reconnaissances to dockyards in Plymouth and Portsmouth and to shipyards in Newcastle, screen tests, a heavy diet of previous British films for casting purposes, and a constant vigilance with regard to naval details. Although a very hard worker, Coward had always been used to having to make little effort where organizing projects was concerned. Since first storming the West End, he had simply conceived an idea in the certainty that no manager or theatre would cavil at the cost, and that if there were anxieties about either the subject-matter or Coward's appropriateness to the main part, they were easily overruled by the promises Coward could make of golden rewards. But in war, even the successful were subject to endless bureaucratic and official anxieties; and in any case, a new career in the cinema required a new apprenticeship. Coward was dauntless and determined and he would not have conceded defeat in the face of these obstacles easily, but there is no doubt that the making of *In Which We Serve* would have been much more difficult had it not been for Mountbatten's support.

After his initial conditions had been met, he lent every assistance. He gave Coward several of the speeches he had made as captain of the *Kelly*. These, including the one in which Coward, as Captain Kinross, welcomes his men aboard at the beginning of the film, were used verbatim. Mounbatten involved himself in the casting: Bernard Miles remembered being summoned to London to attend a screening of a film about the Home Guard in which he had appeared. Mountbatten and Coward were also at the screening. Afterwards, it was the sailor, rather than the actor, who told him that he had got a new job. Concerned that the extras who had been hired did not look sufficiently seaman-like, Mountbatten commandeered two hundred convalescent patients from a naval hospital. He was a perfect partner, and to Coward, a paragon: 'Dickie's militant loyalty, moral courage and infinite capacity for taking pains, however busy he is, is one of the marvels of this most unpleasant age. I would do anything for him.'[9]

Not the least of Mountbatten's qualifications was his capacity for ensuring interest in the most exalted quarters. Thus, Coward's diary, where royal encounters sometimes seem to be the rule rather than the exception, records that in April 1942 the Mountbattens brought the King, the Queen and the two princesses to the set: 'Then I did the Dunkirk speech ... All the time they were perfectly charming, easy and interested and, of course, with the most exquisite manners to everyone. The Queen is clearly the most enchanting woman. The Princesses were thrilled and beautifully behaved.'

It says a lot for Mountbatten's regard for Coward that he was prepared to go to such lengths. After all, he had been parodied, with scant regard for flattery, in *Hands Across the Sea*, only six years before, and *In Which We Serve* attracted some criticism in the Navy. The Admiralty had insisted that Captain Kinross was not Mountbatten, but no one took the disclaimers seriously. Seeing the film at Buckingham Palace in 1942, Mrs Roosevelt was under no illusions at all as to the hero's true identity, and Mountbatten later told Coward that his connexion with the film had led to accusations of self-aggrandisement from his fellow officers. When Coward wrote *Future Indefinite*, between 1947 and 1953, it was inevitable that he would describe the making of *In Which We Serve*. Mountbatten, hoping belatedly to repair some of the damage which the film had done to his reputation, sought amendments in the manuscript; the book as published explicitly exonerates him: Captain Kinross was intended to represent an 'average' naval officer, but Mountbatten was 'very far from being an average naval officer'.

Mountbatten's and Coward's common enemy, Lord Beaverbrook, was determined to be scandalized by the film: by its cost; by the incongruity, as he saw it, of Coward in the main role; by the possible effect on morale and so on. Coward had already had enough of Beaverbrook's criticisms and persecution. He had revenged himself on Graham Greene for daring to criticize him, and now he would do the same with Lord Beaverbrook. *In Which We Serve* therefore opens with a close-up of a *Daily Express* headline promising 'No War This Year'. This gloating reminder of *Express* Newspapers' naïvety outraged Beaverbrook, who redoubled his attacks on the collaborators. Towards the end of 1942, he and Mountbatten were sitting on the same table at dinner, and the press baron rounded on the sailor, angrily accusing him of self-glorification in time of national crisis. His newspapers continued whenever possible to attack Coward also; and although, shortly before Beaverbrook died, there was a sort of reconciliation, it was half-hearted. Coward's diary entry for 16 June 1964 records: 'Max Beaverbrook died on Friday. This long – too long – delayed occurrence requires no comment. God is still presumably in his heaven unless he has been forced to move over.'

Another enemy encountered during the filming of *In Which We Serve* was Cecil Beaton. By then Coward's prophecy, flippantly made in his 1932 revue for Charles Cochran – 'Though Waterloo was won upon the playing fields of Eton/The next war will be photographed, and lost, by Cecil Beaton' – had been vindicated. Beaton had transformed himself, rather like Coward, from being the darling of Mayfair to a patriot for the people.[10] Relations between them had never been easy: they were both too competitive, too catty, and too similar, to refrain from indiscreet observations about each other. When they met in 1942, it was, according to Cecil Beaton's diary, in the usual atmosphere of tension and mutual suspicion, with Beaton, by his own admission, feeling 'intolerant and bitter'. He admonished Coward for what he took to be a lack of interest in his by then very successful career. But he was not prepared for Coward's response:

Don't you believe it, sister, I've been madly interested in you! But I've been a fool, I've misjudged you. The war has shown how wrong I've been. You've done a great job – you've earned great respect in the RAF; and it just shows what a mistake I made. You've been yourself always, and how right you've been! I've been hiccuping off at the outbreak of the war, thinking it was a wonderful thing to give up those two plays that were already in production to do a job that anyone else could have done. You've done much better than I by just sticking to your guns: people respect you for that.[11]

Coward also knew, by 1942, that his assault on posterity had been accomplished.

He admitted to having had such success during the last fifteen years that he wouldn't think it terrible if a bomb killed him today. '*Blithe Spirit* is a bloody good play, and *Private Lives* will always be revived and will go into the history of comedy like a play by Congreve or Wilde.'[12]

Unfortunately, he risked no prophecies with Beaton about the success of *In Which We Serve*.

Coward's confidence notwithstanding, any prophecies would probably have underestimated the acclaim the film received. Its triumphant opening in London in 1942 redeemed anxieties about the film's swollen budget (£200,000), about press discouragement and bureaucratic opposition. And in his diary, Coward allowed himself a moment of brief exultation: enemies like Beaverbrook, and opponents like the Ministry of Information, had been humiliated, and he had contributed to the war effort by 'showing the public what the Navy really is like'.

Mountbatten agreed: 'He produced a film which as far as I was concerned was exactly like life at sea. All the survivors of the *Kelly* agreed that it was quite staggering to find how true the whole film has been.'[13] In the *Sunday Times*, Dilys Powell called it 'the best film about the war yet made in this country or in America'. In the *Observer*, C. A. Lejeune considered it 'one of the most heart-warming, heart-stirring films this country has ever produced, either at peace or in war'. *The Times* was handsomely congratulatory: 'The aftermath of Dunkirk [is] stated theatrically, and the theatrical terms are magnificent.' The *Express*, atoning for its former hostility, found it 'a great film of the Royal Navy'. If the *New Statesman* (an intellectual organ, Coward doubtless noted) complained that the film was 'far too long, too much centred upon Mr Coward', sublime compensation came from the Minister of Information himself: 'I hope you will consider very carefully my suggestion that you should make a film about the Army. I have never seen a really good film made about the Army and I am sure you could make one which would be as rousing a success as *In Which We Serve*.'[14]

Coward's friend, the New York critic Alexander Woollcott, said, 'All your years were a kind of preparation for this,' and in 1943, Hollywood recognized his 'special contribution' with an Oscar. Churchill loved the film, and was repeatedly moved to tears by it. The King himself is said to have wept when he saw it, and his subjects followed suit in their thousands. Joyce Grenfell wrote to her mother: 'It's *terrific*. One of the best I've ever seen. Beautifully photographed, cut, directed and acted and you'll adore it. I cried like a tap all through.'[15] *In Which We Serve* was the most successful film of 1943; and a *Daily Mail* survey of 1945 found it the eighth most popular film of the war years. Finally, it seemed that official, and royal, recognition, of the delight and diversion Coward had given his country, not only during the war but for all his twenty or so adult years, would come.

Diary entries in October 1942 refer to a 'suggestion' made by the King, and relayed by his cousin, and then to a letter of recapitulation sent by Mountbatten, to Coward, who resolved to consider the matter 'very carefully'. It cannot have taken him more than two minutes of soul-searching to realize that he would seize any honour, particularly a knighthood, which is what George VI was proposing; but, by the end of December 1942, Coward knew that an honour was not to be his, and Mountbatten would by then have passed on his suspicion that the proposal had been sabotaged. His disappointment must have been intense, but Coward determined to give the matter no more thought.

Esme Wynne-Tyson, strangely, was as well informed as anybody else about the affair. Her oldest friend other than Coward, Lena Angood, worked in Whitehall in the department responsible for honours. Coward had been passed over, she categorically reported, because of the currency charges, and because of his sexuality.[16]

In Which We Serve is open to several interpretations. Anthony Aldgate and Jeffrey Richards (in their book *Britain Can Take It: The British Cinema in the Second World War*) see it as 'a film of love: love of England ("England may be a very small island, vastly overcrowded, frequently badly managed, but it is in my view the best and bravest country in the world"); love for the Navy ("I love the Navy, I inherited my affection for it, all my mother's family were Navy"); love for Lord Mountbatten.' But the film's images suggest a further interpretation. 'This is the story of a ship,' Leslie Howard intones in the prologue to the film, and the ship clearly represents Great Britain, where discipline, order and understanding and cooperation between ranks and classes is crucially important. And the abiding image of the film – of beleaguered men clinging to a raft while German gunfire surrounds them – is unmistakably emblematic of 1940, when European civilization seemed hopelessly betrayed, and Great Britain alone remained to defend it.

Knowing how to judge the film now is rather difficult. Propaganda – which Cyril Connolly defined as 'the genial guidance of thought by the state which undermines the love of truth and beauty' – is bound to date badly. If today it seems strange to hear Dilys Powell claim that 'the film set new standards in the English cinema', one must remember that the climate of opinion was very different then from what it is now, not least because it was so relentlessly and unsubtly manipulated. There is also the problem of Coward's performance. When, years later, his friend Beatrice Lillie was cast as Madame Arcati in a musical version of *Blithe Spirit*, he said she was as much like Arcati as he was like Queen Victoria. Yet the analogy is no more extravagant than Coward's comparing himself to a naval officer. Even David Lean, who greatly admired his skills in comedy, said that as 'a family man' and an officer he was not convincing. The fact is that Coward remains incontrovertibly Coward throughout, despite his determination, as recorded in his diary, to suppress his most characteristic mannerisms, and despite the experiments with camera angles and lighting which led Ronald Neame to photograph his star from above rather than below. This need not matter, since versatility is not everything in acting, but his presence in a film about the Royal Navy now seems totally implausible (not least because his accent is so clipped as to be inaudible at the best of times, and a sea battle was not the best of times). John Mills, Richard Attenborough and the sublime Celia Johnson are very good. The admiration for the British at war ('There's no use making a fuss, is there?' one character asks another during an air-raid) is consistent and convincing. But more than anything else, *In Which We Serve* seems now to be a monument to its author's determination in the face of opposition, his conviction in the face of improbability, and to the energy of a self-confidence uncomplicated by doubt.

Chapter Five

The encounter with Cecil Beaton in 1942 neatly reversed the meeting between them which had occurred in mid-Atlantic in 1930. On that earlier occasion Beaton had received instruction from Coward. Now, it was Coward who seemed to have something to learn from Beaton, who had not wasted his time in the war by trying to acquire abilities which he did not have. Late in the day though it was, Coward knew in 1942 that he should no longer try and involve himself in good causes for which he had no aptitude: others could dig or fight for victory, but he would not betray his vocation to amuse again: 'If I can make people laugh etc ... I am not doing so very badly ... This is my job really, and will remain so through all wars and revolutions and carnage.'[1]

So he took laughter to the provinces. With *Blithe Spirit* playing to capacity in London, he agreed with Binkie Beaumont to tour England and Scotland with *Present Laughter* and *This Happy Breed*. Along with Joyce Carey and Judy Campbell, his supporting actresses, he endured fuel shortages in huge theatres, erratic wartime trains and rationed bed-and-breakfast food. (By some bizarre logic of war, however, the season was permitted the profligacy of *couture* – Molyneux, as ever – for *Present Laughter*.) The privations they encountered were as nothing, of course, to the privations of millions; but by 1942, when it was hard to remember a time when indiscreet light was not dangerous, and when food was not bought with coupons, the season must have been a tonic, as both plays were new, and Noël Coward was the titan of the English theatre. Joyce Grenfell, having loved *In Which We Serve*, thought him an unparalleled genius: 'What he has got is a complete and colossal ego. But then he has reason to be that way. He is the most talented creature since Michelangelo, I suppose. He can write, act, compose, paint and all well. And now he can make movies, even though he hates them.'[2] She was naturally eager to see him when, between tours herself, she visited Edinburgh, where he was appearing:

... we struck *Present Laughter* which is a perfect piece of escapist froth, quite beautifully played and with such speed and polish ... It's wildly funny and witty and sometimes wise and always a delight to the eye for Gladys [Calthrop] is good at that sort of thing. After nine weeks touring in Northern Ireland it was a lovely jolt to see first-class work and to see an audience that knew what it was all about ... We adored every minute of it and so did the huge house.[3]

As Coward's performance of Garry Essendine became more practised, it became more extravagant also. He introduced variations to mitigate the tedium of a long season, and would regularly end scenes in unscripted recitals of Rostand, whom he was committing to memory as a mental exercise. The tour attracted the sort of coverage – affectionate yet reverential – normally accorded to royal progresses, and Joyce Grenfell was not alone in considering him the polymath of Shaftesbury Avenue. Confronted by the effervescence and diversity of his new brace of plays, local critics, to borrow Kenneth Tynan's famous phrase, stood agape in the lobbies. When the tour culminated in the West End, their metropolitan counterparts were no less impressed, and the plays attracted the attention their novelty deserved. In the *Evening Standard*, Beverley Baxter admitted their author to the pantheon of comic dramatists:

If Mr Coward is not careful he will become a significant and permanent figure in the history of the English stage. That is a sobering thought to many of us who once felt that his gifts belonged to precocity and that the fruit would spoil with ripening ... *Present Laughter* places him in the same gallery as Wilde and Congreve.[4]

In the *Sunday Times*, James Agate was pleased and perceptive. 'One left the theatre thinking of this actor what Lamb said of the Robin Goodfellow of his day: "He is no more an imitator than he is in any true sense himself imitable."'[5] But it was Joyce Grenfell's friend, the critic and writer Herbert Farjeon, who was the most acute: 'If he had not been a successful man, would he ever have written *Present Laughter*? No. However nice his taste in epithets, he would but for success never have acquired that insight into self-dramatization which comes of living up to your fame.'[6]

Amidst this encomium, the *Spectator* was sceptical once again:

In *Present Laughter*, the principal character, Garry Essendine, a portrait of an irresistibly attractive and unfailingly successful author, does not carry conviction. Not because it is unconvincing as far as it goes, but because it does not go far enough. Garry Essendine bears every resemblance to Mr Coward except that he tells us nothing about the real Mr Coward. Garry Essendine is a ghost, and a great comedy must have a real hero and not a ghost.[7]

Of course Coward had not bared his soul: it would have been completely out of his character to do so, and not easily within his capabilities. That is not where the play fails, however. Its problem lies in the fact that it is tailored so completely for Coward: no other actor in any generation could ever portray Garry Essendine as well as his creator, and in that sense, as a bid for immortality, *Present Laughter* might be said to be a self-cancelling conceit.

The season at The Haymarket was not Coward's only activity that year, nor his most remarked. He continued to write songs, and if he was very busy at that time, he was also, suddenly, inspired. He was always at his best as a songwriter when there was something to attack; and in 1943 there was no shortage of targets:

> Don't let's be beastly to the Germans
> When our victory is ultimately won,
> It was just those nasty Nazis who persuaded them to fight
> And their Beethoven and Bach are really far worse than their bite,
> Let's be meek to them –
> And turn the other cheek to them
> And try to bring out their latent sense of fun.
> Let's give them full air parity –
> And treat the rats with charity,
> But don't let's be beastly to the Hun.

Churchill adored this song. Unfortunately, others were less enthusiastic. Coward had learnt already, as a frustrated propagandist during the Phoney War, that an irreverent sense of humour was a liability for the times. Now he was to learn that irony was too subtle a form of expression for the unequivocal requirements of war. The Ministry of Information, still smarting perhaps from the defeats he had inflicted during the making of *In Which We Serve*, immediately refused to pass the song for recording or publication, on the grounds that it contained lines which – sufficiently distorted – might lend comfort to Goebbels.

Coward's wanderlust had been thwarted for two years by the time the controversy surrounding 'Don't Let's Be Beastly To The Germans' broke, and he was longing to leave England. After his brief interlude of officialdom in Paris, he had largely had to create his own war work; and now, armed with a few hastily arranged permits, he decided to entertain troops overseas. He was not going entirely into the unknown, as he had already given a concert and lecture tour in Australia and New Zealand between October 1940 and February 1941, which had raised £12,000 for charity. He had travelled as a guest of the Australian government, and the entire venture had been a great success. (He was subsequently congratulated by the Prime Minister, Robert Menzies.) Years later, in *Future Indefinite*, Coward was to look back on that tour with a surprising degree of modesty: volunteering the observation that his style, technique and stage routines had hardly been perfected with Australian soldiers and farmers in mind, he claimed that he was always dogged by an anxiety that he could not satisfy his audiences. If these were genuine fears, however, he overcame them, and had no misgivings about leaving England again in 1943 to try and earn more perhaps uncomprehending applause. He had resolved to have nothing to do with ENSA (the Entertainments National Service Association), the unofficial body run by his former director, Basil Dean, which aimed to recruit and coordinate entertainers for troops based overseas. Coward would go his own way, and that year his itinerary included Gibraltar, Algiers (where he met Eisenhower), Malta, Cairo, Alexandria, Beirut, Tripoli and Algiers again, and by the time he returned to England he had already undertaken to travel to South Africa.

In Cape Town, in 1944, he was met like a royal ambassador of Englishness by a multitude of thirty thousand. He travelled to Durban, Pietermaritzburg, Bloemfontein, Kimberley, Pretoria and Johannesburg, and then went to Rhodesia. While there, he was cabled by Mountbatten, who asked him to go and entertain the dejected and forgotten troops of the Fourteenth Army in Assam and Burma. By that time, Coward was extremely tired, and the mission which Mountbatten was proposing was certain to be arduous. Mountbatten was in a position to ask favours, of course, after the help he had given with *In Which We Serve*; but the prospect of once more entering the 'orbit of Mountbatten's unpredictable star' left Coward in a state of 'excitement tinged with dismay'.[8] He could plausibly have complained of physical exhaustion and returned to London; but to his credit, Coward accepted the invitation. On the voyage from Mombasa to Ceylon, patriotism overwhelmed him, and he wrote a short story called 'Mr and Mrs Edgehill':

Every morning at dawn and every evening at sunset Eustace performed with correct solemnity, the ritual of the Flag. For this all the boys, in brightly-coloured sarongs, the only moment of the day or night in which they wore anything, stood respectfully to attention. Dorrie stood to attention too, and, once in a while, permitted herself the luxury of a nostalgic tear or two. Thoughts of Home dropped into her mind. The soft wet green of the Romney Marshes; the brightly coloured traffic in Piccadilly on a spring morning; the crowded pavements of Oxford Street; the bargain basement at Selfridge's and the Changing of the Guard.[9]

Mountbatten awaited him in Kandy: 'Although he looked sunburnt and outwardly fit I detected a strain in his eyes.' Coward, too, was soon exhausted by the gruelling conditions and exacting pace of his time in Ceylon and Burma. India, by contrast, was less demanding. He sang in Bombay, Bangalore, Madras and Calcutta, and stayed in the Viceroy's house in Delhi with Lord and Lady Wavell. She, apparently, was 'a dear', but nevertheless proved incapable of reconciling her famous guest either to India's capital, or to the ultimate certainty of its independence. Cecil Beaton, encountering Coward at this time, found him vociferous:

Noël shouted and said he had become more and more imperialistic and would like to beat the black and yellow buggers down the street. 'Why do a lot of intellectuals talk balls and give them self-government? Not fit to look after themselves.' Much too sweeping statements and too sweeping a condemnation of Delhi.[10]

Gandhi's assassination in 1948 struck him, unsurprisingly, as being 'a bloody good thing'.[11] Meanwhile, he and Beaton were as wary of each other as ever, and competed for Mountbatten's recognition. Beaton, leaving a record, has the last laugh:

Noël very excited. [Mountbatten] looked rattled and rugged, untidy, dirty boots. Did not wish to see some of the generals that had been assembled. Dinner went well, was extremely informal. I sat next to Supremo (M) who was in a light mood and only wishing to make jokes. No intention of listening to China's troubles which Mrs Casey had asked me to expound upon, but thoroughly frivolous about our photographing in the glass bed at Faridkot House. Noël galvanized, almost jumping out of his skin, trembling, face contorted. Determination to be amused.[12]

Beaton was particularly delighted to overhear one ADC remark to another: 'It is not so interesting to see what Noël Coward has done for the world as it is to see what the world has done for Noël Coward.' It was all very well for Beaton to be envious and malicious (and there was no doubt some truth in his observations), but the fact remained that Coward had worked very hard and had achieved a great deal. In appalling conditions, with only an accompanying pianist, Norman Hackforth, and a battered upright piano, the 'little treasure', he had entertained thousands. ('Mad Dogs and English-men', which had originally mocked his country's imperial pre-tensions, doubled now as a salute to the British spirit.) When he finally returned to England, his weight had fallen from its normal eleven stones to nine. He broadcast a tribute to the Forgotten Army on the Home Service, and chastised the press for its neglect. He spoke of the terrible conditions in which the soldiers existed, and of their courage: 'We are forever in the debt of these extraordinary men, who are keeping the flame of our national pride and honour burning more clearly in the faraway corners of the world.'[13] The broadcast earned him the thanks and congratulations of the King and Queen. Coward's real reward, however, for this aspect of his war work, was the discovery that he could hold his own as a cabaret entertainer, a discovery that in the peace was to prove something of a salvation.

PART FOUR
ECLIPSE

Chapter One

While Coward had been abroad, David Lean – working again with Ronald Neame and Anthony Havelock-Allan – had filmed *This Happy Breed* and *Blithe Spirit*. Coward was particularly disappointed by the latter interpretation, but did not allow his disapproval to prevent their collaborating again in 1945. He set to work on turning *Still Life*, a one-act play from *Tonight at 8.30*, into a screenplay. The result, *Brief Encounter*, is often today everyone's first, if unwitting, taste of Noël Coward, and quickly took its place as one of the most celebrated of all British films. Its principal tableau, of Celia Johnson and Trevor Howard, behatted, half-shrouded in station smoke, and separated by the window of a train, spoke strongly of an impossible passion intensified by diffidence and thwarted by respectability; and its world, where people spoke beautifully and the trains ran on time, seems now to encapsulate an England as surely lost as that of the Roundheads and the Cavaliers.

Of all the collaborations between Coward and Lean, *Brief Encounter* is the one which allowed the young director the greatest autonomy. To make a feature film out of a short play, Coward had to introduce new material, and he supplies much more information about the lovers. Laura's husband Fred, invisible in *Still Life*, now appears. Whereas the latter's plot proceeded solely through its dialogue, Coward decided that the film should have a narrator, so it is Laura herself who guides us through her affair, beginning with the climactic scene of farewell, and then looking at the events which led up to it. At £270,000, the film was cheap, but the acting was not, and remains perfectly suited to Coward's controlled writing. At his insistence, Celia Johnson made her third appearance in one of his films in as many years, and gave a superb performance. Trevor Howard was unknown before *Brief Encounter*, but it made him a star. Even the comic interludes, with Stanley Holloway and Joyce Carey, as the brilliantly 'refained' Myrtle, imported like Shakespearean low-life to enable us to recuperate from the intensity of the emotions around them, are wonderfully done. Lean and

Coward were accused of cheating in their attempts to convey the charged and intense condition of illicit love – notably in their use of Rachmaninov's Second Piano Concerto – but critics and audiences inclined to the view that the film's merits outweighed its flaws, and some were almost lyrical in its praise. Roger Manvell claimed that 'Its passing express trains have the rush and power of passion, its platforms and subways the loneliness of waiting lovers.'

Nearly twenty years before, in *The Marquise*, Coward had his heroine damn self-sacrifice as 'one of the most sterile forms of self-indulgence in the world'. If he had ever believed that himself, his view had changed. Heroic denial drew the crowds to the box-office; but it was also central to the values of middle-class decency, of respectability, stability, hard work, duty and patriotism, which he had come increasingly to espouse. *Still Life*, the prototype for *Brief Encounter*, was written in 1935. A year later, at the height of the Abdication Crisis, Coward had written to Mountbatten, the King's cousin, asking him to try and take action to control the 'degrading and horrible publicity', adding, in modification of his famous first-night speech from *Cavalcade*, 'I can only think now in the midst of all this scandal and vulgarity, that it's a bloody uncomfortable thing to be English!' By choosing Mrs Simpson in preference to the throne, Edward had let down England's middle classes. But in *Brief Encounter* Alec and Laura are made of nobler stuff, and know instinctively that duty must always prevail. (Only a decade later, in 1955, when another royal matrimonial crisis preoccupied the nation, Coward was happy to discover that Princess Margaret had decided not to marry Group Captain Peter Townsend: 'I am sure she is right to stick by the job. At least she hasn't betrayed her position and her responsibilities.'[1]) But if his public knew that it could look to him for approval of respectability, Coward himself knew that he was a victim of the constricting morality of his age, and was better qualified than most to write about the dangers of proscribed private lives:

Alec: I love you – I love you – you love me too – it's no use pretending that it hasn't happened because it has.

Laura (with tremendous effort): Yes it has. I don't want to pretend anything either to you or to anyone else ... but from now on I shall have to. That's what's wrong – don't you see? That's what spoils everything. That's why we must stop here and now talking like this. We are neither of us free to love each other, there is too much in the way. There's still time, if we control ourselves and behave like sensible human beings, there's still time to – to … (She puts her head down and bursts into tears.)

Alec: There's no time at all.

Although he had reservations about some of David Lean's adaptations of his work, Coward was delighted with *Brief Encounter*, and his diary bestows lavish praise on the film's actors and director, and, half jokingly, on its screenplay. When it opened, it met with little success in Italy, apparently because the Italians did not like Trevor Howard's looks. By contrast, the French were enthusiastic, at least according to Dilys Powell: they loved the idea that anyone could fall in love with Laura, given the preposterous hats she always wore. *Brief Encounter* is still shown regularly on television, and in cinemas, and if one concedes that it would be a much smaller film without its main actors, one must acknowledge also that it reflects uncompromisingly the mood of its time, and that it retains a compelling dramatic strength.[2]

The war was over by the time the film was released in England, and everywhere there was upheaval and readjustment. Goldenhurst was still requisitioned by the army, so Coward bought a cottage, White Cliffs, on the Kentish coast, which was to be his home until the return to Goldenhurst in 1951. (He eventually sold it to his neighbour from Jamaica, Ian Fleming.) More importantly, his emotional life was suddenly and decisively redirected when he met, and fell in love with, a young South African actor called Graham Payn. They had first met in 1932, when the fourteen-year-old auditioned for a part in *Words and Music*, Coward's last revue for Charles Cochran. Suddenly, Payn appeared again in the older man's life towards the end of the war and in 1947 he moved in at White Cliffs.

Coward had always had difficulty in putting his more personal feelings onto paper. Tenses, moods, scenes and even sexes often had to be changed before he was prepared to consider intimating the inner workings of his mind, so it would have been extremely out of character for him to have indulged in frank accounts of his courtship with Payn, even in his diary. Many such confessional documents have been overburdened with details of love; but in Coward's, iron discretion was the rule and whatever attraction Payn held for him, it was either too intimate for him to commit to paper, or too impenetrably personal and subjective. Whatever the charm, it was strong: Payn, who seems to have been universally liked for his sweetness, was still living with Coward when the latter died.

Assuming that everyone would share his high opinion, Coward immediately determined to turn Payn into a stage star, and began the process by giving him a large part in the revue he was then writing, *Sigh No More*, which was designed to celebrate the end of the war. Indeed, the only vestige of the entire venture is its finest song, written for Payn's voice, and for Coward a rather unguarded declaration:

> Matelot, Matelot,
> Where you go
> My thoughts go with you ...
> Though you may find
> Womenkind
> To be frail,
> One love cannot fail, my son,
> Till our days are done,
> Matelot, Matelot,
> Where you go
> My thoughts go with you,
> Matelot, Matelot,
> When you go down to the sea.

Despite this wonderful beginning, Payn, for all his looks and sweetness of disposition, proved no muse, and the attempts to make him a star failed. He was still playing in revivals of *Tonight at 8.30* in Windsor in 1957; Coward could be very determined – and very blind – but even he had to admit defeat, and by the early Sixties he had acknowledged to his diary, if not to his friends, that Payn was without ambition or impetus, 'a born drifter'.

Meanwhile, the news of his arrival and installation horrified Jack Wilson, who had been in America since before the war. On his first post-war visit to England, he interrogated Cole Lesley, who remembered Wilson's bellicose accusation, 'Don't tell me you didn't hate his guts from the moment he walked in the door?' It was apparently irrelevant that Payn's predecessor in Coward's affections had been married for nearly a decade by this time. He was jealous of Payn, perhaps unsurprisingly, and obviously suspected that the new liaison would weaken his financial control over

Coward. The end was finally in sight as far as the great love between the star and the handsome reformed stockbroker was concerned, and Coward was to discover over the next two years how much damage had been done.

Another ending came in that year, 1945. In a Victory Day article commissioned by the *Daily Mail*, Coward had written:

The physical war is perhaps nearly over but the moral war is only just beginning. We as a race are capable, like all other races, of prevarication, muddled thinking, sentimentalism, untimely arrogance and most untimely self-deprecation, but we are also capable, in adversity, of greater qualities than any other race in the world ... Let us try with all our concentrated will to maintain the spirit that upheld us in 1940. Let us remember, disregarding political tact and commercial expedience, that it was our inherited, stubborn integrity that gave the future of the civilized world a chance and a glimmer of hope.[3]

Coward never quite makes clear what the British in victory should do, but it went without saying that electing a socialist government was not part of his scheme. He had made that clear in one of his songs from *Sigh No More*:

> We're the Burchills of Battersea Rise
> And we're faced with a dismal selection again,
> We may find if we swallow the Socialist bait
> That a simple head cold is controlled by the State,
> Though we know Winston Churchill is wise
> And we'd love him to win the election again,
> If he's forced to say 'Yes'
> To the Beaverbrook press
> There'll be loud animal cries
> From the Burchills of Battersea Rise.

There was a great deal about Churchill that Coward did not like, and he had never really forgiven him for his unwanted, if understandable, advice of 1939, to go and sing while the guns were firing. Yet he could not but admire the orator in him; and he was prepared to concede that, for all his failings, he had been the custodian of European freedom, and was without doubt the greatest statesman of the free world (and his greatness comprehended an admiration for Coward's songs). When the Labour Party – 'a shoddy lot of careerists' – won the General Election in July 1945, Coward was outraged: Churchill had not so much been defeated as betrayed, and his downfall, which Coward was convinced would scandalize foreign observers, seemed a terrible portent of uncomfortable change. In 1939, Coward had been at one with his lower-middle-class audience: war was an honourable, if regrettable, course of action, and throughout the hostilities each party had acquitted itself to the satisfaction of the other. The sacrifices had been worth it, and anyway they would be remembered:

> Much will be written
> In future years. Historians will spew
> Long treatises on your triumphant story,
> They'll rightly praise your gallantry and glory
> And probably embarrass you a lot.[4]

There were historical treatises eventually, but Coward was to discover that Britain spent little in expressions of gratitude: there was little of anything – time, money, energy or emotion – to spend. A determination to create a new world was abroad. Churchill had been its first victim; Coward, who also embodied the class-riven Thirties, could easily be its next. As it became established, he felt increasingly ill at ease in post-war Britain. He made no secret of the fact; and relations between him and his native land, formerly so affectionate, gradually cooled in the breezes of the welfare state to a long disillusionment:

> Our far-flung Empire imposed new rules
> And lasted a century or so
> Until, engrossed with our football pools,
> We shrugged our shoulders and let it go.[5]

Chapter Two

Coward's response to this new world was to retreat into the past. Once he had been synonymous with youth and all things audacious and modern. Now he was a nostalgic forty-five. He remembered that while writing *Tonight at 8.30* he had invented a tiny British possession, situated in the southwest Pacific, called Samolo. Now he decided to furnish the island; and a diary entry for November 1945 records an evening spent inventing the history, the climate, even the language, of the Samolan archipelago, as well as establishing its exact latitude and longitude, and soon it had been decided that the principal island could serve as the setting for his first big post-war production, his return to the West End, *Pacific 1860*. Binkie Beaumont had decided that the West End's return to normality should be signalled by a lavish new musical to be staged at the Drury Lane Theatre, the oldest and most prestigious in London. It had been badly damaged by a bomb, but that was nothing that could not be rectified, and he approached the theatre magnate, Prince Littler, whose company owned the building. Coward was commissioned to write a musical. There seemed no reason to imagine that his prodigious gifts for musicals and epics might have staled during the war; and – vital to Beaumont's scheme – he was British, rather than being an imported American genius.

The enterprise was dogged with misfortunes from its inception. Permits to repair the theatre were processed with catastrophic sluggishness, even though Coward took the matter directly to Aneurin Bevan, the Minister of Works. Once they had been secured, shortages of labour and materials led to further delays in the restoration, so that the production opened badly under-rehearsed. Rationing of fuel meant that all the theatrical artifice in the world fell flat when it came to evoking a Pacific paradise in a freezing theatre. There were terrible scenes between Coward and his faithful designer, Gladys Calthrop ('I told her that the sets looked more like Torquay and Draycott Gardens than Samolo'),[1] and friction, most

181

seriously, with the leading lady, Mary Martin. (It eventually transpired that the difficulties which developed between Coward and Martin and her husband, Dick Halliday, had been engineered by Jack Wilson out of spite towards Coward and Payn.) Above all, however, blame for *Pacific 1860*'s failure lay with Coward for producing a bad musical. Set in 1860, it was the story of a love affair between an internationally famous singer and the son of a large family of British plantation owners who considered her unsuitable. It is sentimental, boring and hackneyed. Graham Payn was the male lead, but found that his newest opportunity of stardom coincided with *Oklahoma!* The venture was an expensive disaster; but Coward, slow to recognize his own failings and unused to questioning his genius, had no doubt about where to apportion blame, and did so in his diary. However delightful Mary Martin was, and she charmed Coward, she was unequal, for all her talent, to his 'sophisticated' writing.

A few weeks after the war in Europe had ended, the Allied authorities in Germany had published details of an index of prominent Britons who were to have been eliminated under Nazi rule. Churchill, inevitably, was on the list, and shared the distinction with J. B. Priestley, Alexander Korda, Noël Coward and Rebecca West, who wrote to Coward, the day after the list was made public: 'Just think of the people we'd have been seen dead with.' As much as ten years after the war, Coward was confiding to his diary that the Germans 'are a horrid neurotic race ... none of their contributions to science, literature and music compensates for their turgid emotionalism and unparalleled capacity for torturing their fellow creatures.' But in 1945, inclusion on their index could hardly fail to give grim satisfaction: whatever their other failings, they had not overlooked his contribution to the war effort.

When Paris was liberated, Coward and Cole Lesley had discovered that their flat in the Place Vendôme had been occupied by German officers, although relatively little damage had been done. It was discovered also that their maid, Yvonne, had had her head shaved and been sentenced to ten years' *indignité nationale* for collaboration. They were disinclined to condemn her, or even to lend much credence to the accusations ('all this was none of our business and as far as we were concerned Yvonne had been valiant'),[2] but Coward was struck by the nastiness of the atmosphere in the French capital, and realized how acutely it had suffered. At least in London, there was honour with dilapidation: everyone had been on the same side. But in Paris, suspicions and recriminations were rife. In 1944, he had encountered Maurice Chevalier, who faced accusations of collaboration. He told Coward that he had appeared once in Germany, but in so doing had secured the release of ten prisoners, and that he had been forced to sing on the radio by the Gestapo. Coward, often swift to chide and slow to bless, had decided, uncharacteristically, that the situation was not for him to judge, but the idea of collaboration and the humiliations of occupation stayed in his mind. In 'When William Came', Saki had written about life under a German occupation shortly before the Great War, and now Coward decided to bring that idea up to date. He was still angry about the electorate's betrayal of Churchill, and convinced that it had been his leadership above all which had prevented England from succumbing to totalitarianism and its consequences. A play about an occupied London, about what would have happened without Churchill, would bring home the full extent of their treachery and ingratitude to its audiences.

Perhaps he was suddenly suspicious of the loyalty of those nearer home (Jack Wilson would be an obvious cause of such suspicions), because a contemporary diary entry reveals that he began to ponder the theme of betrayal generally, and to wonder which of his friends, in the event of an occupation, would have died for their principles, which would have compromised and survived without coop- erating, and which would have collaborated and prospered. (This strikes one as being a strange way in which to think about friends, unless one has Coward's ability, which was growing more pro- nounced, to see things in terms of either right or wrong, with no complications or extenuations.) Soon, the preoccupation had assumed theatrical form in his mind: his diary reveals that *Might Have Been*, as the new play was originally called, shaped itself with remarkable speed. Only the title needed to be changed, and suddenly he thought of another way of reminding audiences of the perils of inept leadership, perils which under Churchill they had been able to forget. He decided to call the play *Peace In Our Time*: now merely a quotation, but to the public of 1947, who could remember the day on which Chamberlain had made them that promise, the greatest lie in history. Binkie Beaumont, who had reservations about the project, was as usual to present the play. All details of its contents were withheld, and the entire company was sworn to secrecy.

Coward continued his practice, established in *Cavalcade*, of setting momentous events off-stage, and allowing them to be discussed in front of the audience. *Cavalcade* presented historical fact; but the events which the characters of *Peace In Our Time* discussed in the pub – the play's one setting – were the figments of Coward's melodramatic, and unusually grim, imagination. The royal family, we gather, lives in permanent seclusion at Windsor Castle. Jewish shopkeepers are taken away for questioning. There is a concentration camp on the Isle of Wight. The Nazis shoot Churchill in 1941 (Chamberlain escapes any mention: not because of a softening of Coward's feelings towards him, but presumably because he was beneath contempt). This droll state of affairs is mulled over by a set of types: the kind-hearted Cockney, the grand actress, the cool, polite but ruthless SS officer. Good-hearted Englishness is the dominant tone: 'I've always believed in one thing, Mrs Broughton, and that was that the people of this country were the finest in the world.' Very often, the gossipy parochialism somehow anticipates the world of radio soap opera and *The Archers*.

Point Valaine, the experimental homage to Somerset Maugham which Coward had written in 1934 and seen fail the following year in New York, was finally produced in England in 1947, and Graham Greene risked another rebuke by criticizing Coward again and accusing him of being incapable of reproducing the rhythms of ordinary speech. If that end was either attainable or desirable, Coward failed to demonstrate it in *Peace In Our Time*. In two respects, however, his bizarre new play was remarkable. It shows that he had more political instinct than is regularly supposed, and that he was deeply pessimistic about the future of his country.

Several of the characters are discussing the Battle of Britain, which Britain, of course, lost. Not all of them regret the defeat:

We should have got lazy again, and blown out with our own glory. We should have been bombed and blitzed and we should have stood up under it – an example to the whole civilized world – and that would have finished us. As it is – in defeat – we still have a chance. There'll be no time in this country for many a long day for class wars and industrial crises and political squabbles. We can be united now ...

As successive generations of schoolchildren and historians have looked back at the consequences of the Second World War, contrasting England's painful search for security and purpose in a post-imperial world with the Economic Miracle of the vanquished, such reasoning has become a commonplace. In 1946, it was less orthodox. (Coward had shown the same prescience with regard to Russia. His diaries had recorded the conviction, in 1942, when the Soviets were the darlings of popular opinion, that they were fighting for their own land, and certainly not in defence of individual liberty.)

Peace In Our Time also mounted an attack on one of Coward's 'enemies within'. Its most memorable figure, Chorley Bannister, is described as being an 'intellectual'. He is the editor of an arts magazine called *Forethought*, and is one of the most contemptuously drawn figures in all of Coward's drama. The editorial comment of his magazine has been altered, we gather, to conform to the orthodoxies of this Vichy England, and he eventually becomes a full collaborator. From a writer who admitted to approaching 'the so-called highbrow with a deep-dyed suspicion', this is not at all surprising. But Coward uses the opportunity to deliver his fullest account of his suspicion of thinkers and intellectuals:

You and your kind pride themselves on being intellectuals, don't you? You babble a lot of snobbish nonsense about art and letters and beauty. You consider yourselves to be far above such primitive emotions as love and hate and devotion to a cause. You run your little highbrow magazines and change your politics with every wind that blows.

This scene led to a fierce argument with Peter Quennell, who quite rightly accused Coward of unfairness and provocation. The two men did not know each other very well – they had met through the Flemings – so Quennell could not know that Coward was prosecuting a personal vendetta, as well as expressing a prejudice. They remained on friendly terms (the latter thought the former a 'harmless intellectual'),[3] despite the fact that the model for Chorley Bannister was one of Quennell's closest friends. There was an inadequacy somewhere deep in Coward which made it impossible for him to take criticism, and his diaries reveal that the older he became, the more this inadequacy became entrenched. He admitted to keeping a Black Book in which he listed those with whom he had scores to settle. Inclusion in it was an honour reserved for those who were in a position to make public criticism of him. James Agate wrote some damning (and some favourable) reviews of the plays in the *Sunday Times*. Coward retaliated by writing a hostile poem about Agate. Graham Greene and Lord Beaverbrook were punished. Now *Peace In Our Time* took revenge on Peter Quennell's old friend Cyril Connolly.

Connolly had invited retribution with his acute and honest review of *Present Indicative* a decade before. This, presumably, had brought home to Coward the fact that he was 'a dangerous intellectual',[4] and led him to refer rather lamely to Connolly's novel, *The Rock Pool*, published the year before *Present Indicative*, as 'The Rocky Pool'.[5] By the time Connolly reviewed Coward's autobiography, he was already established as one of the most influential critics of his time. Like Coward, he had served the war effort in his own way. He held one of the 'reserved' occupations which Coward so despised: he was the editor of *Horizon*, and in that capacity proved himself not only to be an editor of genius, and a literary patron of exceptional foresight and wise fastidiousness, but also the guardian of the flame of culture. He was eventually made a Chevalier of the Légion d'Honneur in recognition of the amount of Resistance writing he had published. None of this, however, impressed Coward. Connolly, as well as having committed the unpardonable crime of questioning his genius and public persona, also represented a condition which the self-made often find inexcusable and inexplicable: he was a son of privilege who flirted with the Left. So even after writing *Peace In Our Time*, Coward could not rid his system of its fury against Connolly. In 1953, Ann Fleming again took up her pen to Cecil Beaton:

I decided I mustn't write a letter of groans about Noël! But we had an epic evening ... Noël insisted that Clemence Dane would have more posterity fame than Cyril Connolly, and said that Cyril's only claim to fame was the good fortune he had had in being sent to Eton; it is difficult to protect Cyril but that was going too far. However, seconds later, he laid down that Shakespeare was not an intellectual.[6]

If Connolly was even aware of the attack in *Peace In Our Time*, he should have seen it as an occupational hazard. His friend Evelyn Waugh mocked him as Everard Spruce in *Unconditional Surrender*; and he also featured, not altogether flatteringly, in Nancy Mitford's *The Blessing*. Meanwhile, Coward's attitude towards 'intellectuals' became more obsessive and ludicrous: a diary entry in 1963, recording a Battle of Britain dinner in Manhattan, was full of almost paranoid imprecation and vituperation against the socialist writers and Angry Young Men who, in Coward's opinion, had no respect for the sacrifices and heroism of the war.

Peace In Our Time opened well in the provinces, and at first attendance was good in London. Its critical reception, however, was less auspicious: Coward seemed to reviewers to have lost his way, and in desperation to be writing plays for which he was simply not equipped. Beverley Baxter spoke of a 'crisis for Coward', in the way journalists will, in the *Evening Standard*, and the run lasted a disappointing six months. It was hardly an uplifting evening in the theatre, and not what most audiences expected of Noël Coward. And there was certainly some wisdom in the response of the Lord Chamberlain's reader. Apart from feeling that the word 'bloody' occurred too frequently, he doubted the virtue of the enterprise: 'The fiction inevitably seems pretty poor drama beside the facts of recent history and in my opinion it is a theme which a wise dramatist would avoid.'[7]

The critics were not the only arbiters who seemed to have turned against Coward. In 1947, Ralph Richardson and Laurence Olivier were knighted. With their brilliant interpretations of Shakespeare at the Old Vic, both men had great expectations, though they were no greater than Coward's. What is more, Olivier had been Coward's protégé, and owed his earliest success to him. Whether or not this blatant violation offended Coward, he put a brave face on it: a face which was to set for another twenty-three years, while his juniors were honoured before him. Olivier felt the awkwardness of the situation acutely. He recalled, in his splutteringly honest style:

I found myself quite unable to accept my knighthood without writing to Noël Coward, almost as if asking his permission. It was painfully apparent to all his friends that this honour had been withheld from him for years for what we found to be entirely the wrong reasons; but, I asked him, though I knew that it was wrong for any theatre person to accept it before he had, would he, I wondered, be hurt with me beyond repair if I just had not got what it took to turn it down?[8]

Coward went to New York straight after the opening of *Peace In Our Time*. He had been convinced of his play's success, but it quickly became apparent that, at least by his high standards, he had another failure on his hands. However, if he felt unappreciated in his homeland, America was large with promise, and in his diary he recorded the details of a remarkable overture made by Paramount in 1947: two of its executives, Jules Stein and Charles Miller, told him that in exchange for three commitments, as actor, author or director, they would pay him $500 a week for twenty-three years. No one in England could begin to match such terms; and if Coward had been more committed at that stage to making a lot of money, he would have accepted, and damned the reservations which led him to decline the offer: namely, that he would sacrifice freedom and the respect of many of his English admirers. His integrity still intact, he put the matter out of his mind and continued with the business in hand, which was to keep him in America until halfway through 1948: an ill-advised revival of *Tonight at 8.30*.

Gertrude Lawrence was eager to repeat her performances of 1936, and Graham Payn was to play the parts originally taken by Coward. The venture seemed years out of date, and no one was very interested, on either the East or the West Coast. There were other problems, though, besides the fact that Coward and Payn were flogging a dead horse. Jack Wilson appeared, and there were unpleasant scenes. By now, he was one of the most successful figures on Broadway (he directed *Gentlemen Prefer Blondes* and *Kiss Me Kate*), but he was known to be drinking very heavily, and it was said that, however busy he was, he never rose till noon. He began by claiming that Payn would not be able to appear in any production because his papers were not in order, and generally made fun of Coward and Payn to the rest of the company, damaging morale and making Payn, an inexperienced performer with a huge act to follow, intensely nervous and unhappy. Wilson had been appointed to direct the revivals, but Coward had to relieve him of the job.

Coward also made a shocking discovery through Fanny Holtzmann, Gertrude Lawrence's manager and a well-known show-business lawyer in New York: it seemed that his financial affairs were in complete disarray in America, and that he had been over-paying taxes there for years. Suddenly, in 1947, Coward became aware that Jack Wilson was more than a liability; he could be convicted of breaches of loyalty, of attempts to hinder new productions and successes and, most alarmingly, of financial malpractice. For all his vanities, Coward was a generous and naïve man, and the discovery upset him terribly. The shock was so great that his diary records that he was physically sick; but with composure came the realization that it was 'the end' between Wilson and himself.

That announcement was premature, just as Coward's realization of Wilson's true character was long overdue, for the fact was that he had never been trustworthy. At the beginning of the partnership, verses – a favourite form of communication amongst all the members of Coward's coterie – were written testifying to the fact that Wilson was extravagant, unreliable, and not unimpeachably honest. But Coward had been in love with him, and every weakness had seemed a charming foible, every serious charge, the stuff of affectionate doggerel: 'Darling Baybay, darling Jack/Just a klep-tomaniac.'[9] Cole Lesley quotes several verses, all revolving round Wilson's dishonesty, and written not only by Coward but also by Lorn Loraine. Wilson had not changed, except perhaps in the loss of his looks, but now Coward was prepared to see his failings more clearly.

The partnership was finally dissolved in 1951, but Coward continued to see him, and to be annoyed by him. In 1952, we gather that he is an 'egocentric bore'; in 1954, that he lacks loyalty and moral courage. In 1956, Wilson was so drunk when he and his former lover met that he could hardly stand, and Coward was overwhelmed with the sadness and folly of it all: 'I sat in the front seat of the car weeping silently and remembering the past and how handsome he used to be.'[10] What is unfortunate, but so characteristic, is that although Coward complains throughout the Fifties about Wilson's inexorable decline, he never attempts any explanations for it. Alcoholism was not then fully recognized as a disease, but Coward must have wondered what it was that made someone in otherwise good health, and otherwise good-looking, in the prime of life and very successful, drink himself to death. Was it a congenital weakness? Or that he was not heterosexual and was unhappy in marriage? Or that he was still in love with Noël Coward but felt usurped by Graham Payn? Sadly, Coward was silent in estrangement, and offers no solutions.

Chapter Three

With the failure of *Tonight at 8.30*, Coward, resorting to trusted comforts, decided that he and Payn deserved a holiday. At the beginning of 1948, he learnt in New York that Goldeneye, Ian Fleming's house in Jamaica, was to let, and despite resenting the rent, an exorbitant £50 a week, he took the lease. He had been to the island once before, in 1944, when his boss in intelligence, Bill Stephenson, deemed it a suitable place for Coward to take what he later called 'a nice lie-down'. Accordingly, for two weeks or so, he basked in the hot sun and found time to dash off one of his better comic songs, 'Uncle Harry'. Fleming had also been sent to Jamaica during the war, and it had seduced him entirely: he immediately resolved to build there and Goldeneye rose above an old donkey racecourse near Oracabessa to command a spectacular prospect of the north shore.

In view of the fact that he hated staying in other people's houses, it was inevitable that Coward would find plenty to complain about when he stayed at Goldeneye in 1948, and he duly faulted the cooking, the beds and the design of the house. He made his opinions known to his hosts, but they magnanimously overlooked their exacting guest's remarks, and convinced themselves that they had converted him to Jamaican life. When, at the height of the Suez Crisis, Anthony Eden retreated to Jamaica, Ann Fleming told the *Daily Express*: 'We lent the house to Noël Coward seven years ago after he had had a colossal flop in New York. He went there to lick his wounds. It was very successful.'[1] Uncomfortable or not, Coward could not rest for long, and soon after arriving in Jamaica, he began the second volume of his autobiography, *Future Indefinite*. On this second visit, he was smitten – it is not for nothing that he began his new book by describing the island's gaudy and exotic beauty – and soon he had decided to construct a property of his own. Jamaica was British, and – although even then more or less commutable by air from New York – also very cheap. But Coward already had two properties (with the wartime depredations of Goldenhurst still to be righted) and his finances were in such a state of chronic uncertainty by then that despite being able to acquire much of his site for less than £40 an acre, he had to sell his Rolls-Royce. He never considered himself robbed, however, because out of it all came Blue Harbour, and the land on which he later built another house, Firefly Hill, as an intimate retreat.

He established a routine which took him to Jamaica, along with Graham Payn and usually Cole Lesley, every winter. Prolonged exposure to hot climates had already begun to make his lean and oval face look increasingly oriental, and he soon became known on the island as Chinese Nell. There were often guests: invitations to Blue Harbour were certainly coveted, as presumably were those to Goldeneye, however spartan its charms seemed to Coward. (Indeed, before the days when heliolatry was pronounced harmful, these two pioneers did a lot to make Jamaica, and the West Indies generally, fashionable for rich English and American tourists in the Fifties.) Apart from allowing him to escape the winters of the northern hemisphere, Jamaica gave Coward 'the most valuable benison': 'Time to read and write ... I have always been a staunch upholder of "early to bed, early to rise" ... in Jamaica it is not only possible but automatic; there is nothing to do in the evenings and the morning hours are the loveliest.'[2]

If the island gave him the tranquillity in which to write, it also challenged him to adopt or develop new interests. At the end of the war, Coward had taken up his grandfather Veitch's hobby of painting. Churchill, also a keen amateur artist, converted him from watercolours to oils, and Jamaica gave him his mature style. The English countryside meant nothing to him, so it is unsurprising that the few landscapes he completed in it are flatly green, brown and drab. But his evocations of Jamaica, lagoons, markets and bathing black men, are rainbows of colour and, if they are derivative, they are also celebratory. Coward painted what he thought he saw; but some questioned his willingness to see. Alec Guinness and his wife stayed at Blue Harbour in 1958, before he and Coward flew to Cuba for the location filming of *Our Man in Havana*:

'One marvellous thing about Jamaica,' Noël said, wagging his instructive finger, 'is that there are absolutely no insects and nothing poisonous on the island.' I pointed out something at the side of the pool. 'What's that?' I asked. He gazed at it without seeing before saying, 'I haven't the foggiest.' It was a scorpion. But then his eyes, mostly very observant, were shut to many things he didn't wish to face, or were shut for him. A few days after our arrival Merula and I were robbed while bathing – our watches, my shaving gear, fountain pen and a few odds and ends were lifted from our bathroom. When I told Cole he nearly had a fit – not about our very minor losses but for fear we might tell Noël. 'The Master mustn't know! Promise me you'll never tell him!' We didn't greatly mind but it was a nuisance not being able to claim insurance; also we knew perfectly well who had taken the things and I would like to have got my pen back, but Cole pointed out that any attempt at recovery would cause trouble in the village and there was Noël's reputation as a kindly and tolerant employer to be considered. We knuckled under and from then on I had to keep asking the time.[3]

As the years passed, Coward's eyes had to be closed to more and more. Keith Baxter, invited to stay in 1970, remembered being driven to Firefly Hill from Blue Harbour by Graham Payn:

It was a very bumpy track and we were hurled from one side of the car to the other. Some boys were playing cricket in a field. Graham hooted the horn in greeting. 'Aren't they sweet? Look at them waving – they're shouting "Love to Master"!' To me their cry sounded more like 'Black Power Now', and their waves seemed rather clenched.[4]

Deprived of his watch in Jamaica, Alec Guinness may have forgotten the fact that in colonial possessions – especially tropical ones – time moves differently. In England, colonialism was beginning to be unfashionable (although when Princess Margaret visited Jamaica officially in 1955, the Foreign Office made it quite clear that she was in no circumstances to dance with any blacks), but England, with its post-war disillusionments, was five thousand miles away. From Blue Harbour, Coward was able to observe at close quarters the daily administration of British rule in the West Indies and forget the decline in his country's power and prosperity. Expatriate life has always been a way of shoring up illusions, and angry reactionaries often exile themselves to distant provinces rather than try to accommodate the new politics of the metropolis. Coward was born conservative, and was becoming reactionary before he committed himself to colonial life. There can be no doubt, however, that his political sympathies hardened under the Jamaican sun. A decade after building Blue Harbour, at a time when Britain was shedding its colonial possessions rapidly, he was an unequivocal imperialist:

The British Empire was a great and wonderful social, economic and even spiritual experiment, and all the parlour pinks and eager ill-informed intellectuals cannot convince me to the contrary ... We have done a great deal of good to a great many millions of people, principally by helping them towards common sense.[5]

There was no point, however, in simply having convictions. They had to be declared, so that the wayward and misguided, the progressive and the radical, could be corrected. Coward had already written plays which extolled the English character and commended the existing order of things at home. But so many aspects of the world in which he had grown up were now threatened, not least its history of Empire. *Pacific 1860* had looked sentimentally at the lives of the Victorian plantation owners. Now, with *South Sea Bubble*, he returned to his imperial theme.[6]

The idea of the play, Coward said, was suggested to him by a re-reading of *Vile Bodies*, though the connexion between that novel and *South Sea Bubble* seems tenuous. His new work, like *Pacific 1860*, is set in Samolo. This time, however, we are in the present, or Coward's increasingly idiosyncratic version of it. It is a comedy, based on a bit of tomfoolery at Government House, which is occupied by Sir George and Lady Alexandra Shotter. She was a sort of fusion, he felt, of Edwina Mountbatten and Diana Cooper, a supposedly delightful figure whose delicious naughtiness and irresistible charm unleash mayhem of the most tedious and unfunny variety. Sir George is left-wing, and the butt of the play's heavy-handed moralizing. While Lady Sandra gets into scrapes, politics disturb the island's tranquillity, and two parties contend for the loyalty of the Samolans – the People's Imperial Party and a sort of vague conglomerate calling for independence – but Coward's propaganda leaves us in no doubt about which group most of the natives support:

Boffin: I gather that this island is still a conservative stronghold?

Christopher: On the whole, yes. There are more subversive elements, of course, but most Samolans are still Empire-minded. You see, they've been happy and contented under British rule for so many years that they just don't understand when they're suddenly told that it's been nothing but a corrupt, capitalist racket from the word go.

Sir George is himself a believer in equality and self-determination, but in case the audience might feel any temptation to

193

follow suit, he is put right quickly by Punalo Alani, the leader of the People's Imperial Party, who tells him: 'Your conviction that extreme socialism necessarily implies progress is romantic to the point of fantasy.' Coward had obviously decided not to allow audiences any scope for autonomous decisions at all, and was certainly not going to make the mistake of overrating their intelligence. And those who might wonder why most Samolans are loyal to the PIP and, by extension, to the Crown, soon discover that an island where progressives are kept under control is a paradise. The natives, we gather, 'swim from morning to night. They weave away and make the most lovely waste-paper baskets and never stop having scads of entrancing children who swim before they can walk and have enormous melting eyes like saucers. And whenever they feel a bit peckish all they have to do is to nip a breadfruit off a tree.' With no nonsense about ruling themselves, the natives can glut the market with waste-paper baskets and stagger over the windfall fruit in order to do a quick circuit of the island in butterfly stroke.

Perhaps unremarkably, he had considerable difficulty getting the play staged. Originally he decided that the part of Lady Sandra should be played by Gertrude Lawrence, but somehow she managed to annoy him, and Coward and Binkie Beaumont approached Kay Hammond and John Clements. They rejected it and, despite being close friends, so did the Oliviers. They had not arrived at their plane of eminence by a careless choice of scripts, and told Coward that they thought the play 'old-fashioned' and said that it would do him harm. However, when it was finally produced in London, in 1956, in the same year as the Suez Crisis – a coincidence which must have made its creaking and unconvincing polemic sound more ridiculous than ever – it was Vivien Leigh who played Lady Sandra. As one of the most famous of British actresses, still a beauty, still, just, Lady Olivier, and forever Scarlett O'Hara, she drew large audiences. Although *The Times* found *South Sea Bubble* 'a minor but not unpleasing Coward', most of the younger reviewers inevitably found it difficult to take the play seriously. But it is perhaps not surprising that his middle-class, and by now middle-aged, audience flocked to see it. The Suez Crisis served the bluntest reminder yet of the decline of British military power. Coward, the great reassurer, was giving them a reminder of the glorious past.

In one respect, it was as well for Coward that his plays now shunned innovation and scorned reform. The West End of the late Forties and early Fifties was not an inspiring place for which to write. Those theatres which had not been bombed were in a state of dereliction and, with the popularity of the cinema and the imminence of television, the incentives for speedy restoration were not great. Most of the working theatres were owned by a small consortium of businessmen sometimes known as The Group which was less interested in sponsoring new writers than in filling houses with established stars in tested plays. This monopoly effectively controlled what the public saw, since it was virtually impossible to have a new play produced without its approval, and until the arrival of the so-called 'kitchen-sink' drama of a decade later, nervous conservatism enveloped Shaftesbury Avenue. Kenneth Tynan, looking enviously across the Channel at Europe's experimental dramatists, complained that in the moribund West End the theatre 'was dominated by a ruthless three-power coalition consisting of drawing-room comedy and its two junior henchmen, murder melodrama and barrack-room farce ... the average playwright had ceased trying to hold the mirror up to nature, and the fashionable playwright could not possibly hold a mirror up to anything, since genteel idiom demanded the use of the word "looking-glass"'.[7]

South Sea Bubble was appropriate to this desperate time. But Coward was famous for his versatility: he observed the new popularity of the American musical and decided to venture into the same territory. Sadly, however, the result, *Ace of Clubs*, was nothing more than mediocrity in another discipline. This dismal musical is set in a Soho nightclub, and involves cardboard crooks, a louche if golden-hearted proprietress, cynical but pragmatic policemen, wonderful Londoners, and so on. Graham Payn was, once again, the leading man and had to content himself with one respectable song, 'I Like America', a blandishment no doubt intended for Broadway audiences. The show did not survive long in London, for the simple reason that people had acquired a taste for the exuberance, optimism and excellence of American shows, and taking coals to Newcastle was cheaper than taking musicals to Broadway.

Coward had faced failure before (indeed, since 1945 he had faced little else, except when he appeared as Garry Essendine in a revival of *Present Laughter*) and although he had worked hard at *Ace of Clubs* it had always been designed as a piece of entertainment, an attempt to demonstrate that 'talent and material count more than sequins and tits', rather than as a vehicle of serious instruction. He had always insisted that laughter was very important, and that there was nothing wrong with a theatre which aimed only to entertain. However, even during the war, James Agate had suspected him of having other priorities, and noted that his work had always shown a willingness to abandon pure art for the sterner charms of didacticism'.[8] Now there was less time to observe distinctions between entertainment and education. The world which for his first fifty years Coward knew and valued was disappearing, and audiences must be alerted to the catastrophe. Wit for wit's sake had become a luxury, and in the latter half of his career, Coward increasingly made mirth the handmaiden of reactionary instruction. *South Sea Bubble* had signalled the change in his playwriting policy; its successor, *Relative Values*, confirmed it.

His new play was his finest since the war and enjoyed considerable success when it was first produced at the Savoy Theatre in 1951. For all its polish, however, it is now unrevivable, except as a literary curiosity piece. Nigel, Earl of Marshwood, has fallen in love with a Hollywood actress, Miranda Frayle, and has decided to marry her, to the consternation of everyone, above and below stairs, at Marshwood. Felicity, his mother (to whom, we gather, 'a vestige of the maligned, foolish Twenties still clings'), puts a brave face on the development:

After all, it isn't the first time an English peer has married an actress ... Look at dear Gloria Bainbridge, buried alive in Lincolnshire and absolutely indefatigable, and Lily Grantworth with all those muscular little boys. I think the aristocracy, what's left of it, owes a great deal to the theatrical profession.

The servants are more disconcerted. Crestwell, Coward's spokesman, and a butler in the best dramatic tradition of improbable articulacy, pretends not to mind; Moxie, the Countess's personal maid, is appalled. When the curtain rises, their exchanges establish the play's anxieties about social mobility and the erosion of class barriers:

Moxie: Why couldn't he pick someone of his own class?

Crestwell: Class! Oh dear, I've forgotten what the word means. Remind me to look it up in the crossword dictionary.

Moxie: You may have forgotten what it means but I haven't.

Crestwell: That, Dora, is an admission of defeat. It proves that you have wilfully deafened yourself to the clarion call of progress.

It becomes clear at the end of Act One why Moxie feels so strongly about the arrival of Miranda Frayle and her enforced acceptance by the family: she is her sister. This coincidence, and the fact that it might have remained a secret until that moment, is naturally wildly improbable; but drawing-room comedy was built on improbabilities as much as on a firmly-established social order, as Crestwell's comment, when told of the connexion, implies:

Crestwell: A coincidence in the best tradition of English high comedy, my Lady. Consider how delightfully Mr Somerset Maugham would handle the situation!

Peter: I can think of other writers who wouldn't exactly sneeze at the idea.

Crestwell: If I may say so, sir, our later playwrights would miss the more subtle nuances. They are all too brittle. Comedies of manners swiftly become obsolete when there are no longer any manners.

Miranda Frayle is self-made, like Coward, and she too escaped her background through the theatre. He had shown such a transformation in *Cavalcade*, where Fanny Bridges becomes a well-paid singer rather than following her parents into domestic service. Coward had also drawn other characters who had tried to leave their origins behind: Queenie in *This Happy Breed* and Henry Gow in *Fumed Oak*. But of all his plays, it is the much-earlier *Easy Virtue* which provides the most interesting comparison. In that work, in which the snobbish Whittackers had refused to accept the unconventional Larita, Coward had attacked the inflexibility of English society. In *Relative Values*, written twenty-six years later, it is that very inflexibility which we are called upon to admire. Over the intervening years of his success, self-invention and social-climbing, Coward had become an apologist not only for the paralysis of the working class, but also for what he saw as the birthright of the more privileged.

Yet there is something uneasy in his handling of the situation. It is as though he is aware that, left to its own devices, any audience might decide that it is perfectly reasonable for a peer to want to marry an actress, and vice versa. Accordingly, he manipulates. His spokesman, Crestwell, gets all the best lines. Of one of the other servants, for instance, he remarks: 'He is not happy in his work, my Lady. Like so many of the young people of today he holds very definite views on social equality. He feels that all menial tasks should be done by somebody else.' And we are encouraged to dislike Miranda, who 'kept almost having babies but not quite', and who is quickly but gently put down by the Countess.

Moxie, meanwhile, to spare embarrassment, has been promoted to friend-of-the-family, given some cast-off *couture* to wear, and moved into the Japanese Room. Miranda, too busy acting herself, does not recognize her sister, the implication being that only those who are truly themselves can see clearly, and delivers her version of their childhood, in which drunkenness and poverty were the predominant characteristics: 'I was the lucky one. I always had a conviction, deep down inside me, that somehow or other I should get on, hoist myself up out of the mire, escape from the poverty and squalor of my surroundings. I suppose I must have been born with the will to succeed.' Miranda is doing exactly what Gertrude Lawrence used to do, inventing and dramatizing. As Coward once put it: 'I was born in Teddington, Middlesex, an ordinary middle-class boy. I was not gutter, I didn't gnaw kippers' heads in the gutter as Gertrude Lawrence quite untruthfully always insisted that she did.'

Eventually, Moxie, unable to bear any more of the nonsense, exposes her sister:

I wouldn't have said a word about it if you hadn't started showing off and making out that you were brought up in the gutter. Poverty and squalor, indeed! A London Cockney brought up within the sound of Bow Bells. You were born at Number Three, Station Road, Sidcup, and if you can hear the sound of Bow Bells from Sidcup you must have the ears of an elk-hound!

Coward eventually decides to spirit an old Hollywood flame, Don Lucas, to Marshwood, and he takes Miranda Frayle away with him, leaving the old order unchanged, and an exultant Crestwell to deliver the curtain line:

I give you a toast, Dora. I drink to you and me in our humble, but on the whole honourable calling. I drink to her Ladyship and his Lordship, groaning beneath the weight of privilege, but managing to keep their peckers up all the same. Above all I drink to the final inglorious dis-integration of the most unlikely dream that ever troubled the foolish heart of man – Social Equality!

It would be interesting to know what credentials Coward felt he had either for making prophecies, or for advocating social orders and conditions. He himself certainly contradicted most of what this play represents. Moxie may mean it when she says: 'This idea of play-acting and pretending to be what I'm not won't settle anything. I am what I am and I haven't got anything to be ashamed of.' But Coward could not make the same claim. And a few years later, the contingency which his play had refused to contemplate occurred when an aristocrat, Prince Rainier, married a film star, Grace Kelly.[9]

Even when it was written, *Relative Values* belonged to a bankrupt tradition. Drawing-room comedy has always depended for its vitality on an unquestioned and hierarchical society, and by 1950, with the welfare state a fact of life, there was little point to a new comedy about servants and masters when fewer of either sat in the audience. Nevertheless, the play received good notices: the *Tatler* found it 'a flawless piece of work', while Harold Hobson, the dullest of drama critics, considered it 'the best play Coward has written for several years'. With Gladys Cooper playing Lady Marshwood, and Coward's comic reputation continuing to prove resilient, recent disappointments notwithstanding, *Relative Values* marked his return to popularity. However, it was a popularity based on nostalgia rather than on novelty: the epigrams ring hollow, and the wonderfully polished dialogue, which none of his contemporaries could match, proves nothing, except that Noël Coward, when young so imitated and so innovative, became the Canute of his generation.

Chapter Four

The year which saw Coward's restoration to West End success saw also his return to Goldenhurst, from which he had been exiled since 1940, when the property was requisitioned. White Cliffs had provided him with happiness and with a retreat away from London, but suddenly the time came to leave it: holiday-makers and pleasure-seekers migrated from the capital to the Kentish coast, and the peace and privacy which Coward valued were threatened. He knew that he would miss the view of the sea; but at Goldenhurst there was calm, and also Romney Marsh, the trees and the croquet lawn.

Ian Fleming assumed the lease of White Cliffs. Coward had already proved by his friendship with Mountbatten that he could charm men of action, and his friendship with Fleming was no less improbable. (He too had been a man of action, though he renounced that calling after the war: his life may have been quite tranquil from then on, but his fantasies were not, as his fiction demonstrates.) Although Fleming was known to complain in Jamaica that Coward thought he was God, he still seems to have been extremely fond of him. That in itself need not attract comment, since Coward could be both amusing and generous in deed and spirit. But Fleming, who had enjoyed some notoriety as a ladykiller, was also known to be rather ill at ease in homosexual company, a failing which seems to have amused his wife, Ann:

Ian had a high fever and was fearfully cross, happily Noël Coward came to call and proved himself a Florence Nightingale, changing Thunderbird's [Fleming's] sopping pyjamas, turning the mattress, and fetching him iced drinks. Noël has always found T-B fearfully attractive and jumped at the opportunity to handle him. While Noël fetched ice cubes from the frigidaire T-B's language was something horrible, he blamed me for exposing him to homosexual approaches.[1]

Peter Quennell observed that Coward took great care not to hurt Fleming's 'ticklish *amour propre*', and consequently treated him like a difficult social beauty.[2] The policy obviously worked, since Coward was asked to be a witness at Fleming's wedding to Ann Rothermere, and also to be the godfather to their son, Caspar. And when the Flemings took over White Cliffs, the tone of Ian Fleming's correspondence was nothing if not flirtatious. He was concerned, he says, having inspected

my new mansion and quite honestly it is in a pretty poor way with your pictures down and book shelves removed etc. There are yellow patches on most of the walls and battens up in your workroom which will have to come down and be made good. I gather that as the outgoing tenant the cost of putting this straight should fall on your slim shoulders.[3]

Coward's reply suggested a compromise over the cost of the repairs, and enclosed a cheque for £50. 'If you do not want it I can give you a few suggestions as to what to do with it when you come to lunch on Sunday. With regards and also with smacking great kisses.'[4]

Skittishness and coquetry, whether seriously intended or not, can disarm the most unlikely people, but they are not infallible or universally appropriate. With a sour competitor like Cecil Beaton, there was no incentive for flirtation, and it is interesting to note that Coward resorted to plain speaking when they were together, as though they should both understand each other well enough to dispense with play-acting. When they had discussed their respective careers during the war, they had called a truce once again in their uneasy relationship. They were too alike, Coward had said, to squabble or indulge in backbiting, especially when the rest of the world was potentially hostile towards them both: 'Life's going to be tough for us all for the next years of the war, and much tougher after the war, and it's better that people like us should be friends rather than enemies because we really have so much in common – powers of observation, wit, industriousness and professionalism.'[5] This overture was never likely to lead to undying adoration between the two men, but it did at least prepare the way for a collaboration. Since the earliest stirrings of his ambition, Beaton had always wanted to design a production with Coward, and now that the latter's long-standing partnership with Gladys Calthrop had come to an end, the way was clear. Coward asked him to start work on the costumes and sets for his newest play, *Quadrille*. Beaton was delighted: 'I am utterly enchanted by the play; it has the charm, wit and frivolity of *The Importance* and is more tender and mature than anything you have written.'[6]

After *Relative Values*, it may have seemed to the public, and some of the critics that, even if Coward was now using wit to promote reaction, he had at least regained the confidence and momentum absent in his work of the late Forties. But *Quadrille* failed to make that impression last. The work was written as another vehicle for his friends Alfred Lunt and Lynn Fontanne, whose names and professionalism managed to secure large bookings, but the play suggested that Coward's was now a faltering and exhausted imagination. The story was a comedy of marital disaffection involving English aristocrats and American railroad tycoons set in Belgrave Square, the south of France and a railway waiting-room. Its similarity to a Victorian version of *Private Lives* (it was set in the 1870s) was noted. There is much elopement, some very funny exchanges and an overwhelming sense of suffocation coming mainly from the dialogue. Formerly, Coward's characters had spoken a new dialect of concision, but now their conversation seemed prolix, and if you have little to say, the best policy is always to remain taciturn rather than to gush. But Beaton seemed bowled over not only by Coward's dramatic skills, but also by his working methods: 'Watching *Quadrille* unfold for the first time before an audience was a revelation. Noël is nothing if not a craftsman, and he knew just how to make his play come alive. Many of his laughs came as a pleasant surprise.'[7]

Nothing in the play came as a pleasant surprise to Kenneth Tynan, who accused the drama of suggesting 'Oscar Wilde rewritten on a Sunday afternoon in a rectory garden by Amanda McKittrick Ros'.[8] The combination of Coward's name and the Lunts' following should have guaranteed *Quadrille* a long season, but it closed much earlier than Coward had hoped. In his diary, he complained vaguely, and wondered if all the critics had been right, and he had been wrong. But such an absurd notion was dismissed almost out of hand.

The production marked the last of the collaborations with the Lunts. Indeed, now he had no stars who could inspire him to write comedy and then guarantee a good performance of it afterwards, since just before *Quadrille* opened, news came from New York of the death of Gertrude Lawrence. At the time of her death, she was appearing with Yul Brynner in *The King and I*. In April 1952, Brynner had confided in Coward that he was very anxious about the decline in Lawrence's voice, and that, although she had not been told, there had been complaints from the audience that she could not sing. The next thing Coward heard, in September 1952, from the newspapers in England, was that she was dead.[9] The cancer which claimed her had been undetected, and so moved swiftly, and when the lights of Broadway and the West End were dimmed in valediction, she was only fifty-four. His diary records Coward's typical reaction to death, lachrymose effusion mixed with brisk efficiency:

I dined with Gladys, and then came home and wrote an obituary for *The Times*. This was agony and I broke down several times, but pressed on and finished it. ... Poor, darling old Gertie – a lifelong friend. With all her overactings and silliness I have never known her do a mean or unkind thing. I am terribly, terribly unhappy to think that I shall never see her again.

The postscript which Coward added to the official obituary in *The Times* upset the Lunts, implying as it did that their role in Coward's success had been subordinate to hers:

Whether we have been acting together or not, we have been integrally part of each other's lives ... I wish so very deeply that I could have seen her just once more playing in a play of mine, for no one I have ever known, however brilliant and however gifted, has contributed quite what she contributed to my work. Her quality was, to me, unique and her magic imperishable.

There is no doubt that English comedy lost a great star with Lawrence's premature death, but it is less certain that Coward lost a close friend. In his autobiographies the focus seldom strays away from Coward himself, but when it does, Lawrence is given little time or attention. Since the beginning of the war, she had spent most of her time apart from Coward in America; and by her second marriage, in 1940, to Richard Aldrich, a theatrical producer, she had become an American citizen.

It is therefore possible to believe that when he was writing Lawrence's obituary, Coward was acting bereavement slightly, if only for his own benefit. Peter Quennell recounted a story which bore this out. Two friends of his, who also knew Coward well, dropped in on him the day that Lawrence died:

Earlier they had read reports of the great *comédienne*'s death; but the news had slipped their minds; and they drove happily towards his door. They had reached their destination and were preparing to ring the bell, when the door was flung open; and, silhouetted against the light, there stood Noël, wearing a black or, at least, a very dark dressing-gown, his arms extended from the threshold. 'You *darlings*,' he cried, 'I *knew* you'd come ...' Not until several minutes had passed – minutes of speechless embarrassment – did they understand his tragic welcome and begin to fall into the dignified consolatory parts he had intended they should play. His own part – heart-broken but still hospitable – he enacted to perfection. With a few sighs and some faint autumnal smiles, he produced a tray and glasses; and, standing, they drank a silent toast in beloved Gertie's honour.[10]

Quennell went on to qualify the unappealing implications of sham and melodrama of this story by adding: 'I do not suggest that his sorrow was insincere, but that sincerity and insincerity are relative terms as applied to any well-known actor.' Joyce Grenfell had also recorded her disapproval of the exaggerated sentimentality and spurious emotions of the theatre when watching Coward with some of his colleagues at a party: 'Whatever is easiest and pleasantest they do and all romance is divine. They don't think and they don't read and they accept the third-rate too easily for me.'[11] But, as *Present Laughter* had already suggested, Coward knew all about the constant temptation to perform.

In 1952, George VI died and Coward astonished some of his friends by sending letters of sympathy to each member of the dead King's family. Ann Fleming admitted, perhaps unnecessarily, that she found being 'catty' about Coward irresistible while 'he continues to pose as intimate friend of the royal family':

When we arrived last night he said with great drama, 'My Dears, I have despatched my letters to the Queen, such a relief as the formalities one must observe obscure the feelings, but between the conventional beginnings and ends I was able to put in my whole heart.'[12]

His attentions appeared to do him little good in royal circles, however, when John Gielgud was knighted in the Coronation Honours of 1953 and Coward, who had influenced him and played an important part, through *The Vortex*, in projecting him to early fame and success, was again overlooked. As before, when Olivier was honoured, Coward curbed any justified complaints he could have made, and contented himself in his diary with the magnanimous reflection that he was happy for Gielgud because he had deserved the honour for so long. But the same was true of Coward himself. In Coronation year he found himself participating in a salute to the new Elizabethan age when he appeared, at Binkie Beaumont's suggestion, in a revival of George Bernard Shaw's *The Apple Cart*, with Margaret Leighton. The part was originally promised to Alec Guinness, who refused to take it over when Coward left after his usual three months. The play undertook an examination of the role and purpose of the monarchy, and its timely revival was generally well received. Coward, whose principles of self-discipline and professionalism always led to his being word-perfect at the first rehearsal, acquitted himself well, even though it was his first appearance in a play by another playwright since 1928. The stress of appearing in someone else's work, and carrying conviction while speaking someone else's words, must have been considerable for him, but he had resolved not to succumb to stage-fright again, and his diary made a note of that determination.

Also in 1953, he decided to adapt Oscar Wilde's *Lady Windermere's Fan*, first produced in 1892, as a 'musical play'. It was an odd choice. The play – while being characteristic of him – is not Wilde's best, and could certainly be improved, but drawing-room comedy does not make particularly promising material for musicals. What is more, Coward was out of sympathy with Wilde for most of his life. After being introduced to his work by Esme Wynne, he read him extensively in later life during the course of his self-education. However, his admiration for *The Importance of Being Earnest*, which was profound, was qualified by a general disapproval of the man, and he devoted a lot of intolerant energy to enumerating Wilde's failings in his diary. An encounter with the unexpurgated *De Profundis* prompted a stern catalogue of charges: folly, conceit, self-deception, and a complete lack of humour which seemed doubly unforgivable when linked with such brilliant wit. Perhaps in Coward's mind Wilde sinned as Connolly had also sinned, by being privileged with a great education and many other advantages which he then appeared to throw to the winds. Coward's conclusion, that he could have made life at Reading gaol less excruciating with the odd 'warm little human joke' with his warders, seems unbearably smug and unsympathetic, particularly when one considers that he himself could have been indicted on similar charges. He too had wit, but showed a surprising lack of humour when his work was criticized. When it came to self-deception, he had only to recapitulate his experiences with Jack Wilson, which had seen solvency sacrificed to good looks and charm, to reflect that he was quite Wilde's equal. And, whatever he may have thought, it is hard to imagine that Victorian ideas of penal reform sanctioned 'warm little jokes' with prison warders. Wilde annoyed because he had flown in the face of convention, rather than courting it, as the more cautious Coward had done, and in so doing, brought homosexuality into renewed disgrace, a disgrace from which it took most of Coward's life to begin to recover. Whether or not it could be argued that Wilde had squandered his first-rate intellect – and Coward disapproved of waste – there is no doubt that he died a failure, and Coward hated failures. He felt that Wilde was 'one of the silliest, most conceited and unattractive characters that ever existed', and when talking about wit, he would often make the point that monologues, however glittering, were boring, and that the best comic dialogue avoided epigrams in favour of ordinary comments that became funny by virtue of their context. So Wilde, implicitly, was belittled; but despite such efforts, Coward could never escape the knowledge that anyone who set out to write witty plays in English would be measured, however unfairly, against the Irishman, and would be found wanting.

Wilde was intrigued by the idea of people who led double lives (unsurprisingly: during his lifetime, it was an inescapable aspect of the homosexual condition) and the device features in more than one of his plays. In *Lady Windermere's Fan*, Mrs Erlynne has a double life, as the disguised mother of Lady Windermere. But she is also that familiar figure from nineteenth-century drama, the woman with a past, the outsider with a guilty secret. Coward had already indicated his interest in this predicament when he wrote *Easy Virtue* in 1924. Then, the situation closely paralleled his own, as he made his way into a society to which he did not belong by birth. In 1953, however, with social acknowledgement long since achieved, he had nothing new to say on the matter, and his policy – of merely substituting Coward for Wilde wherever possible – led to his incorporating the best bits of Wilde (and some of his more boring passages) and adding a few anodyne songs. *After the Ball*, as the adaptation was called, ignored completely the opportunity to make Lady Windermere herself as interesting and appealing as Mrs Erlynne and, not entirely undeservedly, failed to appeal in the theatre.

While Coward's fortunes were languishing, in 1953 his second biography appeared and was obviously intended by its author, Robert Greacen, to bring about some sort of rehabilitation of Coward's reputation. Greacen made some valid points. Speaking of Coward's 'half sentimental, half astringent' personality, he said, 'For too long he has had to pay the penalty of the artist whose work can be enjoyed by people of varying intelligence.' His book was certainly not without its inaccuracies. Forgetting the distinction between honesty and forthrightness, he remarked – of a man whose life was based on performance – that 'one of Noël Coward's most enjoyable qualities is candour'; and he tactfully dismissed Coward's dissemblings of 1918 by saying, 'As a private soldier in the Artists' Rifles he failed to achieve distinction.' (This was at least more accurate than the assertion made in the first study of Coward's life, by Patrick Braybrooke, that he had volunteered for service.) On the whole, Greacen seemed a somewhat uninspired apologist: and even Coward, who was never slow to welcome attention, confided to his diary that the biography was neither incisive nor interesting enough. It is a publication of its time, and so inevitably is pre-occupied with concerns about its subject's permanence:

Coward has had rewards in plenty ... but somehow the prizes he esteems most have been slowest in coming. He can make money, and stir hearts, proletarian, suburban and aristocratic. He can walk with kings and duchesses, and chat without condescension to able-bodied seamen. He can raise laughs in any company. But those who 'decide' whether a writer is lightweight or heavyweight, those who estimate the pros and cons of probable 'permanence' have had doubts about Coward and they see the trace of a snigger on his face. Even the *salons des refusés* inhabited by the livelier and more rebellious spirits have not opened their doors to him with any show of enthusiasm. Is this because success is suspect?[13]

Success has always been suspect in England, and it was to be another ten years before Coward's 'permanence' was conceded.

However, if his position as a playwright seemed uncertain at this time, Coward remained a star, and received acclaim in other areas. He had learnt a lot in the war, and had contributed generously to the war effort, but the most important development occurred while he was toiling to entertain troops with his songs. He had learnt, without knowing it, the uneducable art of cabaret entertainment, and in 1951 he was prevailed upon to appear at the Café de Paris for a month. He was to be paid £750 a week, a sum which later rose to over £1,000. He confessed to nerves in his diary, but need not have worried, because the first night was a triumph, royalty was in the audience and the applause was loud and long. The success of the occasion was such that the season became an annual event until 1954. His repertoire drew mainly on his songs of the Twenties and Thirties, which by then had acquired a period charm. He had no voice, of course, but audiences had known that for thirty-odd years. What they were going to see was a master of comic timing, elegantly autocratic gestures and nuance, clad in that ensemble of dinner jacket and deep tan, which more than anyone else he had made fashionable. Unfortunately, there is little surviving film of Coward in cabaret; recordings can testify that he sang 'Mad Dogs and Englishmen' at virtuoso speed, but they can do nothing to evoke his brilliance as a live performer. Critics were, on the whole, unequal to the occasion. The reviewer from the *Evening News* seemed entirely bemused: 'For nearly an hour this quizzical, faintly oriental-looking gentleman with a shocking voice held spellbound an audience that included Princess Margaret and the Duchess of Kent.' Only remarkable critics can do justice to remarkable performers, and happily for Coward, and for posterity, Kenneth Tynan went to the Café de Paris.

Tynan had already earned considerable fame and notoriety. Aged twenty-three, he had published his first volume of essays, *He That Plays the King*, and soon afterwards he became the *Observer*'s principal theatre critic. His career in that field was often said to be the most brilliant since Hazlitt's and, by the time of his premature death in 1980, his showily brilliant reviews and profiles had immortalized many entertainers whom he considered capable of giving 'high definition' performances, and now constitute an important chronicle of the post-war English theatre. In the Fifties he sponsored the theatrical experimentation which was to dethrone Coward and Rattigan and drawing-room drama. He had already been very damning about some of Coward's work, but he was an admirer nevertheless and was instrumental in ensuring Coward's revival a decade later. The essence of Tynan's greatness as a critic was his ability to praise: his writing at its best transcended the sterile polemic of criticism versus creativity, because rather than destroying, as critics are popularly supposed to do, he preserved, capturing live performances forever with an aphoristic impressionism. Only twenty-four years old when he went to the Café de Paris, he could already command formidable powers of description:

To see him whole, public and private personalities conjoined, you must see him in cabaret ... he padded down the celebrated stairs ... halted before the microphone on black-suede-clad feet, and, upraising both hands in a gesture of benediction, set about demonstrating how these things should be done. Baring his teeth, as if unveiling some grotesque monument, and cooing like a baritone dove, he gave us 'I'll See You Again' and the other bat's wing melodies of his youth. Nothing he does on these occasions sounds strained or arid; his tanned, leathery face is still an enthusiast's. All the time the hands are at their task, affectionately calming your too-kind applause. Amused by his own frolicsomeness, he sways from side to side, wagging a finger if your attention looks like wandering. If it is possible to romp fastidiously, that is what Coward does.[14]

The season was a remarkable reinvention, and added another aspect to the much remarked variety of his talent and accomplishment: playwright, actor, lyricist, painter, scriptwriter, film star, and now cabaret entertainer. It also led presently to another remarkable offer from America.

Coward had never believed in resting on his laurels and, however busy and acclaimed he was in his new career, the writing had to continue. Apart from *Pacific 1860* and *Quadrille*, both of which had been set in the past, and *Peace In Our Time*, which had been set in a sort of limbo, Coward's post-war plays, *South Sea Bubble* and *Relative Values*, had both damned aspects of contemporary life. In 1954, Wilenski's *Lives of the Impressionists* gave him another target. His own paintings had already declared Coward's loyalty to figurative art, so it was not at all surprising that while he found Wilenski's analysis of Manet, Cézanne and Renoir interesting and illuminating, he could muster neither understanding nor sympathy for his remarks about abstract art. When he had written *Hay Fever*, Coward was surprised that no one had had the idea first, and his feelings about contemporary art may have been the same: here was a subject begging for satirical treatment, and an irresistible temptation to Coward.

The play which resulted, *Nude With Violin*, was a confirmation of his reactionary position, and made easy fun of the excesses of modern art, and the bubble reputations which are dictated not only by artistic fashion, but also by dealers, critics and the other parasites of genius whom Coward had long since condemned. The dramatic situation of the play was simple. One of the great masters of twentieth-century art, Paul Sorodin, has just died in Paris. Instead

209

of leaving a will – and when the play begins, relatives have already arrived to divide what they assume is his vast estate – he leaves behind a letter declaring that all his work was painted by someone else, and not only one person, but by 'a Russian tart, an ex-Jackson girl, a Negro Eleventh-Hour Immersionist and a boy of fourteen'. The basis of the comedy, such as it is, lies in the manoeuvrings of Sebastien, Sorodin's valet, with the relatives, the press and others with a vested interest in preserving and enhancing Sorodin's reputation.

Sebastien, we gather, is fluent in fourteen languages, 'including dialects'. (When the play was finally produced, in 1956, the valet was played by John Gielgud, who thus began his tradition of playing superior servants, a tradition he was later to turn to such lucrative advantage.) Through Sebastien, we learn that Sorodin had much in common with Coward. He too had a Jamaican period: 'Yes, all those fat negresses, all that primitive simplicity and glorious colour as well.' He too 'loathed cant, jargon, intellectual snobbism, and the commercializing of creative talent. Successful art-dealers, critics and so-called experts were his *bêtes noires*.'

Nude With Violin is a disingenuous play because Coward was advocating a conservatism that not even he entirely endorsed. He bought art for pleasure rather than for investment: he had a Boudin which was much loved. Other acquisitions show that he was on appreciative terms with important twentieth-century masters. In 1946, he bought a Vlaminck for £1,000; and in the Thirties, when Beatrice Lillie paid $8,000 for a Modigliani, Coward immediately loved it and offered her $10,000. He described his own painting as 'Touch and Gauguin'.[15] However derivative it seems – and it has been described as Lowry transferred to the tropics – it makes an important point about Coward. He painted stylistically rather than naturalistically, and understood that art was a matter of a personal vision rather than objectively true depiction. The conservatism (or wisdom, depending on one's point of view) of *Nude With Violin* was as much deliberately provocative as genuinely believed; and Coward could be confident that remarks like 'It isn't a portrait at all. I mean it isn't like anyone or anything' would cause trouble. In *Still Life*, he had once said that painters and writers should have a deep and unsentimental desire to do good. Now, it seemed, they were nothing but pranksters and charlatans. Sebastien observes: 'I don't think that anyone knows about painting anymore. Art, like human nature, has got out of hand.' Determined to ridicule his enemies, as he saw them, Coward resorted to irony of the most laborious kind:

Jane: Do art critics really know?

Jacob: Of course they do. They are most of them men of the highest character.

However, by the time the play comes to a close, it has developed into an attack, not just on twentieth-century art, but on formlessness in all self-expression. Almost all areas of contemporary artistic endeavour now appeared to Coward to be sham, and those who furthered the careers of the fakers were equally culpable. There are many entries in his diaries in the Fifties and Sixties where Coward's conservatism seems almost a parody of itself; but his preoccupation with the decay in standards and the commensurate increase in charlatanism was genuine. It was all a huge conspiracy. If one person simply spoke out, everyone would be exposed. *Nude With Violin* does not end with exposure, merely with its possibility: 'Tens of thousands of industrious people who today are earning a comfortable livelihood by writing without grammar, composing without harmony and painting without form, will be flung into abject poverty or be forced to learn their jobs. Reputations will wither overnight.' The other side too is given its say: 'This God-damned philistinism, this dumb, ignorant hostility to anything that's progressive in Art – it gets one down sometimes.' But as with *Relative Values*, it is the voices of reaction which are given the best lines. Most audiences are conservative, while critics usually try hard to be avant-garde. When it was finally produced, in 1956, *Nude With Violin*, like its recent predecessors, received terrible notices, but enjoyed long runs in England and on the West Coast of America.

Chapter Five

Having begun the project in 1948, Coward finally completed the second volume of his autobiography, *Future Indefinite*, in 1954. Cole Lesley felt that the book gave one a feeling – unintentionally and certainly unnecessarily – of self-justification, as though Coward felt that he must in some way prove his patriotism and his support for the war. If *Present Indicative* was often a silly and inaccurate book, its successor seemed unreal and pompous. The account of his war activities could be compressed into half the space; and a kind editor might have questioned some of the more effusive declarations about England:

I did love England and all it stood for. I loved its follies and apathies and curious streaks of genius; I loved standing to attention for 'God Save The King'; I loved British courage, British humour, and British understatement; I loved the justice, efficiency and even the dullness of British colonial administration. I loved the people – the ordinary, the extraordinary, the good, the bad, the indifferent, and what is more I belonged to that exasperating weather-sodden little island with its uninspired cooking, its muddled thinking and its unregenerate pride, and it belonged to me whether it liked it or not.

He probably wrote this long-winded, enthusiastic yet laboured passage (and the others that are like it) in good faith: where patriotism was concerned, he had the zeal of the convert. But to say that he liked virtually all his compatriots, just because they were English, was merely idiotic; and to claim that he and England were spiritually inseparable was the sort of remark that returned to haunt him in 1956. In one respect, however, *Future Indefinite* showed a melancholy candour, and any younger generation of theatre-goers who happened for whatever reason to see *Nude With Violin* might have agreed with Coward's appraisal of himself at this period: 'I am now an ageing playboy, still witty, still brittle and still sophisticated, although the sophistication is, alas, no longer up to date, no longer valid. It is a depressing thought, to be a shrill relic at the age of fifty-two, but there is a little time left, and I may yet snap out of it.'

The most overwhelming intimation of mortality came in the year that *Future Indefinite* was published. Coward by then had two families, one of blood, and one of close, cohabiting friends, and of the former only his mother survived, his Aunt Vida having died, aged ninety, in 1946. Vida's life as a spinster may have been lonely, and there were certainly many violent quarrels with her sister Violet, but her end, according to her nephew at least, was easy: she died in her sleep, and he could reflect that death was kind to the old. By the time he came to writing a play about the approach of oblivion in 1959, however, he could not be quite so sanguine about it, because by then he had suffered a loss without equal in his life. Violet Coward was an old woman when the Second World War broke out, and it must have occurred to her son that she could not live much longer. But indomitably she did, withstanding evacuation to New York, deprivations on her return to belligerent London and prolonged separation from her son. With extreme old age, however, she became an object of unbearable pathos to him. Dutifully, he had installed her in a flat in Eaton Square, within easy reach of the studio in Gerald Road, but his diary reveals that he came almost to dread his visits there: she had become virtually deaf and blind, and he knew that she could neither recognize him when he appeared, nor hear or understand when he spoke. In 1954, she celebrated her ninety-first birthday, and shortly afterwards, and dramatically, during a solar eclipse, she died:

I know it to be the saddest moment of my life. Owing to my inability to accept any of the comforting religious fantasies about the hereafter I have no spurious hopes that we shall meet again on some distant Elysian shore. I know that it is over. Fifty-four years of love and tenderness and devotion and unswerving loyalty. Without her I could only have achieved a quarter of what I have achieved, not only in terms of success and career, but in terms of personal happiness. We have quarrelled violently over the years, but she has never stood between me and my life, never tried to hold me too tightly, always let me go free. For a woman of her strength of character this was truly remarkable. She was gay, even to the last I believe, gallant certainly. There was no fear in her except for me. She was a great woman to whom I owe the whole of my life.[1]

His literary facility was remarkable, enabling him to write rapidly and to order. The day after the death of his mother must have been, as he says, the saddest moment of his life: but the speed and ease with which he wrote meant that he could produce this true and coherent epitaph, the most memorable entry in his diary, at a time when less ordered men would have been content to let silence, or inarticulacy, prevail. Violet Coward had been the rock of his life, and the motor of his precocious promise. Without her, it is conceivable that he would have become a star, but he would not have set foot so early upon the path that led to stardom, nor would he have trodden so direct and unencumbered a route without her encouragement, her vicarious ambition and her brand of snobbishness which blended suburban competitiveness with a contempt for convention.

If Coward lived in the past where his country was concerned, in his own life he had no interest in nostalgia. He used his memory for learning a part or a song, but never for escaping to distant miseries or joys. Repeatedly, his diaries reveal that once epitaphs are written, their subjects have no hold on him: with the possible exception of his mother, he seldom thought of people once they were dead. And although he could easily recount the vicissitudes of his own extraordinary life, the sensations and emotions which accompanied each development do not interest him. At the height of his success at the Café de Paris, a diary entry reveals that he found himself listening to some of his old recordings, and the inability to remember the associations of the songs he describes indicates how completely the present lost its vivid appeal the moment it slid into the past.

In the course of that four-year triumph, he discovered that his voice – or rather, his singing – was to be his salvation. In 1954, he learned that he was £19,000 overdrawn, and he recorded being absolutely furious, not least because he had been given no intimation or warning of the situation. Large earnings were due later in the year, and Coward tried to comfort himself with the argument that things were less acute than they appeared. But retrenchment was definitely inescapable.

It is unlikely that he was ever reimbursed for the monies he had spent while in government service during the war. Since then, he had been involved in some very costly – and often abortive – productions (*Pacific 1860*, for example, had been given a budget of £40,000), and he had been given no warning by Jack Wilson about supertax.[2] In addition, he had many dependants – his mother before

214

her death, Cole Lesley, Graham Payn, Lorn Loraine – and two fully staffed houses in England, and one in Jamaica, to maintain. His accountant had used his life insurance as collateral to secure the overdraft. Coward, one of the most highly-paid and successful of all entertainers, was now middle-aged and without anything saved against retirement.

Again, that remarkable luck which attended his professional destiny came to his rescue. During his last season at the Café de Paris, he was approached by a New York theatrical agent, Joe Glaser, who offered him a short season in 1955 in Las Vegas. Coward had hardly heard of Las Vegas, and Wilbur Clarke, the owner of the Desert Inn, had hardly heard of Coward. But this was no time for equivocation, since the terms were remarkable: for a total of fifty-six performances to be given twice nightly over a period of a month, he was to be paid, with American handsomeness, $35,000 a week.[3]

There were anxieties about whether his voice would withstand the strain of such a long period of hard exercise, particularly one undergone in such a savage climate (the famous photographs, commissioned by *Life* magazine, of a dinner-jacketed Englishman smoking in the Nevada desert, were taken when it was 129 degrees). He took voice relaxation lessons, and, a lifelong and heavy smoker, tried to reduce drastically his consumption of cigarettes. Norman Hackforth, his loyal English accompanist, had been unable to secure a work permit, so a new pianist, Pete Matz, was found. Lack of familiarity with Coward's technique and the fresh arrangements which he provided for all the songs, meant that extra rehearsing was needed, and there were worries that the Midwestern gamblers who flocked to Las Vegas, and who would constitute the bulk of the audience, would not understand 'Mrs Worthington', or 'Mad Dogs and Englishmen'. The venture was very much to be a test of Coward's skill, but his standards had always been rigorous; and he was confident that professionalism would understand professionalism, and that he would not disappoint his employers, bizarre though they sometimes seemed. He noted in his diary that the casino owners and their myrmidons were devoted to their mothers (as he had been), often kind and often sentimental, but that they were also unscrupulous and could be cruel without compunction. He was particularly fond of Joe Glaser, however, the agent who had approached him in London, and was sure that he was honest 'according to his neon lights'. It would be fascinating to know what these desert impresarios thought of the natty Englishman, with no voice but great charm, whom they had imported from so far away, but sadly they left no comment. They cannot have been dissatisfied, however, for his season at Las Vegas was one of the pinnacles of Coward's career. One scandal sheet complained that he was the 'highest paid British tulip ever imported into the United States', but it was the only dissenting voice: audiences were appreciative, Frank Sinatra was laudatory on the radio, and stars boarded private aeroplanes and flew from Beverly Hills for the spectacle. Pete Matz said it was Coward's very exoticism which appealed to the audiences Coward had worried he might bewilder: farmers and workers from the Great Plains loved the idea that they were being charmed and confided in by what they took to be an embodiment of aristocratic Europe.[4] A record survives – Cole Lesley thought it was the best Coward ever made – which indicates that the balance he found between sentiment and comedy, between 'A Room With A View' and his brilliant version of Cole Porter's 'Let's Do It', was exactly right.

At about the same time, Coward received news that he had been offered nearly half a million dollars by CBS Television for three one-hour 'specials' to be shown live from New York to Los Angeles. The fee was to cover all production costs; but he was confident of netting about a quarter of a million from the arrangement. The first of the three, made with the star from *Pacific 1860*, Mary Martin, was called *Together with Music*, and was broadcast in 1955. It was followed later by edited versions of *This Happy Breed* (with Coward playing Frank Gibbons, and Edna Best as his wife), and *Blithe Spirit* (with Coward as Condomine, Lauren Bacall as Elvira, and Claudette Colbert as Ruth). Middle America was offered wholesome entertainment: a patriotic paean and a drawing-room comedy which, if a little sophisticated, was at least without the offending sexual preoccupation of *Private Lives*. All three were a great success, and Coward again found himself overwhelmed with plaudits.

If he had ever doubted the truth of the old adage, that there was no success like American success, he would question it no longer. His attitude towards the United States was often ambivalent, and as recently as 1950, he had complained in his diary that the Americans seemed increasingly vulgar; but now he felt loved again, and cherished as he had not been for a long time. He gauged the magnanimous response of the American press to his achievement, and it compared tellingly with the carpings of English critics. He basked in new acclaim, and inevitably began to reckon the extent of England's dereliction: 'My own dear land, which for years has robbed me of most of my earnings, withheld all official honours from me ... abused me ... and, frequently, made me very unhappy.'[5] He had always admired success, an admiration which seemed increasingly unfashionable in England. Now it seemed that, despite his patriotism, his English humour, his pride in England's past, he had more in common with America's meritocracy, and its belief in handsome rewards for handsome talent.

Chapter Six

A number of considerations combined in Coward's realization that he no longer wanted to live in England. He had always disliked the climate, and for many years had escaped its winters whenever possible. (English food, that other national affliction, seems scarcely to have impinged: provided he could eat chocolate, and also smoke in order not to put on weight, he was indifferent to what he ate.) But the prevailing moral and intellectual climate, which seemed so different from that of his youth, he found less tolerable. Like most of his generation, he had been brought up to believe in prosperity through hard work rather than state benefits, and whatever the merits of his background, it had denied him that sympathy with the theories of equality sometimes found in the educated middle classes. He neither liked nor understood the welfare state of post-war Britain, and he made that fact clear in his plays. In 1956, the year that he left England, John Osborne's *Look Back in Anger* launched a zealot's onslaught on the genteel pieties of the West End. Inevitably, Coward did not like Osborne's work, nor the values (or lack of them) which he represented. As he later put it: 'There's always room for low-life plays, but the attitude that you can only have a good play if it's about people dying in dustbins is absurd. Duchesses are quite capable of suffering.' He obviously had a great many admirers still in England, and he could continue to command large audiences. But those who pontificated in the newspapers seemed disinclined to admit those facts: increasingly, Coward saw himself, and his plays, denounced as pointless and archaic, and more and more, England seemed admirable for what it had once represented, rather than for what it had become. Furthermore, it was very expensive. His average annual tax bill lay somewhere between £25,000 and £50,000. When he learnt that his income tax for 1955 came to £20,000, even though he had only spent eight weeks there in the entire year, he decided that he could not afford to live in a society which, as he saw it, was determined to succour the mediocre at the expense of the exceptional.

His position was of course entirely sound, and there was no need for him to indulge in self-justification, nor to remind himself, as he did in his diary, that at fifty-six, he had nothing to show for a lifetime of astonishing success and unremitting industry apart from a little property, his talents and his health, none of which could be considered indestructible. Where choosing inept financial advisers was concerned, he was not entirely blameless, but he was right to insist that he had worked too hard to suffer a straitened old age. He was equally correct to insist that his decision to live outside England, when it was finally taken, had nothing whatever to do with patriotism. By 1955, he knew that he earned his living in America and did his work in Jamaica; and, with the death of his mother, he no longer had any reason to return to England regularly. His decision was not anti-patriotic, merely economically realistic. *Past Conditional* seems almost to have been begun so that he could justify his exile to posterity:

I feel it to be the primary duty of a creative and talented Englishman, or indeed a creative and talented Chinaman for the matter of that, to continue with his work wherever he sees fit and, by doing so, contribute perhaps a little to the sum total of his country's proud artistic record. I cannot feel that my obdurate refusal to pay taxes which I consider to be both exorbitant and unjust, need in any way prevent me being of value to my country whether I decide to live in Switzerland, the Galapagos Islands or Kathmandu.

But Fleet Street did not see it that way.

At first, Coward hoped that he would get away with establishing separate companies that could manage Gerald Road and Goldenhurst. However, once 'The Great Decision' had been taken, it became apparent that the severance from England would have to be absolute, and that his homes for the last two decades and more would have to go. Again, as with the death of friends, there was no repining and no living in the past, and once he had taken the decision, he was able to make a clean break. As though nostalgia was a protocol, his diary observes a couple of brisk reflections on the transient nature of all sublunary things, and then returns with practicality to the business in hand. Lorn Loraine was instructed to sell both his houses, and eventually accepted offers on his behalf of £5,000 for Goldenhurst and £11,000 for Gerald Road. Both Gladys Calthrop and Joyce Carey attempted to dissuade him from going, but they discovered that a financially secure future weighed more with him than they had realized. Following the advice of his accountants and solicitors, he resigned his presidency of the Actors' Orphanage and his membership of the Athenaeum as concessions to the limited time he would henceforth be allowed in England, and to demonstrate that his intentions were serious. He also sold most of his small collection of paintings.

Coward's property in Jamaica remained unaffected by the decision, but he had to find somewhere else to establish residence. Bermuda seemed ideal. Like Jamaica, it could guarantee hot weather but, unlike Jamaica, it offered shelter from English taxes. Like Jamaica, it was a British possession, which to Coward was a crucial consideration. As he later told his detractors: 'I am in no way saying goodbye to England, I would never become an alien citizen and am only going on being as British as I can be in two British colonies.' Whatever its nominal allegiances, however, Bermuda was an off-shore island of the United States, and promised easy commuting to Manhattan. He went to look at property, and found Spithead Lodge, which had belonged to Eugene O'Neill, and was the birthplace of his daughter, Oona, later Lady Chaplin, and Coward's future neighbour in Switzerland. The house seemed outrageously expensive at £23,000, but he hoped that he could get it unfurnished for about £5,000 less, and duly bought it.

Ian Fleming had warned him that his departure for tax exile would provoke great hostility, but Coward was more naïve. He may have reflected that any remaining hopes he had of receiving a knighthood were irreparably damaged by his decision: it might be absurd to insist that all knights should be heterosexual but it was also believed, more reasonably, that they should not desert their sovereign. (In 1959, Alec Guinness and Michael Redgrave, both his juniors by several years, were honoured.) But if Coward did think that far ahead, it is unlikely that he foresaw the animosity of the press. The furore was enormous, not least because many of the newspapers believed, erroneously, that he was abandoning England with taxes outstanding. (He had settled his debts with the inland revenue after the season at Las Vegas.) And his countless patriotic pronouncements, for which he had been famous for two decades, inflamed Fleet Street and returned to haunt their author.

It was as though he had been convicted of treason. On one occasion, reporters followed him onto the *Queen Mary* (he could not disembark, because he was not allowed to set foot on English soil), and enraged him by interrogating him for over an hour and a half. He was able to report that he had curbed his temper throughout, but that the amount of unwanted public attention he was receiving was enough to make Marilyn Monroe jealous.

Churchill had told him to save what he could, but Lord Salisbury tried to cut him. *Punch*, meanwhile, remembered its Marvell, and in 'I'll Never See You Again', made mocking rhymes of a patriot's career:

> Where the remote Bermudas ride,
> He who once sang of 'London Pride'
> Descended from a westbound 'plane
> And rais'd a breathless, cultured strain:
> 'What should I do but sing the praise
> Of this entirely splendid place
> Where my design for living's free
> Of all responsibility?
> For see how present laughter thrives
> In our expatriated lives:
> Here, wafted in on every breeze,
> Come cavalcades of royalties,
> Which gather in my bank in stacks
> Unravag'd by the income tax!
> So by this venture I am freed
> From thraldom to that happy breed
> Who in the island of their birth
> Still work, and pay, for all they're worth.
> Now a new loyalty I'll own
> In which we serve ourselves alone.[1]

But he knew better than to allow these outbursts to unsettle him. Besides, unpopularity had its compensations. In 1958, he confided in Cecil Beaton that he was saving £30,000 per annum by being domiciled abroad. And a couple of years after that, an ecstatic diary entry records a conversation with the Queen and the Queen Mother, who counselled him not to be annoyed or overwhelmed by the retribution of the press, and fostered his conviction that as a 'cosy royal snob' he should cherish such moments of regal understanding far more than any honour. Perhaps anyway he could yet enjoy prosperity and official royal recognition.

Now that his time in England was rationed, it became more

221

difficult for Coward to see his plays in performance. He could not see Vivien Leigh in *South Sea Bubble* in London, and only saw *Nude With Violin*, which had finally been produced, because he prevailed upon Binkie Beaumont to open the adaptation in Dublin, where he was beyond the jurisdiction of the Inland Revenue. The new play moved to Shaftesbury Avenue, where *South Sea Bubble* was still playing, and ran in London for over a year, with John Gielgud being replaced by Michael Wilding. Although its critical reception had been muted, Coward obviously decided that the play was amusing enough to warrant an American production, and decided to play Sebastien in New York in 1957. The play was not very well received on Broadway. Walter Kerr remarked: 'It is delightful to have Mr Noël Coward back in the theatre. It would be even more delightful to have him back in a play.'[2] But the production was transferred to the West Coast, business was brisk, and it prospered until the following spring.

It was a momentous season for Coward, not least because he also fell in love again. Whether or not he and Graham Payn had an understanding which allowed for amorous adventure, the world of the theatre (where charm and desire are feigned every night, and attractiveness is paramount) is littered with broken marriages and well-publicized divorces, so Coward's lapse would not have been remarkable even if anything had happened. But it did not. He speculated in his diary that as a result of a diet, and a leaner figure, he was more attractive both to himself and to others, but not for the first time he deluded himself. The man in question, William Traylor, had a small part in the play. He was then a struggling actor of twenty-seven, Roman Catholic and heterosexual. Coward may well have become more attractive to himself, but his leaner figure did not seduce Traylor, who became very distressed by his overtures.[3] And if it was a miserable time for Traylor, it was unhappy for Coward as well: a rather melancholy entry in his diary records the painful imaginings, the inescapable obsessiveness and the annihilation of self-respect which unrequited love entails. Characteristically, however, he makes no mention of the name of the man, where they had met, why he was attractive, what had gone wrong, or any of the other secrets such a journal might be expected to contain.[4]

Caution and discretion were second nature to him. Although he wrote about homosexuals, he never wrote about homosexual love, and one feels that even if the moral climate had been different he would not have trusted himself to deal with the matter. For writers, however, all experience is material for their art, or at least is supposed to be, so he wrote a short story, called 'Cheap Excursion'. It is about a young actor who unwittingly inspires a hopeless passion – but the broken heart belongs to his leading lady:

I don't care how high my position is, or how much I trail my pride in the dust. What's position anyway, and what's pride? To hell with them. I'm in love and I'm desperately unhappy. I know there's no reason to be unhappy, no cause for jealousy and that I should be ashamed of myself at my age, or at any age, for being so uncontrolled and for allowing this God-damned passion or obsession or whatever it is to conquer me, but there it is. It can't be helped. No more fighting – no more efforts to behave beautifully. I'm going to see him – I'm going now – and if he is unkind or angry and turns away from me I shall lie down in the gutter and howl.[5]

Chapter Seven

It was in indication of the fullness of his existing career, and of his allegiance to the theatre, that after the triumph of *In Which We Serve*, Coward did not rush into a career in the cinema. The proposal made by Paramount in 1947 had already indicated that he would easily have found lucrative employment in Hollywood, but, with the exception of *Brief Encounter*, he had had no involvement with the film world until 1949, when he adapted another play from the *Tonight at 8.30* series, *The Astonished Heart*, and played the principal part, that of Christian Faber. If he had hoped to repeat the success of the earlier adaptation, however, he was to be disappointed, since the film was reviewed with indifference in New York and hostility in London, and the presence in it of both Margaret Leighton and his favourite actress, Celia Johnson, failed to tempt the public. (Ian Fleming and Violet Coward both denounced the film categorically.) After this lacklustre venture, there was a further hiatus of six years before Coward allowed himself to be inveigled into a film studio: having seen the film of *Oklahoma!* he declared that if the cinema 'could make acres of green corn look so lovely, it could do the same for me', and he joined a large cast of well-known actors playing cameo roles for £100 a day in Mike Todd's film, *Around the World in 80 Days*.[1] (His role, as Roland Hesketh-Baggott, was described by the script as 'superior and ineffably smug'. He remarked, perhaps inevitably, that 'It was clearly type-casting.')[2] That venture whetted his interest in the cinema, and in 1956 he confided to his diary that he wanted to make another film, and one that did not involve prolonged periods spent in water. (*The Astonished Heart* had called for him to be soaked with rain. In *The Scoundrel*, the character he played drowned. And *In Which We Serve* required almost amphibian accomplishments.)

As ever, he was fortunate, since this new interest happily coincided with changes in his circumstances. He knew that with advancing age it would become increasingly difficult for him to undertake large parts in the theatre, even while restricting himself to three-month seasons. And although he would still be accessible to his admirers on records, films offered a greater and more attractive exposure. Moreover, since his success in Las Vegas and, more importantly, on American television, his standing in the United States was higher than it had ever been, and Hollywood echoed with his renown. With the greater degree of financial cunning which may have resulted from his debacle with the Inland Revenue he realized, now that his own plays were no longer guaranteed successes, that he could not afford to reject the absurdly lucrative contracts the film studios began to offer, however bored he was by the mechanics of filming, and however inclined he was to dismiss what he considered the easy stardom of the film world. As before in his life, need and opportunity fell beautifully together; and at nearly sixty, Noël Coward became a film star.

In 1959, he appeared as the King in *Surprise Package* and as Hawthorne in *Our Man in Havana*. (Ann Fleming went to see her Jamaican neighbour's performance and took a friend: 'Cecil Beatnik [Beaton] was determined not to laugh at Noël Coward, very difficult because he was very funny.'³) In 1963, he was in *Paris When It Sizzles*; in 1965, in *Bunny Lake Is Missing*; in 1967, in *Boom*; and in 1968, perhaps most famously, he played Mr Bridger in *The Italian Job*. He worked for directors of the calibre of Carol Reed, Otto Preminger and Stanley Donen; and as often as not he stole the thunder of the film, even though he shared the screen with actors as popular as Michael Caine, Audrey Hepburn, William Holden, Elizabeth Taylor, Alec Guinness, Laurence Olivier and Yul Brynner. And if the films which Coward made in his twilight are remarkable, the ones he did not make are more remarkable still: he rejected the principal parts in *The King and I*, *My Fair Lady* and *The Bridge on the River Kwai* (perhaps because this last would have entailed more filming in wet conditions).

He decided, while enjoying this late flourishing of fame and success, that it was foolish to own two houses in the tropics and none in Europe. Having adored the sun, he realized in Caribbean seclusion that he wanted climatic variety; moreover, although most business could be resolved in New York, he still needed to visit Europe regularly. In 1959, he decided to sell Spithead Lodge in Bermuda, having reached the conclusion that the south of France would suit his needs: it was warm, it was smart, it was near to London. However, he could find nothing that suited, and instead bought a house near Montreux, in Switzerland. (It cost £12,000; happily, the year in which he bought it he had been paid £35,000 and expenses for *Surprise Package*, and £1,000 a day for *Our Man in Havana*.) He eventually became a Swiss resident, which meant that all his earnings went straight into Crédit Suisse and attracted less than 8 per cent tax.[4] The financial security which seemed to have evaded him for so many years, and which had been a recurring problem, only intermittently considered, since he had gone into management with Jack Wilson nearly thirty years before, was finally assured. He would not die in poverty.

Not everyone liked Château Coward (or Shilly Chalet, as it was also known). Rebecca West was reminded irresistibly of Margate. Cecil Beaton had been told that it was 'very typical of Coward, lots of signed photographs, a house that might have been brought from Eastbourne'. Certainly, it lacked the grace of Beaton's house, Reddish: 'It is true the house suits Noël perfectly. It has no real character, is ugly, decorated in the typical theatre-folk style, but it is warm and comfortable and it works.'[5] He could have added that it was light, it commanded views of Lake Geneva and the distant Alps, and its winters provided the starkest possible contrast to Jamaica. Moreover, there was fellowship: the rich, the famous and the itinerant – kindred spirits – were numerous and accessible. Joan Sutherland and David Niven lived nearby, as did Queen Victoria's granddaughter, Victoria Eugenia, Queen of Spain. She appears with great regularity in Coward's later diaries, where she is invariably described as being 'merry as a grig', though how she managed such merriment in proximity to Lausanne is never made clear.

From this cosmopolitan eminence, Coward kept an eye on the aspects of England that continued to interest him, principally the theatre and London's social life. The new school of English playwrights which was then flourishing continued to confuse him; but John Osborne, the most successful of them, seemed to Coward to present a clear case of grotesquely exaggerated ability, and was roundly denounced in his diary. It was all too easy, it seemed to Coward, to criticize governments and traditions, but there had to be some substance and some skill other than in writing invective. To the veteran playwright, Osborne, the angriest of the angry young men, seemed conceited, envious, publicity-hungry, a careless technician and more dissatisfied than angry; in other words, rather a spurious figure. Two years before Coward passed that judgement – he would bide his time before delivering a major attack on the so-called 'kitchen-sink' dramatists – he had seen his lifelong friend, and the greatest actor of his time, Laurence Olivier, recognize (and so bless) the modern English school by accepting a part in Osborne's *The Entertainer*. A personal triumph for Olivier, the play was otherwise denounced. It took a family of down-at-heel vaudevillians as its protagonists, and made the decaying music-hall in which they were doomed to try and draw audiences a symbol of Britain's vanished purpose and resigned acceptance of decline. Coward was not particularly interested in dramatic symbols, certainly not if they shadowed forth national decay, and blamed it, as the new playwrights often did, on Britain's colonial past, her class divisions and so on. But he was interested in performers, and, in 1959, he began work on a new play which was also about ageing and failing vaudevillians. Like Osborne's work, *Waiting in the Wings* was heavily didactic; unlike it, however, and typically of Coward, it was about 'behaving beautifully', and determined to prove the possibility of 'rising above' the sadness of old age. 'The play as a whole,' he announced, 'contains the basic truth that old age needn't be nearly so dreary and sad as it is supposed to be, provided you greet it with humour, and live it with courage.'

He was a youthful sexagenarian by the time that *Waiting in the Wings* was produced. He had kept his figure and certainly his energy, and when he made his decision to write about retirement, he knew that that was one step he would never voluntarily take. Equally, however, he was aware of the chill, footless years. It was to his friend Ann Fleming that Evelyn Waugh wrote: 'You will lose someone you love every year now for the rest of your life. It is a position you have to accept and prepare for.'[6] Coward knew that too; but while he found it relatively easy to come to terms with getting older, the regular and irretrievable loss of friends was much harder to bear. He reminded himself that every happy day should be counted as a dividend, and every moment should be lived to the full – a pledge he had always honoured more than most. But the general tenor of his intimations of mortality is a hope that he will not follow his mother and survive into decrepitude. Although Violet Coward's last years had been cruelly protracted, she had at least been spared hardship, loneliness and obscurity, and Coward knew that his decline would also be free of such anxieties. Nevertheless, the terror of such a possibility somehow haunted him, and in *Waiting in the Wings*, he attempted to confront it.

The play is set in The Wings, a retirement home for actresses. All the residents have been reduced to poverty and obscurity: so its situation brings its author's preoccupations full circle, since *I'll Leave It To You* examined the possibility of escaping those conditions. The inhabitants of The Wings are not without companionship, but they are deprived of privacy, the commodity Coward had so jealously guarded all his life. Furthermore, in a state of total dependence, they are robbed of the power to achieve. The plot of *Waiting in the Wings* reflects their helplessness, hovering between the actresses' attempts to organize a solarium extension to the home, and the resolutions of various fraught relationships.

Plotlessness was by now a hallmark of Coward's work; but his previous characters had had the capacity for action. Judith Bliss, for instance, his first portrait of a retired actress, does not actually 'do' anything, but her retirement, we sense, is chosen and enjoyed. For the inmates of The Wings, it is enforced and resented. Coward realized that one of the ways in which we measure time is by action and achievement. When those things become impossible, time drags and becomes meaningless:

Perry: ... when people get old they can recall, say, Queen Victoria's Jubilee, and not be able to remember what happened last week.

Cora: Nothing did.

Coward's own life had been full and active, and he knew that he would find it difficult, when the time came and he was infirm and inactive, to take comfort in the traditional consolations of old age. And if he had finally ensured financial provision for those years, he had resisted, almost defiantly, all opportunity to equip himself with any philosophy that might make light of inaction and oblivion. But a lifetime of contemplation still leads to the grave, and before he adapted one of Keats's greatest sonnets, 'When I Have Fears', he knew at least that he preferred hard memories to metaphysics: 'I console myself with vanished years / Remembered laughter, remembered tears, / And the peace of the changing sea.'[7]

The characters of *Waiting in the Wings* have nothing left but memories, and also, Coward intimates, one remaining lesson to learn, that old age has a lot to do with one's state of mind:

Maudie: Who was it who said that there was something beautiful about growing old?

Bonita: Whoever it was, I have news for him.

Estelle: Since I've been here I somehow can't remember not being old.

Bonita: Perhaps that's something to do with having played character parts for so long.

John Lahr remarked that 'the notion of stars being forgotten, of performers' "magic" no longer able to protect them from the vagaries of life, touched something deep in Coward', and *Waiting in the Wings* has more grief and regret in it than any other play he wrote. He had been able to pretend in some of his later plays that disagreeable developments like social equality, the collapse of the Empire, or modern art did not exist, but old age and death could not be gainsaid:

Miss Archie: I hate welcoming new arrivals, they always look sort of lost.

Cora: That's nothing to what they look after they've been here for a few months.

Bonita: Why do you say that, Cora? You know you don't really mean it.

Cora: Perhaps I was trying to be funny.

Maudie: There's nothing very funny about arriving here for the first time. I know I cried myself to sleep for a whole week.

Estelle: But you're happy here now though, aren't you? On the whole, I mean?

Cora: Are you?

When the play opened in London, some of the reviews suggested that Coward had misunderstood his ageing actresses or, worse still, had patronized them. But he treated them with respect and sympathy, and the comedy, when it occurs, is apposite and plausible. Sarita Myrtle, one of the older inhabitants of the home, is showing distinct signs of senility:

Sarita: Out, damned spot! Out I say! One, two: why then, 'tis time to do't.

Miss Archie: You must *not* quote *Macbeth* in this house, Miss Myrtle. You know how it upsets everybody.

Later, a stranger, Zelda Fenwick, tries to make small talk about the home with Sarita, but discovers she is wasting her time:

Zelda: It's a very nice house, isn't it?

Sarita: Capacity.

Along with these nice exchanges, Coward also allows himself a short outburst of propaganda about the contemporary theatre: 'The Lyceum melodrama at least gave you your money's worth. An honest bit of blood and thunder's a lot more healthy than this modern creeping about in the pitch dark and complaining.' But he did not allow these asides to deflect him from his main purpose, and he took *Waiting in the Wings* very seriously. Having worked hard at it over a prolonged period, he confided to his diary that he was sure of its eventual success. It seemed to him to be a compelling and disciplined construction, and he defied the critics to be displeased. Later, he recommended *Waiting in the Wings* 'more seriously than any [play] I have written for many years, to the reader's most earnest attention'.[8] Unfortunately, reviewers were unable to share the author's confidence and enthusiasm; and although the new play opened well in Dublin, Liverpool and Manchester, it was attacked with vicious relish when it came to London. In the *Sunday Times*, Harold Hobson mumbled some faint praise, reserving most of his column for commendation of Coward's famous charity and *esprit de corps*. But in the *Daily Mail*, Robert Muller was not to be appeased: 'I tried to think of something agreeable to say about what I had just seen, and I couldn't think of anything ... The writing is flat; the comedy fatigued; the dramatic voltage is fatally low. It makes for a very long evening.' In the *Daily Express*, Bernard Levin, a rising star in the younger generation of theatre critics, found it 'the most paralysingly tedious play I have ever seen' and described the play as 'an exercise in grisly nostalgia so awful as to defy analysis, a defiance reinforced by the fact that Mr Coward has achieved what I would have said was impossible, and written a play that is about nothing'. This was absurdly immoderate. Levin was still a relatively inexperienced theatre critic, and to claim that *Waiting in the Wings* was the most tedious play he had ever seen was a mark of that inexperience. There are maudlin scenes, stock figures (especially that of Deirdre O'Malley, the Irishwoman) and a general lack of dramatic tension resulting partly from the powerless and sedentary life the play depicts, but it is hard to imagine why the play so offended the critical mentality, unless one concludes that Coward was attacked by the younger generation of journalists simply because of what he represented. Sheridan Morley[9] may have had a point when he remarked: 'Here at the beginning of the forward-looking Sixties, almost five years after the arrival of Osborne at the Court, was a drama by Coward who'd been around as a playwright for the last forty years about a lot of old actresses who'd been around for even longer.' After a good start, public interest waned in the face of such critical hostility, and the play was soon forced into closure.

Although Coward cared far more about critical opinion than he was ever prepared to admit publicly, he was usually able to put his private feelings about it into some sort of extenuating context. This time, however, he felt very bitter: his hopes had been so high, and he could only console himself in his diary with the explanation that he was hated so much because he had been successful for so long.

To compound his disillusionment, the production marked a serious breach with Binkie Beaumont. In 1957, Coward had begun to feel disenchanted with him when he had proposed extortionate terms for the American production of *Nude With Violin*. However, that had been forgotten, and Beaumont was offered *Waiting in the Wings*, as he had been offered all of Coward's plays since the beginning of the war. He did not like it, and demanded a complete rewrite. Coward was prepared to perform some surgery, but felt that Beaumont's demands were unreasonable. They quarrelled, and Coward eventually made arrangements for his new play to be presented by a different management. Later, it transpired that Beaumont had acted treacherously, rather than merely unreasonably. He had told Coward that Gladys Cooper and Edith Evans – both considered for the cast – had disliked the play, when in fact they had never even been shown it. Coward also discovered that Beaumont had tried to discourage potential investors.

The rift healed and Tennent's, Beaumont's company, was to present his last play, but the old intimacy was never quite regained and Coward could only remark in his diary, rather late in the day, that business and friendship were a bad mix. But if he had been less naïve, he would have learnt that lesson with Jack Wilson.

Chapter Eight

Nineteen-sixty saw also the publication of *Pomp and Circumstance*, Coward's only novel. The story is once again set in Samolo, and had been begun several years earlier and repeatedly neglected.[1] Finally, however, Coward managed to complete it, and the book became a best-seller in England and the United States. Like *South Sea Bubble* before it, *Pomp and Circumstance* is set in the present (as seen by Coward), and the central joke around which its plot revolves is that of an impending royal visit which is meant to be a closely guarded secret and instead is common knowledge. Few writers, however snobbish, could have been as cool and brassy about a reverence for royalty as Coward. To insist, as he had done in his diary a few years before, that there was no point in having a constitutional monarchy without being 'a cosy royal snob' was one thing; to write an entire novel about the preparations for a royal visit to an imaginary British possession as the disestablishment of Empire quickened was quite another. *Pomp and Circumstance* is a very banal novel: its principal characters are flat, its secondary ones caricatures, and the plot, such as it is, is quite remarkably uninteresting. The most animated passage in the entire book concerns royalty, and if the novel has any enduring value, it is as a document of one of its author's more unsophisticated public passions:

Royal snobbery, in moderation, is rather a good thing, I think, and I am all in favour of it. The Crown is a symbol and as such is, or should be, of tremendous importance. We are used to the tradition of royalty and have been brought up to believe in it and respect it and love it. I, being thoroughly British, and sentimental to the core, would hate to live in a country in which there was no royal pageantry and no chance of seeing the Queen drive by. This I know can be described as reactionary emotionalism which perhaps it is, but reactionary or not I feel it very strongly ... I want the symbol to go on shining, to go on being out of reach, and I am thankful to say that in our country and its colonies and dominions, it still does, in spite of all efforts to belittle it.

Quentin Crewe, in his review, said that *Pomp and Circumstance* offered positive proof that its author had signed off from the real world.[2] One could claim, equally confidently, that its existence confirms the theory that labels and first impressions stick. Coward found early fame as a cynic and as a tormentor of the so-called Establishment, and that, roughly speaking, is still how he is imagined today, despite his longing to see the Queen drive by.

As he collected his royalties, Coward could more or less ignore critical abuse. Whether or not he had signed off from the world, he found it increasingly discouraging to follow events in the world of the arts. In August 1960, just before *Waiting in the Wings* provoked blunt denunciation in London, he saw *Waiting for Godot*, arguably the most influential and controversial play of the Fifties, and was appalled. Samuel Beckett is one of the most overrated playwrights of recent times, but in the mid-Fifties, critics were competing to praise and champion him, so that Kenneth Tynan was not condemned for hyperbole when in 1955 he announced that the play 'appealed to a definition of drama much more fundamental than any in the books'.[3] To Coward, Beckett's play seemed annoyingly contrived in its madness, formless and incoherent, and that judgement was recorded in his diary, where denunciations of modernism were becoming ever more frequent. Had it not been for the anger he felt about *Waiting in the Wings*, he would probably not have abandoned the sensible course of public indifference to critical hostility which he had followed since the late Forties, and his thoughts on such matters might have remained his private property. But suddenly, in 1961, his temper snapped and he mounted the pulpit in the *Sunday Times* to deliver a series of homilies over three weeks about the contemporary theatre.

'These Old-Fashioned Revolutionaries' addressed the new school of playwrights. 'The Scratch-and-Mumble School' addressed the younger generation of actors. And the series was concluded with 'A Warning To The Critics', which Coward described in the newspaper as a 'valedictory' message to his 'old enemies'. In the interests of justice, the *Sunday Times* persuaded Robert Bolt to speak for the defence. The essence of Coward's first article – written, like its sequels, in a tone of Olympian detachment – was the importance of consideration for the public. Coward claimed that the preoccupations of the new generation of playwrights were too overtly political, and their manner of writing too unsubtly propagandist, to achieve widespread commercial acceptance. 'The first allegiance of a young playwright should be not to his political convictions, nor to his moral or social conscience, but to his talent,' he insisted. That was well said, but he had been writing propaganda in the theatre for years, in support, variously, of the established social order, the British Empire, artistic conservatism, even his own persona, and was therefore not the best-placed to announce that: 'Political or social propaganda in the theatre, as a general rule, is a cracking bore.' He was inconsistent also when he stated that 'a beginner should first write about the class he knows best', since he himself had certainly not served his dramatic apprenticeship by bringing the lower middle classes to the stage. But he made one extremely valid criticism of the class bias of the new generation:

The fact must be faced that a very large proportion of English people, even in our tax-ridden Welfare State, contrive to live, if not graciously, at least comfortably. The men manage to earn reasonable salaries in offices, banks, shops and factories; the women manage to run houses or flats, have children, bring them up and educate them and, on the whole, live fairly contented lives. For all the eager young talent of our day to be encouraged to dwell exclusively on the limited and monotonous problems of a fast diminishing proletariat seems to me to be not only foolish but very definitely old-fashioned.

Coward had not written about 'normal' life: those of his plays set in the suburbs now seem patronizing, while Elyot and Amanda came closer to the aspirations of most middle-class theatre-goers, rather than to the reality. But he was right to criticize the relentless pessimism of the new school: in the late Fifties and early Sixties, many English people had 'never had it so good', but their new prosperity went unmentioned in the theatres. (A similar criticism might be made of the repetitive British cinema of the Eighties, with its strident and one-sided view of 'Thatcher's Britain'.)

The second article, to the actors, concerned standards. 'I was young myself once,' Coward remarked, as he embarked on a tirade against actors who appear in dirty clothes for auditions. He advises all aspiring stars to remember that 'the Common Man, unless written and portrayed with genius, is not, dramatically, nearly so interesting as he is claimed to be'. It is important, Coward insists, for all actors to learn to play characters from as wide a social spectrum as possible, rather than concentrating on workers: 'To perform small grey plays in small grey theatres with the maximum of realism and the minimum of make-up is a great deal easier than to play classic drama or modern comedy with enough style and technical assurance to convince an audience of 1,500 to 2,000 people.' Perhaps he was right, but again he was being rather disingenuous. Although he was a superb exponent of modern comedy, he had never shown any interest in classical drama, and his acting career had been remarkable for the narrow range of types he had chosen to play.

The third article was about critics. Coward, as ever, was in no doubt about his loyalties. 'Like the cobra and the mongoose, the artist and the critic have always been and will always be Nature's irreconcilables ... A dramatic critic is frequently detested, feared, despised, and occasionally tolerated, but he is seldom loved or envied.' None of this piece rings true. Coward claims indifference to critical opinion, as he had done for most of his career:

My personal attitude to the dramatic critics, after fifty years of varying emotions, has finally solidified into an unyielding core of bored resignation. Every now and then the outer edge of this fossilized area in my mind can be twitched into brief sensitivity by an unexpected word of praise or a stab of more than usually vicious abuse, but these occasions are becoming rarer and rarer ...

He insisted that the only reason he was addressing reviewers was because he worried about the future of the theatre, a future he considered jeopardized by critical prejudice against traditional theatrical forms. But the article rapidly turned into a prolonged complaint against critics' 'manners', and a repetition of the stale argument that all critics are failed playwrights.

The series as a whole probably did Coward no harm, but it can certainly have done him no good. It sounded bombastic, its arguments appeared contradictory, and it was somehow not right for him to descend to such an arena. Kenneth Tynan retorted famously that: 'The bridge of a sinking ship, one feels, is scarcely the ideal place from which to deliver a lecture on the technique of keeping afloat.'[4] And that, indeed, was what Coward's remonstrance was about: a series of regrets for the theatre of his heyday, its acting styles, its dramatic conventions, its assumptions and its audiences.

He never came as close again to conceding publicly the possibility that he might be out of date: all stars have their pride, and it is founded on a belief in the immortality of their charm. Privately, however, Coward had already wondered if he had anything left in common with the age in which he lived: pornography, squalor, garishness and vulgarity – as far as he was concerned, the pilot-stars of post-war culture – held no appeal, because he was still addicted to charm and glamour, and he began to wonder, not entirely flippantly, if he should spend the remainder of his years sorting his memories. Life, however, had always been kind to him, and he was not to die out of fashion, or out of favour.

The productions continued. 1962 saw the arrival in New York of *The Girl Who Came to Supper*, Coward's adaptation of *The Sleeping Prince*, which Terence Rattigan had written as a tribute to the coronation of Elizabeth II. In 1964, there was a musical adaptation of *Blithe Spirit*, called *High Spirits*. The most important production of the early Sixties, however, was *Sail Away*, a musical comedy set aboard a liner making an Atlantic crossing. The production propelled Elaine Stritch to stardom, and did good business in America in 1961, and in England a year later. Its finest lyrics are still popular ('Later Than Spring', for instance, or 'Why Do The Wrong People Travel?'), but the piece as a whole has fallen into obscurity. However, its arrival in London prompted some surprising and important reassessments amongst English journalists. The *Tatler*, of all institutions, urged reappraisal:

There are critics, of course, who seem defeated, even exasperated by Mr Coward's long run of success, but their ideas are beginning to date as fatally as they say Mr Coward's do. 'Book, music, lyrics and direction by Noël Coward.' We have been reading that line on programmes for more than thirty years. We even take it for granted that this extraordinary man of the theatre should be capable of doing that, and doing it with more than skill; with intelligence, with wit and with the true theatrical panache. In this notoriously denigrating kitchen-sink phase we seem to be going through, Mr Coward has no master in sheer professional competence ... Finally, and throughout, there is Mr Coward. Surely it is time we realized there is nobody in the theatre, in ours or anyone else's, quite like our own Noël Coward.[5]

A month later, writing in *The London Magazine*, John Whiting found little to excite him in *Sail Away* ('big band stuff, with the subtlety of a steamroller in the Hammersmith Palais-de-danse'), and he castigated Coward for having discarded the frivolity and insolence of his earlier persona in order to lecture the new egalitarians of post-war Britain: 'Democracy was upon us all, but it lay heaviest on Mr Coward ... He did something which has proved disastrous to him as an artist of the theatre: he raised his voice. The mob was at the gates and he made the mistake of trying to address it.' But he insisted that Coward was 'a major artist of the theatre', and sought to place him in a historical context where, validated by time, his achievement might be judged: 'Who doesn't love his youth? For that is what Coward is to men of my age. *Private Lives*, *Conversation Piece*, *Operette*, *Tonight at 8.30*, *The Scoundrel* and all those songs we sang to our girls driving back in the red MG from the Thames pub on a summer night in 1936.'

Coward had changed over the years of his fame and success, most noticeably in the way in which he had tried, laboriously and didactically, to come to terms with his eclipse in the Fifties. But time and fashion had changed more, and now he was to gain by their inconstancy. As Frances Gray remarked, 'his songs were rediscovered by a new generation. They suited the Sixties pre-occupation with style and the flip satire which was fashion's response to the break-up of the British Empire.'[6] 'We have had him with us for sixty glorious years,' Whiting reckoned. 'We had better accept him.'

James Roose-Evans was a young director who had presented a festival revival of *Private Lives*. Like most of the young of his time, he had never seen any other Coward, having grown up during the latter's post-war adversity, but he liked the play enough to consider putting it on again at the Hampstead Theatre. In the earnest days of the early Sixties, the revival could have been a catastrophic failure; but its small cast meant that it could be produced without daunting expense, and the play had been so neglected since the war that in 1963, Roose-Evans was more or less proposing a première for his generation. Aware, perhaps, that any attempted rehabilitation of Coward might fall badly flat, he made the mistake of importing notes of 'contemporary significance' into the production, but these gestures seem to have been discreet enough not to have affected the tenor of the production, and he found himself with a hugely-acclaimed revival on his hands. The success took everyone by surprise. Even Coward, never the most modest of geniuses, was unprepared: 'There has been a revival of *Private Lives* in a tiny theatre in Hampstead and it has had rave notices! Some critics even praised the play!'[7] The reviews were, indeed, virtually unanimously encomiastic. It was as though a playwright of genius had just been born, rather than merely restored. Harold Hobson, in his characteristically boring column, proclaimed the evening one of 'exuberant and untroubled pleasure' and, admiring Coward's sense of balance, considered the play 'one of the rare jewels of modern comedy'.[8] *Queen* realized that *Private Lives* was 'a classic of light comedy, timeless and brilliant'.[9] In the *Financial Times*, T. C. Worsley saw that it was as much of its time as *The Way of the World* and *The Importance of Being Earnest* were of theirs, and in so doing, implied the play's position in the tradition of classic and enduring comedy.[10] He rebuked 'the young' for using Coward's name as shorthand for all that was 'passé', and argued that the play greatly benefited from that most unfashionable of qualities, sound structure. Bernard Levin was, once again, silly, though this time, at least, he was also complimentary.[11] Critics, as Coward well knew, are powerful, especially when pronouncing in concert. Happily, for the first time in many years, the chorus spoke in his favour. The production was the success of the season and transferred to the West End: one post-war generation learnt something of another, and it was Noël Coward who presided over the introduction.

Success bred success. The revival prompted Kenneth Tynan, always an admirer for all his damaging notices, and now literary adviser, or 'dramaturg', at the newly-established National Theatre, to persuade Laurence Olivier to invite Coward to direct a revival of *Hay Fever* for the 1964 season. The gesture was widely interpreted as being the repayment of a debt by Olivier, who had found early fame in the first production of *Private Lives*, thanks to Coward. The playwright himself made no mention of favours being redeemed and, instead, was all gratitude. To Tynan, he remarked, 'Bless you for admitting that I'm a classic. I thought you were going to do nothing but Brecht, Brecht, Brecht.' And when he arrived to start rehearsals, he confirmed his reputation as one of the charmers of his time: 'I am thrilled and flattered and frankly a little flabbergasted that the National Theatre should have had the curious perceptiveness to choose a very early play of mine and to give it a cast which could play the Albanian telephone directory.' Judith Bliss was to be played by Edith Evans, a neighbour when Coward's family had moved to Ebury Street. During the rehearsals, she persistently upset Coward's rhythms, and Coward himself, by saying, 'On a very clear day you can see Marlow.' Finally, Coward could bear it no longer. 'Edith, the line is "On a clear day you can see Marlow." On a *very* clear day you can see Marlowe *and* Beaumont *and* Fletcher.'[12] The production was again a huge success, and proved different things to different men. To Coward, it was a vindication of his anti-epigrammatic style and his onslaughts against the 'kitchen-sink' school (as well as of his star quality):

When I tapped out this little comedy so exuberantly on to my typewriter in 1924 I would indeed have been astonished if anyone had told me that it was destined to re-emerge, fresh and blooming, forty years later ... One of the reasons it was hailed so warmly by the critics in 1925 was that there happened to be an ardent campaign against 'Sex' plays and *Hay Fever*, as I remarked in my first-night speech, was as clean as a whistle. True there has been no campaign against 'Sex' plays lately; on the contrary rape, incontinence, perversion, sadism, psychopathology and flatulence, both verbal and physical, have for some time been sure bets in the race for critical acclaim. I was therefore agreeably surprised to wake up on the morning after the first night at the National Theatre and read a number of adulatory and enthusiastic notices. Such (almost) unanimous praise has not been lavished upon me for many a long year and to pretend that I am not delighted by it would be the height of affectation.[13]

To Kenneth Tynan, the success vindicated his championing of Coward, and ratified his standing as an international playwright worthy of regular revival – the central aim of the National Theatre's constitution.[14] To Ronald Bryden, writing in the *New Statesman*, the success of the revival proved a further point:

Who would have thought the landmarks of the Sixties would include ... the emergence of Noël Coward as the grand old man of British drama? There he was one morning flipping verbal tiddlywinks with reporters about 'Dad's Renaissance' ... the next, he was there again, a national treasure: slightly older than the century on which he sits, his eyelids wearier than ever, hanging beside Forster, Eliot and the O.M.s, demonstrably the greatest living English playwright.[15]

Coward's reputation was established for the remainder of his life, and has not dramatically altered since. But despite being what Terence Rattigan called 'nationalized', he still had to wait another six years for official recognition.

PART FIVE
RESTORATION

Chapter One

While this restoration was underway, his friends were beginning to die. But of those who did not live to see his return to favour, some were more sincerely mourned than others. As long ago as 1954, Coward had written of Jack Wilson in his diary: 'Nowadays I have no contact with him at all ... He meant so much to me for so many years and now I find even a discussion of the weather a strain.' It was one of many testy epitaphs written well in advance of Wilson's death, like the ever-ready obituary kept in waiting by a diligent editor; and when the end finally came, in 1961, their lives had diverged to such a degree, and Wilson's mental and physical condition had deteriorated so much, that Coward could hardly even pretend to sadness. Wilson was only sixty-one when he died – his widow, Natasha, was to survive him by twenty years – the victim of his unquenchable alcoholic's thirst. If there was no occasion for surprise (as his former lover observed, he had in effect died years ago), there was also little sympathy: as far as Coward was concerned, Wilson had committed the most selfish form of suicide, inflicting protracted torment and suffering on those around him. With his death, he vanished without trace. There were no children to mourn him; and, if Coward was to be believed, all his friends had slowly fallen away, alienated by his cruel drunk's tongue. But the second most important figure in Coward's first forty years could not be banished quite so easily and entirely from the memory, and Wilson's shadow fell briefly over Coward's last play, *A Song at Twilight*, written in 1965.

It had ended sadly and messily, it had cost Coward a lot of money; but in the years before Graham Payn came along, the liaison with Jack Wilson had also given him happiness: if it was indeed better to have loved and lost, then Coward was fortunate to have known him. Certainly, he was lucky compared to many homosexual men of his age. We easily forget now that England used to be much more puritanical and repressive, that otherwise law-abiding men (unless wealthy or worldly enough to go abroad) risked blackmail, prosecution, ostracism and imprisonment with every illicit embrace. The society of the theatre may have been relatively tolerant and liberal, but it was still subject to the forbidding morality of the larger world, and actors and stage designers alike, no matter how idolized or successful, were only sensible to remember that jurisdiction. Many accordingly led lives of mingled acclaim and inhibition, as Cecil Beaton later implied:

Even now I can only vaguely realize that it was only comparatively late in life that I would go into a room full of people without a feeling of guilt. To go into a room full of men, or to a lavatory in the Savoy, needed quite an effort ... To feel that one was not a felon and an outcast could have helped enormously during the difficult young years.[1]

Not all homosexuals could observe the unremitting discretion and self-discipline such a moral climate made necessary, and Coward certainly knew men who fell foul of the statute books. In 1955, he had noted glumly in his diary that a magistrate's court in London had ruled overwhelmingly against repealing the laws against homosexuality, and concluded that the decision would expose British law to international ridicule. He also reflected that the decision would have implications in all British territories, and that even giving a lift to a stranger in his car was a hazardous undertaking.

It is hard to imagine that Wilson's death was the catalyst, but suddenly, in the early Sixties, Coward gave a lot of thought – in view of his rigid conservatism, his political apathy and the judicious discretion with which he veiled his private life – to the necessity and desirability of greater sexual licence, and wrote three works, in three different media, which argue for reform. The most important of these was his last full-length play, *A Song at Twilight*, which was really a study of hypocrisy, though by the time it was presented the Swinging Sixties were sufficiently established for it to be interpreted as his endorsement of the new liberalism.

Before then, however, in 1962, he wrote 'Me and the Girls', a short story which took the form of a dramatic monologue of a dying cabaret dancer looking back over his life. Fluent, like all Coward's short stories, rather than inspired, it nevertheless sustains well its tone of camp backstage reminiscence, and is unequivocal in its position:

I never was one to go off into a great production about being queer and work myself up into a state like some people I know. I can't think why they waste their time. I mean it just doesn't make sense does it? You're born either hetero, bi or homo and whichever way it goes there you are stuck with it. Mind you people are getting a good deal more hep about it than they used to be but the laws still exist that make it a crime and poor bastards still get hauled off to the clink just for doing what comes naturally as the song says. Of course this is what upsets some of the old magistrates more than anything, the fact that it *is* as natural as any other way of having sex ...[2]

The following year, he wrote 'Not Yet the Dodo'. He described it as 'an epic poem about the English upper middle class', and in its sub-Betjemanesque way, it is:

> In the countryside of England
> Tucked snugly beneath the Sussex Downs
> Or perhaps a mile or two away
> From gentle cathedral towns
> There still exist to-day
> A diminishing few
> A residue
> Of unregenerate characters who
> Despite two wars and the Welfare State
> And incomes sadly inadequate
> Still, summoned by Sunday morning chimes,
> Walk briskly to church to say their prayers
> And later, in faded chintz arm-chairs,
> Read of divorces, wars and crimes
> And, shocked by the trend of world affairs,
> Compose,
> In a cosy, post-prandial doze,
> Tart letters of protest to *The Times*.
> These people still tap the weather-glass
> And prune their roses and mow their grass
> Representative
> For so long as they live
> Of the English upper middle class.[3]

General and Lady Bedrington, the upper-middle-class couple who command the poem's attention, were stationed throughout the Empire before the war, and are intended as portraits of the respectable middle classes who constituted Coward's audience of the Thirties, Forties and Fifties – the audience which had to be kept in ignorance of his sexuality. By the early Sixties, however, things

245

have changed, and the upper-middle-class Bedringtons have a son called Barry (his name jars with inappropriateness throughout; there are other names which rhyme with 'marry'). They visit him while in London to attend a royal garden party, and discover that he is living with an Irishman. 'Not Yet the Dodo' is really a second-rate endeavour but, once again, Coward is unequivocal:

> They both knew more and they both knew less
> Than either of them admitted.
> To them, the infinite, complex
> And strange divergencies of sex
> Were based on moral capriciousness
> And less to be blamed than pitied.
>
> They both agreed that there'd always seemed
> A 'difference' about Barry.
> He'd never plagued them with sudden scares
> Involving dubious love affairs;
> Preserving himself, so they fondly dreamed,
> For the girl he would finally marry.
> . . .
>
> 'I don't know what this is all about
> But Barry's the one I care for.
> I don't mind whether he's strange or not
> Or goes to bed with a Hottentot.
> It's no good us trying to puzzle out
> The what, the why and the wherefore.'

Meanwhile, in the course of this gentle proselytism, he set to work on the new play, determined, in so doing, to write a huge part for himself. At its inception, this idea – of 'an acting orgy swan-song' – took the form of three short plays, set in a hotel suite in Switzerland, to be called *Neutral Territory*. However, by the time the project reached Shaftesbury Avenue, *A Suite in Three Keys*, as it was called, comprised two one-act plays, *Shadows of the Evening* and *Come Into the Garden, Maud*, and one short but full play, *A Song at Twilight*. It was one thing, Coward well knew, to abandon his lifelong discretion about homosexuality and embark on a little quiet campaigning in a short story and then in a poem, but it was entirely another to appear on stage before an audience night after night and do the same thing. An author distances himself from disagreement and attack when he publishes his opinions in books or magazines;

at any rate, there is something less *physical* about his vulnerability. The same is not true of the live polemicist: by appearing on stage, even disguised as someone else, Coward was exposing himself in a way which was entirely uncharacteristic. But the stories which lay behind *A Song at Twilight* were ready-made and, in their respective ways, more bizarre than any fiction. And the way in which they became known to Coward at exactly the time when he was looking for material for a new play seemed too neat a coincidence to overlook.

He never knew Sir Max Beerbohm, although he had known Constance Collier, Beerbohm's one-time mistress, all his professional life. The dandy and exquisite died in 1956 and, a few years later, Coward was delighted to read in David Cecil's biography of Beerbohm of how the old man's exile at Rapallo had been horribly interrupted when Constance Collier had arrived unannounced to torment him. This situation seemed to have great comic possibilities. Coward was haunted also by the correspondence between George Bernard Shaw and Mrs Patrick Campbell, which he had read in 1953. He had, of course, known both of them: perhaps something could be spun out of Mrs Pat's request to Shaw for permission to publish some of his letters? Coward had also known Somerset and Syrie Maugham for many years, and had continued to see the ageing novelist whenever they had coincided in the same city: his diary reports that he had lunch with Maugham in 1953, and came away hoping that he too would be as charming and vivacious when he was eighty.

However, Maugham's charm was tarnished when in 1962 he decided to publish his memoirs in an American magazine. (His English publishers, Heinemann, had rejected *Looking Back* as 'the ravings of a lunatic', but that consideration did not stop the *Daily Express* from serializing it.) It was in particular Maugham's vicious attacks on his wife, Syrie, which outraged so many of his friends and acquaintances. As one of the leading decorators of the Thirties, she had pioneered the fashion for white interiors, and had worked at Goldenhurst. Maugham's sudden, capricious and bitter betrayal scandalized Coward, whose watchwords had always been loyalty and discretion, and he decided that he never wanted to see him again. By the early Sixties, Maugham was anyway a wretched and pathetic figure: the sinister rejuvenation treatments he had been receiving for several years meant that he had the mind of a near ninety-year-old inside the body of a man in his sixties. (Coward had already suggested to Binkie Beaumont that they call Maugham 'the Lizard of Oz'.⁴) Furthermore, his lifelong struggle to come to terms with his homosexuality, and then to conceal it from his enormous public, had made him a cruel and bitter figure. Coward needed no instruction where this process was concerned: and it is telling that when Gerald Haxton, the love of Maugham's life, died it was to Coward that the latter had written to express his feelings. Coward later admitted that the first stirrings of inspiration, for a play about a famous writer with a secret homosexual past, occurred to him in 1944, when Haxton died. Now, two decades later, when the story might just be acceptable in Shaftesbury Avenue, it coalesced in his mind with other thoughts on Shaw and Beerbohm. He had hoped to write a comedy, but *A Song at Twilight* turned out to be a melancholy and serious West End farewell.

Maugham's biographer, Ted Morgan, said that the novelist's public humiliation of his wife so upset Coward that he 'channelled his indignation in the direction of what he did best, writing plays. He did to Maugham what Maugham had done to Hugh Walpole in *Cakes and Ale*, but posthumously.'⁵ That is only partly true, because *A Song at Twilight* is not really an attack on Maugham. Nor is it a homosexual's study of homosexuality. In one way, it is a play which sets out to demonstrate the importance of discretion (an importance Coward had never throughout his life doubted): how terrible would it be to be famous *and* vulnerable to blackmail? Beyond being a melodrama about secrecy, it is also a play about the creative price any artist or writer must pay when he sacrifices truth to appearances. And from there, *A Song at Twilight* attacks the social conditions which make that disguise necessary. In a sense, therefore, it was a play which was sympathetic to Somerset Maugham's predicament, if not to his behaviour or personality. Nevertheless, Robin Maugham, his nephew, was sufficiently annoyed when he saw the script by what he considered hostile references to his uncle, and also by what he saw as gratuitous revelations about his closely-guarded sexuality, to threaten Coward and Binkie Beaumont with libel proceedings. Happily, Maugham died on Coward's sixty-sixth birthday: in law, you cannot libel the dead, and the way was clear for Coward's West End swan-song.

A Suite in Three Keys was presented by Binkie Beaumont. This time, perhaps to atone for the difficulties he had created over

Waiting in the Wings, he lavished every attention on Coward and did nothing to qualify the impression that the star's return to the West End was an event of great theatrical importance. Beaumont's biographer, Richard Huggett, recounts a significant story:

Anxious to get the maximum publicity for what Binkie privately knew would be Coward's last appearance on the London stage, and to contradict rumours that Coward was dying, he arranged a massive photocall in the theatre. Edward Burrell, the stage manager, remembers that Coward sat on the sofa in the middle of the stage while all the Tennent staff, the staff from the Queen's, Apollo, Lyric and Globe, plus actors from other theatres who had heard he was there, all appeared in an orderly queue and filed past Coward to pay their respects. 'I have never before seen such bowing and scraping, such unashamed sycophancy,' he said, 'most of them called him "Master" and some actually kissed his hand. It was just like an exiled emperor returning home.'[6]

However, despite the excitement the project generated, finding a director proved difficult. At first, Glen Byam Shaw was approached, but he declined because he thought Coward would prove too grand to take direction and because he feared also that Coward would set his supporting actresses, Irene Worth and Lilli Palmer, 'against him'. Vivien Matalon was then approached, and asked Coward whether he wanted a stage manager or a director: 'I have always had a great respect and admiration for you. During your years of wilderness and exile I supported and defended your good name, and I don't want to work in any capacity which might lead to disillusionment.' Coward replied unequivocally: 'It's been eleven years since I last acted on the stage and I'm frightened.'[7]

To begin with, Coward was full of enthusiasm for the skill and professionalism of Worth and Palmer, but again his judgement proved premature and there were terrible scenes during rehearsals. Lilli Palmer was told that her acting put him in mind of 'the German silent cinema of the Twenties and Thirties – you provide a gesture for every word'.[8] As often before, Coward, with his strict self-discipline, found himself disappointed by the relative inefficiency of other actors, and there were bitter complaints made to his diary about how angry he was that they had not learnt their words and had thus betrayed his grand and spectacular scheme to open all the plays on consecutive nights.

In the event, Coward found himself forgetting his lines on stage for the first time in his career, and was consequently reliant on the discreet prompting of the actresses. (They may have been as disillusioned with Coward's behaviour as he was with theirs, since he was notoriously dictatorial with actresses. Cicely Courtneidge pronounced him 'cruel as hell'.[9] Edith Evans said, 'Nothing will make me work for him again.'[10]) To add to the director's problems, *Come Into the Garden, Maud* required Coward to play the part of a hen-pecked American husband. Given that his acting abilities in English roles were easily taxed, the casting seemed optimistic. He had no qualms, however: 'It's so easy to play Americans. All you have to do is say "Hi, folks" very loudly, and then do the rest in English.'[11] But the season seemed to be a guaranteed success. As Richard Huggett remarked, 'realism and plausibility was the work of lesser talents. Coward, the living legend, was back in the West End and there were many thousands of play-goers who were glad of it.'

Soon, Coward was able to file a satisfied and happy report in his diary: the reviews contented him; his performance on the opening night was free of stage-fright; he had received letters of thanks and congratulation; he felt adored by each audience; and, above all, he was back with a vengeance in the world which he had always claimed. And as box-office takings settled at a handsome £10,000 a week, Peter Lewis in the *Daily Mail* sighed gratefully: 'As the curtain fell last night I felt oddly elated, as if I had recaptured the flavour of an elusive drink that one tasted when young but which had never been mixed quite right since. I know the name of it ... not mannerism, not bravura, not histrionics, but style.'

There are four characters in *A Song at Twilight*: Sir Hugo Latymer, a novelist; his German wife, Hilde; his former mistress, Carlotta, an actress; and the 'startlingly handsome' waiter, Felix. The curtain rises to disclose the obviously routine struggle for the upper hand between the long-suffering Hilde and her disagreeable but famous husband. Coward's superbly slick, if slightly verbose, exposition establishes their mutual incompatibility and dependence, and reveals the cruel expertise of Sir Hugo's malevolence. The facts necessary for the play's development are painlessly and discreetly established, the principal one being the expected arrival of Carlotta, whom Sir Hugo has not seen for many years. What can she want? Is he right to feel uneasy? Latymer is clearly not a self-portrait, although Coward gives his character several of his prejudices: his dislike of the cinema – 'I have had no less than three novels and five of my best short stories massacred by the cretinous medium. I refuse to have any more of it'; his dislike of modern youth – 'grubby, undisciplined and ill-mannered'; and his dislike of Germans – 'turgid mysticism, Santa Claus, Christmas trees and gas chambers'. Hilde, the guardian of his reputation and the bulwark of his camouflage, leaves when Carlotta, the dangerous past, arrives. Coward enjoys writing the initial skirmishing between them, and then gives us the reason for her sudden arrival:

Hugo: ... What is it that you want of me?

Carlotta: Permission to publish your letters.

Hugo: Letters! What letters?

Carlotta: The letters you wrote to me when we were lovers. I've kept them all.

...

Hugo: I believe that some years ago Mrs Patrick Campbell made a similar request to Mr George Bernard Shaw and his reply was, 'Certainly not. I have no intention of playing the horse to your Lady Godiva.'

Carlotta: How unkind.

Hugo: It would ill become me to attempt to improve on Mr George Bernard Shaw.

The skirmishing continues and Carlotta, realizing that her former lover will not surrender, offers to return his letters. But she cannot let him have the others.

Hugo: Others? What others?

Carlotta: Your letters to Perry.

Hugo (visibly shaken): My letters to Perry! What do you mean?

Carlotta: Perry Sheldon. I happened to be with him when he died.

Hugo: What do you know about Perry Sheldon?

Carlotta: Among other things, that he was the only true love of your life. Goodnight, Hugo. Sleep well.

Now, the curtain-line seems laboured and too self-consciously provocative. In 1966, however, this was sensational stuff, and Coward can have been guaranteed close attention throughout Act Two, which turns out to be a rather prolix argument between Hugo and Carlotta about dishonesty, hypocrisy and self-preservation. We gather that he has written an autobiography which one academic considered a 'superlative example of sustained camouflage'. It annoyed Carlotta: 'But why the constant implications of hetero-sexual ardour? Why the self-conscious, almost lascivious ref-erences to laughing-eyed damsels with scarlet lips and pointed breasts?' Coward himself could not be convicted of such hypocrisy, at least: whatever the other faults of his autobiographies, self-conscious references to scarlet lips and pointed breasts are not among them. At the same time, however, he had carefully fostered a public persona of the heterosexual cad, and he had done so for the same reasons as Hugo Latymer, reasons of self-preservation.

Carlotta, suggesting that Hugo has 'vitiated his considerable talent by dishonesty', reveals the reason for her annoyance: 'You might have been a great writer instead of merely a successful one.' And she accuses him of treachery over his former lover. Like Jack Wilson, he seems to have been a weak and addictive personality:

Hugo: He was a bad debt. He became an alcoholic. And alcoholics bore me.

Carlotta: And whose fault was it that he became an alcoholic?

Hugo: His own.

Carlotta: Do you really think you can shrug off the responsibility as casually as that?

Hugo: You are implying, I suppose, that my tyranny drove him to it.

Carlotta: Not your tyranny. Your indifference.

Hugo: Rubbish. Perry took to the bottle because he liked it and because he was a weak and feckless character.

Carlotta: And yet you loved him. You loved him for quite a long while. Your letters prove it.

Coward did not drive Jack Wilson to drink; but he shared Latymer's intolerance of the excesses of drinkers. The argument between Carlotta and Latymer fizzles inconclusively. Hilde returns unseen and eventually declares that she knew about her husband's past all along. She is loyal to him, despite his deserts, and hostile towards Carlotta for her attempted blackmail. Perry, she insists, was a worthless and ineffectual character. The letters are returned,

Carlotta vanishes, and the curtain descends as Latymer contemplates the tyrannies of love.

Coward was very pleased with *A Song at Twilight*: 'far and away the best-constructed play I have ever written, and when I played it I knew as an actor that as a writer I had served myself very well; there is an almost mathematical precision to it that in no way detracts from the reality of it.'[12] Generally, the reviews, for what they are worth, were unimpressed. Penelope Gilliatt, writing in the *Observer*, noted that: 'If it hadn't been for the new plays that Coward has railed against as imperilling the theatre's popularity, this work presumably couldn't have been written, let alone licensed.'[13] Harold Hobson, by remarking that Coward was 'taking a glance in the direction of John Osborne', made the same point. The dialogue was considered wooden and unlikely (with some justification), and no one seemed interested in its author's pleas for tolerance. Writing a year after the play was first presented (and ten years after the Wolfenden Report had said that the laws against homosexuality were a charter for blackmail), John Russell Taylor claimed that Coward was making a valiant attempt to swing with the Sixties.[14] John Lahr saw it differently: 'Inspired by and looking like Somerset Maugham, Coward acted out his own obsession with reputation and the creative price he'd had to pay for a lifetime of subterfuge.'[15]

Lahr's interpretation can only be sustained if one considers Latymer to be a self-portrait, and it is true that there are parallels. Unlike his protagonist, Coward was still without a knighthood. However, he shared Latymer's fear that any declaration about his sexuality would endanger his sales and income (hence the condition he imposed on Sheridan Morley's biography) and believed in discretion irrespective of one's sexuality:

Any sexual activities when over-advertised are tasteless and for as long as these barbarous laws exist it should be remembered that homosexuality is a penal offence and should be considered as such, socially, although not morally. This places on the natural homo a burden of responsibility to himself, his friends and society which he is too prone to forget.[16]

Wilde had violated this code a few years before Coward's birth, and his behaviour and subsequent disgrace had lent an urgency to the concealments of later homosexual writers. But Sir Hugo Latymer is not Coward. He, after all, could not express love at all, and had suppressed the promptings of the heart, whereas Coward, by his own admission, was 'no good at love' because he destroyed it 'with over-articulate tenderness'.[17] Rather than being a self-portrait, Latymer is a reparation for the way in which Coward had treated homosexuals before. Here, after the lisping caricatures who flit so coyly through the pages of his short stories ('the nice young men who sell antiques' of his version of 'Let's Do It'), is a rounded character realized with respect and grudging admiration.

Maugham, the inspiration of the play, paid for his concealment by becoming bitter, vindictive and disliked. Coward's old enemy, Osbert Sitwell, paid by failing to produce a masterpiece,[18] and Terence Rattigan yearned to write about the workings of the heart, but could not.[19] Coward was a very different sort of writer. When Lahr talks of 'the creative price he'd had to pay', he implies that Coward betrayed his gifts and failed. But he did not; and the plays of his that are most interesting to us, the ones that are still theatrically vital, are exactly those which deal with cloaked eroticism and obliquely-expressed emotion: *Blithe Spirit, Design for Living, Private Lives, Present Laughter*. The qualities which mark them as being quintessentially Coward – the waspish humour, the deployment of charm which conceals a longing to be loved, the scepticism about the permanence of human love, the fascination with glamour, the implicit dread that the party will come to an end – betray a homosexual sensibility. It is the plays of Coward's where he could speak directly – the patriotic vehicles and the clumsy advocations of imperialism – that now appear dated and embarrassing. One could almost say, therefore, that it was the strictures of the Lord Chamberlain and the intolerance of society that created the strange climate which forced Coward's wit and dramatic imagination to produce their best and bravest flowers. *A Song at Twilight* is about the problem of unused talent but that is not Coward's problem.

Chapter Two

On 16 December 1965, the day on which Somerset Maugham died, and the occasion also of Coward's sixty-sixth birthday, the ageing embodiment of youth took stock in his diary. Although he had never been very preoccupied by the world outside the theatre, and had never shown much interest in the glory of human achievement other than his own, even he marvelled at the changes that had occurred in the world since his birth. There had then been horse-buses in Teddington, he reflected, while cars had been curiosities, aeroplanes unknown, and space travel had been beyond the imagination. Noël Coward began to be aware of growing old during his sixties, and the robust health which he had taken for granted for so many years began to decline. From the mid-Fifties, he had relied on the ministrations of Doctor Ed Bigg at the Passavant Hospital in Chicago. The diaries reveal regular and comprehensive tests at the clinic, but in 1959 he developed phlebitis: 'My monotonously beautiful right leg swelled up like a pink sausage and I had to be carried about like a parcel. Fortunately I have an Italian houseboy who is quite square like a biscuit box and *likes* carrying wardrobes up and down stairs.'[1] Then, in 1962, Bigg advised him that an artery in his right leg was closing. Smoking was forbidden and, equally alarmingly, exercise prescribed. Later that year, in Lausanne, it was decided that he should undergo surgery to have a plastic artery inserted. Before the operation could be performed, however, Coward, accompanied by Rebecca West, consulted Professor Paul Niehans who explained, no doubt to his famous patient's relief, that the knife was not always the solution. Instead, he proposed to inject Coward with placenta, in the belief that new cells would then form fresh arteries. The patient needed little persuasion; and although it would mean stopping drinking and smoking, he entered Niehans's clinic.

This therapy provoked merriment: Coward was worried, he claimed, about being injected with non-U ewe, and Cole Lesley sang 'I've got ewe under my skin'.[2] The course of injections proved a deliverance, temporarily at least, and Coward was spared a major operation which, though he did not know it at the time, might easily have killed him. In 1965, he underwent surgery to have the jowls under his chin removed. This operation, relatively minor though it was, established that, despite being dogged by serious illness, Coward was still healthily narcissistic, sufficiently so indeed to become one of the first men to undergo cosmetic surgery. It was six months before he learnt from the doctors that instead of suffering to be beautiful, he had nearly paid a greater penalty: he had 'died' under the anaesthetic, since his heart had stopped beating for forty-five seconds. Vanity has its reasons; and one of them no doubt lay with the consideration that it was a star's duty always to look his best. But it was a narrow escape.

Total inactivity had been alien to Coward all his life. He knew nothing about resting, and very little about not rising to new challenges, and not long after that operation he decided to take a holiday in the Seychelles, then a more hazardous undertaking than it sounds today. He developed a form of amoebic dysentery which left him very frail (he was never restored to full health again) and the production of *A Suite in Three Keys* had to be delayed because he was so badly weakened. Throughout the season in London, he complained of great pain, and his doctor Ed Bigg later discovered an enormous kidney stone. In 1968, Princess Marina's memorial service allowed Cecil Beaton ample time to scrutinize old acquaintances: 'A shock to see some near contemporaries for the first time in so long, particularly Noël Coward. He has become a fat old turtle with slits for eyes – no upper teeth – the lower lip bulging outwards – hunched – bent – the lot. How sad. He was once the very spirit of youth.'[3]

But old age, for Coward at least, did have its compensations, and his seventieth birthday was marked by what he termed 'Holy Week', which involved a season of his films at the National Film Theatre, television productions of his plays, and a party which the BBC gave for him at The Savoy. Most importantly, however, Mountbatten's long campaign to secure official honour for him was finally rewarded: he had talked the Queen, Prince Philip and Princess Anne into attending *A Suite in Three Keys* – though *A Song at Twilight* cannot have been ideal royal entertainment – and Coward's diary mentions that Mountbatten 'went on' one evening about his old friend, and the greatest entertainer of his age, receiving some sort of honour. Coward concluded that Mountbatten was more concerned that the omission be made good than he was himself.

By the time he had lunch at Clarence House with the Queen Mother and her daughters, the matter had been settled. The Queen Mother and the Queen, oblivious to the pleas of his doctors, had opted for bejewelled smoking accessories – a cigarette-box and a cigarette case – as birthday presents, while Princess Margaret gave him cufflinks. After these tributes were presented, the Queen proffered another:

'If I offered you a knighthood, would you accept it?' And I said, 'Of course, Ma'am, I should be very honoured and very touched.' I bent down to kiss her hand, disappearing from view, and Princess Margaret, who was at the other end of the table, thought I'd disappeared entirely.[4]

Accompanied to the Palace by Gladys Calthrop and Joyce Carey, he became Sir Noël, and later he remarked, rather disarmingly: 'I loved being knighted.'[5] The elevation, sanctioned – improbably, some remarked – by a socialist Prime Minister, was less an acknowledgement of Coward's status as 'one of the few remaining guardians of the English language'[6] than a reward for the entertainment he had given to so many over so many years. Esme Wynne-Tyson, who remembered him expressing his intention to be famous sixty years before, and who had suffered the slings and arrows of his frivolity and teasing with fortitude since resigning the theatre a half century before, was reminded in a letter of his new dignity: 'You must *never* sit in my presence – unless I happen to have thrown you onto the sofa – and you must *always* address me as Sir Poj.'[7]

The honour came none too soon, because his health began to fail badly. He liked cigarettes, and would not surrender them. Exercise had always been a bore: arterio-sclerosis became acute, and movement a painful challenge. Cecil Beaton found a further deterioration when he visited Switzerland:

I found Noël in a scarlet jacket hunched and crumpled in a chair, looking very old and resigned and fatter. He seemed surprised to see me although, no doubt, as he later said, he had been looking forward to my visit. A glass of brandy and ginger-ale was within reach and the cigarettes at hand. Noël is only a little over seventy. He suffers from a bad leg; the circulation cannot be relied upon and if he walks he can be in great pain. As a result, he doesn't walk, and spends most of his time in bed. This is not good for anyone. But Noël has aged into a very nice and kind old man. He is really a darling, so trim and neat, his memory unfailing. His intelligence was as quick as ever and within a few moments we were enjoying each other's jokes and laughing a lot ... In the lift, recently built for Noël's comfort, he plopped himself down on the stool and said, 'It's awful. I'm so old!'[8]

Mountbatten visited him in 1971, and also marked the decline:

It really was an extraordinary meeting. When I came in Noël leant forward, put both his hands in the arms of his chair and made a motion as though he was going to get up. I asked him not to get up and he replied that he couldn't, anyhow, even if he tried, he was merely trying to look polite; Noël seems in a really bad way. However, he was spritely compared to Charlie [Chaplin], who sat on the sofa by me and practically never uttered or moved. Alfred Lunt was gay, wearing very dark glasses, but I discovered he was completely blind. His wife, Lynn Fontanne, was really the only hale and hearty person, but of course she is getting pretty old too.[9]

Throughout the latter half of his diaries, there are many entries which express Coward's hope that he will be spared a lingering old age. The thought appalled him, strengthening him in his decision not to forsake any agreeable vices, and he elected to smoke rather than face senility.

Binkie Beaumont died suddenly, aged sixty-four, on 22 March 1973. His death was a great shock to Coward, and Cole Lesley has written poignantly about his sadness and about his frequently reiterated hopes that Beaumont would have made provision for his servants, Anna and the evocatively-named Elvira. Four days after Beaumont's death, Noël Coward, succumbing to a heart attack, followed him. He had not known 'the wasted hand on the coverlet and the loved ones gathered round',[10] and by the standards of his family he did not reach a great age. But he had contemplated eternity without regret: 'I have had ... "a talent to amuse" and ... have been able to make many millions of my fellow creatures laugh, which ... is not a bad accolade to retire to the grave with.'[11] At his death, *Private Lives* was running in London, along with *Cowardy Custard*, an anthology of the songs and sketches. In New York, *Oh, Coward* was offering a similar tribute.

Coward's will, which had been drawn up in London in 1971, was published in June 1973, and stressed his Swiss domicile: 'I have abandoned my English domicile of origin and any domicile of choice that I may have acquired in the islands of Bermuda, that I intend to live and die in Switzerland, that I regard Switzerland as my permanent home and that I have no intention of ever permanently residing again in England.' There were many small (and less small) bequests. For instance, Gladys Calthrop received his Boudin; Laurence Olivier, 'my cabochon amethyst buttons, links and studs'; Doctor Ed Bigg, 'my Nonesuch of Dickens'. Binkie Beaumont was to have received emerald and sapphire jewellery. Coward left £20,000 in England, but the bulk of his assets were in Switzerland and the West Indies. Under Swiss law, the size of the estate was undisclosed, but it was divided, after the named bequests had been made, between Cole Lesley and Graham Payn. It was the end, but it was not oblivion.

Sheridan Morley's biography was reissued with its subject's death. Less than a year after Coward's death, his next biographer, James Pope-Hennessy, died in macabre and grotesque circumstances.[12] In 1979 a scrapbook compiled by Sheridan Morley, Cole Lesley and Graham Payn appeared, promising 'unpublished material from Coward's own archive'. Most importantly, in 1982, the Noël Coward Estate published his diaries, and the editors, Graham Payn and Sheridan Morley, insisted that the journals had been left materially untouched: 'We have not seen a duty to preserve the reputations of those living or dead; nor have we seen it as any part of our duties to censor anything.' Their only concessions, they insisted, had been to the laws of libel, which had necessitated 'minor but still regrettable cuts'. It is hard to doubt their word.[13] Coward was self-editing, and it would have been completely out of character for him to have committed intimate secrets to a journal which he must have known would one day be published. (It is no accident that the book's tone often suggests its author's awareness of an audience which, though unseen and unheard, was nevertheless attentive.)

The critical consensus was that the diaries' appearance had done nothing to enhance Coward's personal reputation, and there was general disappointment about their lack of intimate and confidential detail. David Holloway, in the *Daily Telegraph*, commended them as an 'important record of the theatre and films between the end of the war and 1969', but found much, inevitably, that was 'repetitious and unimportant'. B. A. Young, in the *Financial Times*, was almost hurt: 'I would much rather not have read them, but instead gone on believing that Sir Noël was a thoroughly delightful person.' *Punch* found the diarist who emerged 'blinkered' and 'smug'. Only Adam Mars-Jones in the *Sunday Times* saw the situation clearly when he lamented 'a diarist who would rather be dull than vulgar, and for whom self-analysis was always an indiscretion'. Diaries and autobiographies are literary self-portraiture, and the first requirement of that art is the ability to be honest with oneself. But Coward could never muster sufficient indifference to the outside world to practise the candour vital to confessional writing: ever the showman, one senses that even in private he was too conscious of his public, too anxious about embarrassment in the stalls and unrest in the gallery to expose a rogue emotion.

This self-consciousness, this awareness that he was always on display and always performing, never left him and gave focus to his waking hours. Having been the centre of attention in his restless mother's confining world, he could never again settle for being ignored, and the remainder of his life was spent wooing bigger audiences and louder applause. Nothing else really mattered to him. As a result, his spangled career, for all its acclaim and commotion, was strangely uneventful and lacking in emotional and intellectual development. He glimpsed this truth, only to misinterpret it, when he wrote: 'My personality only really changed once, and that was when I was twenty-four and I became a star and a privileged person.'[14] The external circumstances of his life may have changed then – from indigence and obscurity to affluence and fame – but his personality remained constant, especially in its admiration for the morality of his suburban background, and its conviction that contentment lay in financial prudence, conservatism, ambition and determined hard work.

Coward found fame in his earliest plays when he appeared to ridicule those virtues. Yet he teased respectability so effectively only because he understood it (after all, it is the watchword of the suburbs) and as he grew older, he became increasingly conservative and increasingly conformist. That in itself is a familiar development. In Coward's case, however, it revealed more than the usual process of intellectual mellowing, or a reversion to parental values: it revealed a longing for acceptance. If he liked standing apart from the crowd, and enjoyed its admiration, he longed also for its approval. This instinct – almost a professional requirement in the theatre, and the troubling impulse in many homosexual destinies – dominated him, and lent his life its peculiar tension.

Coward struggled to disguise this dilemma – of how to be an outsider but not an outcast – and also to resolve it, by playing the child, because children are exempt from the rules of adult society. With naughty precocity he teased the serious world, and his best plays taunt the proprieties of their time. Eager to be indulged, he took an ingenuous delight in the trophies of acclaim, though characteristically he could not resist turning them to playful and insolent account: 'The legend of my modesty grew and grew. I became extraordinarily unspoilt by my great success. As a matter of fact, I still am.'[15] But children can have cunning too; and if Coward was the favourite of fortune, he was astute enough to use its dispensations to impress, secure in the knowledge that the public has expectations of its stars, and that it would admire his life of limousines, pampered travel and silken adornment almost as much as he did. Once he had decided on a performance, Coward always delivered it with panache, and there was a great sophistication to this provocative immaturity, a sophistication Kenneth Tynan saluted in 1953, when he remembered that one of Coward's earliest professional appearances had been in a play about a little boy who would not grow up: 'Forty years ago he was Slightly in *Peter Pan* and you might say that he has been wholly in *Peter Pan* ever since.'[16]

The problem was that this cunning immaturity and the spectacle of success which accompanied it obscured Coward's achievement, as he himself was the first to realize: 'It is fairly natural that my writing should be casually appreciated because my personality, performance, music and legend get in the way.'[17] To his contemporaries, his life and persona were more compelling even than his writing; and because he featured so prominently in the chronicles of the Twenties and Thirties, he has come to seem indistinguishable from those years, even representative of them. When Rebecca West tried to analyse his self-creation, she saw him above all as 'the immortal spirit of the charming Twenties', while to Stella Gibbons, he was more symbol than man: 'He seems to me to incarnate the *myth* of the Twenties.' This association persists, and continues to distort Coward's fame and to define it. At its best, his dialogue, which renders the longing for love tragi-comically, is of an exemplary freshness and clarity and needs no props with which to plead. As though it is impenetrably archaic, however, directors imagine that audiences will not understand it without the visual support of cigarette-holders and tuxedos, and we have yet to meet the Elyot and Amanda of the jean generation.

Today the voice and the manner and the dress and the wit which dazzled a generation are fading in living memory. Yet Noël Coward endures triumphantly in the popular imagination. His unusual name has the power of a spell to conjure glamour and style in prosaic and amnesiac minds, and those who know neither the inimitable voice nor its words recognize his quizzical smoker's face. That is a remarkable achievement, and one which hardly any other popular English writer can boast. But few had such a spectrum of talent to proclaim, or such single-mindedness, or such a fascination with fame, or such a solipsistic energy.

Notes

INTRODUCTION
1. *New York Times*, December 1970.
2. *New York Times*, December 1969.
3. *Harper's Bazaar*, August 1960.
4. This valediction was repeated by Sir Bernard Miles, Director of the Mermaid Theatre, where *Cowardy Custard* had been running for a year when Noël Coward died.
5. Noël Coward, *Past Conditional*, Methuen, London, 1986.
6. Quoted, Cole Lesley, *The Life of Noël Coward*, Jonathan Cape, London, 1976.

Part 1: Obscurity
CHAPTER 1
1. Noël Coward, *Present Indicative*, Heinemann, London, 1937.
2. William Marchant, *The Privilege of His Company: Noël Coward Remembered*, Weidenfeld and Nicolson, London, 1975.
3. Coward's wit and humour were quintessentially English, and reflexive mockery was integral to them.
4. Quoted, Sheridan Morley, *A Talent To Amuse*, Heinemann, London, 1969.
5. Quoted, Hugo Vickers, *Cecil Beaton*, Weidenfeld and Nicolson, London, 1985.
6. Quoted, Dick Richards (ed.), *The Wit of Noël Coward*, Leslie Frewin, London, 1968.
7. 'Personal Reminiscence', Noël Coward, *Collected Verse*, Methuen, London, 1984.

8. V. S. Pritchett, *A Cab At The Door*, Chatto and Windus, London, 1968.
9. *Present Indicative*.
10. Ibid.
11. Quoted, Lesley.
12. Ibid.
13. Ibid.
14. *Past Conditional*.
15. Noël Coward, *The Collected Short Stories*, Dutton, New York, 1983.
16. 'A Private Life', A documentary of the life of Noël Coward, BBC TV, 1983.
17. Loelia, Duchess of Westminster, *Grace and Favour*, Weidenfeld and Nicolson, London, 1961 (introduction by Noël Coward).
18. Quoted, Lesley.
19. Quoted, Cole Lesley, Sheridan Morley and Graham Payn (eds), *Noël Coward and His Friends*, Weidenfeld and Nicolson, London, 1979.
20. *The Complete Works of Saki*, Penguin, London, 1967, introduced by Noël Coward.
21. 'Boys' Weeklies', George Orwell, *Collected Essays*, Secker and Warburg, London, 1961.
22. *Present Indicative*.

CHAPTER 2
1. Quoted, Patrick Garland, *Vogue*, July 1973.
2. *Present Indicative*.
3. Ibid.
4. Quoted, Morley.
5. Quoted, *Noël Coward and His Friends*.

6. Quoted, Charles Castle, *Noël*, W. H. Allen, London, 1972.
7. Noël Coward, *Diaries*, Weidenfeld and Nicolson, London, 1982.
8. Anonymous writer in *The Times*, 1958.
9. Quoted, *Present Indicative*.
10. Ibid.
11. *Noël Coward and His Friends*.
12. Ibid.
13. Quoted, Morley.
14. 'Me and the Girls', *The Collected Short Stories of Noël Coward*.
15. Sheridan Morley, *Gertrude Lawrence*, Weidenfeld and Nicolson, London, 1981.

CHAPTER 3
1. As related by Esme Wynne-Tyson, courtesy of Jon Wynne-Tyson.
2. Ibid.
3. Ibid.
4. Ibid.
5. Quoted, Morley.
6. Ibid.
7. Ibid.
8. Ibid.
9. Noël Coward to Esme Wynne-Tyson, courtesy of Jon Wynne-Tyson.
10. Noël Coward to Esme Wynne, courtesy of Jon Wynne-Tyson.
11. See *Who Was Who 1971–1980*.
12. Her son, Jon Wynne-Tyson, remembered that they greeted each other like long-lost brother and sister when she visited Coward backstage when he was appearing in *The Apple Cart* in 1953. And Wynne-Tyson's play, *Marvellous Party* (Calder, 1989), imagines a reunion – in Las Vegas, of all settings – at which they look back on their youth, are tempted to analyse the reasons for the parting of their ways, and embark on a fast and furious return to childhood.
13. Esme Wynne-Tyson, courtesy of Jon Wynne-Tyson.
14. *Present Indicative*.
15. There is one version of this poem in the *Collected Verse of Noël Coward*. This quotation is from an unpublished variation.

CHAPTER 4
1. Quoted, Lesley.
2. *Present Indicative*.
3. Ibid.
4. *Past Conditional*.
5. Lesley.
6. *Present Indicative*.
7. Quoted, Lesley.
8. *Present Indicative*.
9. Ibid.
10. Quoted, Morley.
11. Remembered by Esme Wynne-Tyson, courtesy of Jon Wynne-Tyson.
12. Quoted, Morley.
13. Ibid.
14. Ibid.
15. *Present Indicative*.
16. Noël Coward, *Diaries*.
17. *Present Indicative*.
18. Quoted, Morley.
19. Ibid.
20. *Present Indicative*.
21. Ibid.
22. BBC Radio, 1966. Quoted, John Lahr, *Coward the Playwright*, Methuen, London, 1982.
23. Samuel Hopkins Adams, *Alexander Woollcott*, Hamish Hamilton, London, 1946.
24. Quoted, Morley.

CHAPTER 5
1. Quoted, Morley.
2. *Present Indicative*.
3. According to Cole Lesley.
4. John Pearson, *Façades. A Biogra-*

phy of Edith, Osbert and Sacheverell Sitwell, Macmillan, London, 1978.
5. Ibid.
6. Ibid.
7. Ibid.
8. Ibid.
9. Cecil Beaton, *Self Portrait with Friends: The Diaries of Cecil Beaton*, Weidenfeld and Nicolson, London, 1979.
10. *Present Indicative*.
11. Ibid.
12. 'The Youngest Generation', reproduced in *A Little Order* (a selection of the journalism of Evelyn Waugh), Eyre Methuen, London, 1977.
13. The *Spectator*, 13 April 1929, reproduced in *A Little Order*.
14. Quoted, Morley.
15. Raymond Mander and Joe Mitchenson, *Theatrical Companion to Noël Coward*, Rockliff, London, 1957.

Part 2: Fame
CHAPTER 1
1. *Present Indicative*.
2. Correspondence of the Lord Chamberlain's Office, British Library/Crown Copyright.
3. Ibid.
4. Ibid.
5. Ibid.
6. Quoted, Lahr.
7. Correspondence of the Lord Chamberlain's Office.
8. John Gielgud, *Early Stages*, Macmillan, London, 1939.
9. Basil Dean, *Seven Ages: An Autobiography*, Hutchinson, London, 1973.
10. Quoted, Morley.
11. The *Sunday Times*. Quoted, John Russell Taylor, *The Rise and Fall of the Well-Made Play*, Methuen, London, 1967.

12. Kenneth Tynan, *A View of the English Stage*, Methuen, London, 1975.
13. Quoted, Castle. Sybil Thorndike remembered 'one awful scream, driving up Sloane Street one day. He was in front of us in an open taxi and we were coming along in our old car making a terrific noise, trying to attract his attention, and he screamed at us: "Stop it, stop it!" He didn't recognize us. We rocked with laughter. But he was nervous, you know. He had awful nerves.'
14. Tynan.

CHAPTER 2
1. Dean.
2. Patrick Braybrooke, *The Amazing Mr Coward*, Archer, London, 1933.
3. In conversation with the author, January 1990.
4. Alan Jenkins, *Remembering the Thirties*, Heinemann, London, 1976.
5. According to Michael Thornton, writing in the *Evening Standard*, January 1990. See also Michael Thornton, *Royal Feud: The Queen Mother and the Duchess of Windsor*, Michael Joseph, London, 1985.
6. Coward had an alternative explanation, which he ventured years later to Truman Capote, of all people: 'He (the Duke of Windsor) pretends not to hate me, but he does, and it's because I'm queer and he's queer but, unlike him, I don't pretend not to be.' Thornton.
7. Sir John Gielgud to the author, February 1991.
8. Esme Wynne-Tyson, courtesy of Jon Wynne-Tyson.
9. There seems to be a discrepancy. Perhaps it is just another of Coward's inaccuracies in *Present Indicative*. Whether the affair began in London or New York, however, Gielgud's memory is not uninter-

esting. He said that he was in 'considerable awe' of Coward at this stage, and that the latter 'never discussed his love life with me, even when we became good friends'. Coward need not have feared censure from Gielgud, yet the moral climate was such, and his discretion was such, that many things were left unsaid. It is interesting to note, though, that Wilson was wearing exactly what his lover became famous for wearing – dinner jacket and carnation – and that his beauty was paraded. He and Coward must have made an impressive pair. Sir John Gielgud in correspondence with the author, February 1991.

10. John Lahr is appropriately reminded of Evelyn Waugh's dictum: 'Manners are especially the need of the plain. The pretty can get away with anything.'

11. *Present Indicative*.

12. Cecil Beaton, *Diaries*.

13. Repeated in Marchant.

14. Cecil Beaton, *Diaries*.

15. Quoted, Morley.

CHAPTER 3

1. Correspondence of the Lord Chamberlain's Office.

2. Esme Wynne-Tyson, courtesy of Jon Wynne-Tyson.

3. Cecil Beaton, *Diaries*.

4. Correspondence of the Lord Chamberlain's Office.

5. Quoted, Morley.

6. Ibid.

7. Quoted, Lesley.

8. Braybrooke.

9. Ibid.

10. Quoted, Morley.

11. Ibid.

12. Quoted, Lahr.

13. *The Collected Short Stories of Noël Coward*.

14. 'Let These People Go', *Collected Verse of Noël Coward*.

15. Lahr.

16. *Present Indicative*.

17. Quoted, Morley.

18. According to Gray.

19. Cole Lesley's figure.

CHAPTER 4

1. *Present Indicative*.

2. 'P and O 1930', *Collected Verse of Noël Coward*.

3. Quoted, Richard Huggett, *Binkie Beaumont, Eminence Grise of the West End Theatre, 1933–1973*, Hodder and Stoughton, London, 1989.

4. Cecil Beaton, *The Glass of Fashion*, Weidenfeld and Nicolson, London, 1954.

5. Coward seems secretly to have been less satisfied with her performance than their audiences. Watching a revival of the play just before he died, he preferred Maggie Smith's interpretation: 'Much better than Gertie. She always wanted to be the perfect lady but Amanda is common and that's what Maggie captured so well.' Quoted, Huggett.

6. Correspondence of the Lord Chamberlain's Office.

7. Joyce Grenfell, *Darling Ma: The Letters of Joyce Grenfell*, ed. James Roose-Evans, Hodder and Stoughton, London, 1988.

8. Quoted, Lesley.

9. Quoted, Morley.

CHAPTER 5

1. Quoted, Humphrey Carpenter, *The Brideshead Generation*, Weidenfeld and Nicolson, London, 1989.

2. *The Glass of Fashion*.

3. The architectural historian. Quoted, Lahr.

4. Socialite, and mother of Nancy Cunard.

5. *Chips: The Diaries of Sir Henry Channon*, (ed. Robert Rhodes James), Weidenfeld and Nicolson, London, 1967.

6. Quoted, Lesley. Lawrence seemed a figure of almost mythic significance to a number of writers of the Thirties: Auden and Isherwood contemplated his greatness and wisdom for several years, and Terence Rattigan later wrote a play about him. Coward's admiration for him was not therefore exceptional, though it is hard to imagine in what way, except as a war writer himself, Lawrence was qualified to comment on *Post-Mortem*.

7. *The Times* obituary of Coward noted that '*Cavalcade*'s sincere, sentimental patriotism converted to Coward's cause many theatre-goers who had distrusted the flippancy, the facility and the witty light-heartedness of his earlier work.' *The Times*, 27 March 1973.

8. BBC Radio, 1972. Quoted, Lahr.

9. The inscription he put inside the copy of *Cavalcade* which he sent to Esme Wynne-Tyson, after the play's success was assured, 'With love from a National Hero', has a facetious ring to it. And in 1973, Lyndon Wynne-Tyson told his son: 'Noël wrote *Cavalcade* with his tongue in his cheek as a send-up of the British Empire. He was as surprised as anyone when the public, perhaps influenced by the General Strike atmosphere, took it literally.'

CHAPTER 6

1. In *A Talent To Amuse*, Sheridan Morley writes that Coward 'organized a boardroom *putsch* which in spite of some severe opposition from other members of the committee, succeeded in putting the Orphanage onto a basis of business efficiency rather than sentimental charity.'

2. John Lahr thinks the play failed. 'While he succeeded in providing the Lunts and himself with an actors' lark, Coward failed to find a proper metaphor for his ideas. The issues of abnormal sexuality and success are never fully integrated into the play.' *Coward the Playwright*.

3. Coward, incidentally, enjoyed considerable acclaim amongst French audiences, who at one time or another saw *Weekend* (*Hay Fever*), *Les Amants Terribles* (*Private Lives*), *Le Printemps de Saint Martin* (*Fallen Angels*), *Joyeux Chagrins* (*Present Laughter*), *Au Temps des Valses* (*Bitter-Sweet*) and *Jeux d'Esprit* (*Blithe Spirit*).

4. Laurence Olivier, *Confessions of an Actor*, Weidenfeld and Nicolson, London, 1982.

5. Jeffrey Brown Martin. I am indebted to his monograph, *The Screenplays of Ben Hecht*, University of Michigan, Ann Arbor, 1978.

6. Basil Dean, *Mind's Eye: An Autobiography: 1927–1972*, Hutchinson, London, 1973.

7. See John Elsom, *Post-War British Theatre*, Routledge Kegan Paul, London, 1979.

8. Jeffrey Brown Martin.

9. Remembered by Esme Wynne-Tyson and repeated to her son, Jon Wynne-Tyson.

Part 3: The War

CHAPTER 1

1. Quoted, Lesley. Corroborations of Coward's anti-appeasement sympathies occur occasionally in his autobiographies. Thus, *Past Conditional* describes his attending

one of Mussolini's rallies in Rome. '... hundreds and hundreds of Fascist youths marched up and down and back and forth shining with zeal and drilling themselves to a lather. They were on the whole a handsome lot but the expression of dedicated fanaticism on their moist young faces was fairly irritating. A few weeks previously I had spent a weekend in Kent with Anthony and Beatrice Eden. Anthony, just returned from some summit conference or other, had given me a blow by blow description of Mussolini at an official lunch party given in Anthony's honour.'

2. In its obituary of Binkie Beaumont, *The Times* quoted Tyrone Guthrie's remark that Beaumont 'could make or break the career of almost any worker in the British professional theatre'. His power was indeed immense, and in the Forties and Fifties it fuelled vindictive and unfounded allegations, spread by jealous impresarios and actors excluded from his productions, of a homosexual 'ring' which resolved all decisions of importance. As arguably his most important ally during those years, Coward was vulnerable to such allegations.

3. Quoted, Mander and Mitchenson.

4. Quoted, Huggett. Huggett adds: 'Binkie had no wish to remember his middle class, Nonconformist Welsh background, in fact he could not forget it quickly enough, and if that made him a snob then so be it.'

5. Noël Coward, *Play Parade*, Vol. 4, Heinemann.

6. *Darling Ma*.

7. Lahr also points out that Coward lived a star's life, and that although he may have been born into the life he depicts in *This Happy Breed*, he had forgotten altogether its material realities. 'Gibbons's attitude well served the star mentality which depends on the idea of the extraordinariness of the few standing out from the ordinariness of the many.'

8. Marchant. Sheridan Morley mentioned that the latter and Coward were lovers. Certainly, there is a sense that something in Marchant's book has been left unsaid. If Morley is correct, Marchant was far from being an impartial judge of Coward's character.

9. Mark Amory (ed.), *The Letters of Ann Fleming*, Collins, London, 1985. As an example of his sometimes insistent social manner, Ann Fleming referred to a poem, 'Don'ts for my Darlings', in which Coward gave the Flemings advice for their future married happiness. She wrote to one friend: 'I have suffered considerably from his reading it aloud in front of strangers.'

10. Peter Quennell, *The Wanton Chase*, Collins, London, 1980.

CHAPTER 2

1. Noël Coward, *Future Indefinite*, Heinemann, London, 1954.

2. Ibid.

3. Ibid.

4. Sir Campbell Stuart, *Opportunity Knocks Once*, Collins, London, 1952.

5. *Darling Ma*.

6. *Sunday Express*, August 1940.

7. F. J. Bellenger, Labour.

8. I am indebted in these pages to Anthony Aldgate and Jeffrey Richards, *Britain Can Take It: The British Cinema in the Second World War*, Blackwell, Oxford, 1986.

9. Quoted, Anthony Holden,

Olivier, Weidenfeld and Nicolson, London, 1988.
10. Ibid.
11. 'Lie In The Dark And Listen', *Collected Verse of Noël Coward*.
12. William Stephenson, *A Man Called Intrepid: The Secret War, 1939–1945*, Charnwood, London, 1976.
13. Ibid.
14. Quoted, Lesley.

CHAPTER 3
1. *Future Indefinite*.
2. Shelley's 'Ode to a Skylark' begins: 'Hail to thee, blithe spirit!/Bird thou never wert –/That from heaven or near it/Pourest thy full heart/In profuse strains of unpremeditated art.'
3. Noël Coward, *Play Parade*, Vol. 5, Heinemann, London, 1958.
4. Whether or not Coward's self-education had made him aware of the fact, he was following a literary tradition here. The Elizabethans distrusted those who set themselves up as spectators of life and rejected participation in its comedies and tragedies – thus Francis Bacon's magisterial pronouncement: 'In this theatre of man's life it is reserved only for God and angels to be lookers on.'
5. Kenneth Tynan noted: 'I cannot think that it will ever be possible to explain to a Belgian or Italian audience exactly why Budleigh Salterton is funny and Henley-in-Arden is not', *Profiles*, Nick Herne Books, London, 1989.
6. Quoted, Richard Huggett. Huggett says that Beaumont pointed out that both *Twelfth Night* and *Macbeth* had survived for three centuries, and that Coward could not guarantee that *Blithe Spirit* would be popular in the twenty-second century. He could not; but

so far, time seems reluctant to prove him wrong.
7. She asked for the epitaph, 'A Blithe Spirit', to be inscribed on her gravestone.
8. Quoted, Frances Gray, *Noël Coward*, Macmillan, London, 1987.
9. The *Spectator*, 11 July 1941.
10. *Collected Verse of Noël Coward*.

CHAPTER 4
1. See Philip Ziegler, *Mountbatten*, Collins, London, 1985.
2. *Future Indefinite*.
3. The details of this report were first published in *Sight and Sound*, 1990.
4. Noël Coward, *Diaries*.
5. Coward describes his position in *Future Indefinite*.
6. Quoted, Castle.
7. See Aldgate and Richards.
8. Quoted, *Sight and Sound*, September 1991.
9. Noël Coward, *Diaries*.
10. In Martin Green, *Children of the Sun*, Constable, London, 1977, we read: 'Instead of débutantes, reflected upside down in tin foil, or apparently beheaded, he showed the nation bandaged babies, courageous old Cockneys, and unselfconsciously heroic firemen and trawlermen, portrayed with reverent pathos and in the simplest settings.' Green also maintained that between them Beaton and Coward 'did more than anyone else to fix the official image of cheery, hearty, proletarian England at war'.
11. Cecil Beaton, *Diaries*.
12. Ibid.
13. Quoted, Castle.
14. Quoted, Aldgate and Richards.
15. *Darling Ma*.
16. Lena Angood must have been trustworthy and highly-consid-

ered: her career in Whitehall was eventually rewarded with an MBE.

CHAPTER 5
1. Noël Coward, *Diaries*.
2. *Darling Ma*.
3. Ibid.
4. *Evening Standard*, 1 May 1943.
5. *Sunday Times*, 2 May 1943.
6. *John O' London's Weekly* 21 May 1943.
7. The *Spectator*, 7 May 1943.
8. *Future Indefinite*
9. *The Collected Short Stories of Noël Coward*.
10. Cecil Beaton, *Diaries*.
11. Noël Coward, *Diaries*.
12. Cecil Beaton, *Diaries*.
13. Quoted, Aldgate and Richards.

Part 4: Eclipse
CHAPTER 1
1. Noël Coward, *Diaries*.
2. Writing in the *Daily Telegraph* in 1987, Jeffrey Richards remarked: 'It was fashionable to the swinging 1960s to mock the well-bred anguish of the lovers and the film's exaltation of restraint over unbridled passion, duty over self-indulgence, and concern for others over immediate self-gratification. But in the AIDS-conscious 1980s, when fidelity and monogamy are the flavour of the decade, *Brief Encounter* may not quite seem the antique that its "liberated" detractors claimed. Irrespective of the whims of fashion, *Brief Encounter* remains both documentarily and emotionally true.'
3. *Daily Mail*, 9 May 1945.
4. 'I've Just Come Out Of England', *Collected Verse of Noël Coward*.
5. 'Not Yet The Dodo', *Collected Verse of Noël Coward*.

CHAPTER 2
1. Noël Coward, *Diaries*.
2. Lesley.
3. Peter Quennell in conversation with the author.
4. Ibid.
5. Ibid.
6. *Letters of Ann Fleming*.
7. Correspondence of the Lord Chamberlain's Office.
8. Laurence Olivier, *Confessions of an Actor*.
9. Quoted, Lesley.
10. Noël Coward, *Diaries*.

CHAPTER 3
1. She was not particularly complimentary either about Coward's behaviour while the Edens were in Jamaica: 'Noël Coward appeared last night with a party of persons called "Perry", "Terry", "Binkie" and "Coalie"; he seems most annoyed he was not received by the Edens, he sent them a basket of caviare, cutlets, Earl Grey tea and Romary biscuits, and apparently gossiped with the detectives. I tried to appear disinterested but drank in everything he said – very low to gossip with detectives, and I should have told him so. Nothing he said is repeatable, it was distressingly intimate and conceivably true.' *The Letters of Ann Fleming*.
2. *Future Indefinite*
3. Alec Guinness, *Blessings in Disguise*, Hamish Hamilton, London, 1985.
4. Quoted, *Sunday Telegraph*, 21 October 1990.
5. Noël Coward, *Diaries*.
6. The play was also known, at various stages, as *Island Fling* and *Home and Colonial*.
7. Tynan, *A View of the English Stage*.
8. When reviewing *Present Laughter*

and *This Happy Breed* in the *Sunday Times* in 1943.
9. An observation made by Frances Gray in *Noël Coward*.

CHAPTER 4
1. *The Letters of Ann Fleming*.
2. Quennell, *The Wanton Chase*.
3. Quoted, John Pearson, *The Life of Ian Fleming*, Jonathan Cape, London, 1966.
4. Quoted, Lesley.
5. Cecil Beaton, *Diaries*.
6. Quoted, Morley.
7. Cecil Beaton, *Diaries*.
8. *Curtains*, Kenneth Tynan.
9. In its obituary, *The Times*, 8 September 1952, said that she danced 'with magical lightness', and that in *Private Lives* she gave a 'brilliant and sustained piece of high comedy acting'.
10. Quennell, *The Wanton Chase*.
11. *Darling Ma*.
12. *The Letters of Ann Fleming*.
13. Robert Greacen, *The Art of Noël Coward*, Hand and Flower Press, England, 1953.
14. Tynan, *A View of the English Stage*.
15. He also admonished Cole Lesley: 'Monet, Monet, Monet, that's all you think about.'

CHAPTER 5
1. Noël Coward, *Diaries*.
2. According to Joyce Carey, 'A Private Life', BBC TV.
3. This sum seems to vary. Cole Lesley settled for $35,000. Sheridan Morley argues that it was $40,000. The *Daily Telegraph* obituary, 26 March 1973, mentions £13,000, and in his diary, Coward, who should have known, talks of $15,000. But only the avaricious would insist on exactitude here.
4. 'A Private Life', BBC TV.

5. Noël Coward, *Diaries*.

CHAPTER 6
1. *Punch*, 1956.
2. Quoted, Morley.
3. Traylor died in 1990 in Los Angeles. Coward's New York representative, Charles Russell, is reported – *Daily Express*, 26 January 1990 – as saying that he attempted suicide in his despair over Coward's attentions.
4. At least in the *Diaries* as they are published.
5. *Collected Short Stories of Noël Coward*.

CHAPTER 7
1. Quoted, Castle.
2. Ibid.
3. *Letters of Ann Fleming*.
4. According to Coward in his diary.
5. Cecil Beaton, *Diaries*.
6. Quoted, *The Letters of Ann Fleming*.
7. 'When I Have Fears', *Collected Verse of Noël Coward*.
8. *Play Parade*, Vol. 6, Heinemann, London, 1962.
9. In Morley.

CHAPTER 8
1. He mentioned the novel in a letter dated 3 March 1960, to Esme Wynne-Tyson: 'It has been hanging over me like the sword of whoever it was for ages. It is so light and *uns*ignificant that I think they will have difficulty in getting it between covers.' Courtesy of Jon Wynne-Tyson.
2. In the *Sunday Express*.
3. Tynan, *Curtains*.
4. Ibid.
5. The *Tatler*, 4 July 1962.
6. Gray.
7. Noël Coward, *Diaries*.

8. The *Sunday Times*, 5 May 1963.
9. *Queen*, 17 July 1963.
10. The *Financial Times*, 4 July 1963.
11. The *Daily Mail*, 4 July 1963: 'May their names be blessed for evermore, and may a thousand flowers bloom at every step they take, and may they be heaped with gold and silver and precious jewels and pelted day and night with caviare and roses and bottles of champagne.'
12. Quoted, Kenneth Tynan, *Profiles*.
13. Quoted, Lesley.
14. In 1973, the year of Coward's death, Tynan challenged Cyril Connolly's uncharacteristically obtuse judgement of 1937, that 'one can't read any of Noël Coward's plays now ... they are written in the most topical and perishable way imaginable, the cream in them turns sour overnight.' 'His best work has not dated, by which I mean his most devotedly ephemeral ... with the passage of time, the profundities peel away and only the basic trivialities remain to enchant us.'
15. Quoted, Lesley.

Part 5: Restoration
CHAPTER 1
1. Quoted, Vickers, *Cecil Beaton*.
2. 'Me And The Girls', *The Collected Short Stories of Noël Coward*.
3. 'Not Yet The Dodo', *Collected Verse of Noël Coward*.
4. Quoted, Huggett, *Binkie Beaumont*.
5. Ted Morgan, *Somerset Maugham*, Jonathan Cape, London, 1980.
6. Huggett.
7. Ibid.
8. Ibid.
9. Quoted, Castle.
10. Ibid.

11. Quoted, Huggett.
12. Quoted, Marchant.
13. The *Observer*, 17 April 1966.
14. Russell Taylor.
15. Lahr.
16. Noël Coward, *Diaries*.
17. 'I Am No Good At Love', *Collected Verse of Noël Coward*.
18. In *Façades*, the Sitwells' biographer, John Pearson, described this predicament as it related to Osbert Sitwell: 'During a lifetime as a homosexual, he had learned to be too blank, too bland in his relations with outsiders. The mask goes on, the terrible discretion starts, the inner self is not revealed. Ironically, his sexual status, which conferred so many incidental benefits upon him as a writer, seems to have deprived him of his masterpiece.'
19. *The Deep Blue Sea*, of 1952 was originally to have been about the death of Rattigan's adored Kenneth Morgan, but Binkie Beaumont would not allow it. *Ross*, his 1960 treatment of T. E. Lawrence, and *Man and Boy*, of 1963, both sublimate their homosexual content. See B. A. Young, *The Rattigan Version*, Hamish Hamilton, London, 1986.

CHAPTER 2
1. In a letter to Esme Wynne-Tyson, March 1960, courtesy of Jon Wynne-Tyson.
2. Quoted, Lesley.
3. Cecil Beaton, *Diaries*.
4. Quoted, Castle.
5. Ibid.
6. Quoted, Marchant.
7. In a letter to Esme Wynne-Tyson, 19 January 1970.
8. Cecil Beaton, *Diaries*.
9. Quoted, Ziegler.
10. His definition of ideal death, as described to Judy Campbell, who

had acted with him in *Blithe Spirit*, *This Happy Breed* and *Present Laughter*.

11. In a letter to Esme Wynne-Tyson, 9 March 1960.

12. Lusting, it was later speculated, after the advance he was thought to have received for the biography, his assassins broke into Pope-Hennessy's flat, gagging and binding him. A servant surprised them, there was carnage, and Pope-Hennessy died in hospital, having inhaled blood. Cecil Beaton, who was to have helped with the biography, spoke for many in the *Observer* when he 'wondered why oh why James with such talent, charm and good looks had gone the way he had'. Quoted, Vickers.

13. Though as late as 1991, Sheridan Morley was still publicly defending his integrity as an editor against charges of expurgation.

14. Noël Coward, *Diaries*.

15. *Present Indicative*.

16. George Sanders, another international Englishman, considered that all actors were Peter Pans: 'Acting is for children – who else can take this posturing seriously?' He might also have said that that hunger for fame which seems to haunt so many actors, and certainly obsessed Coward, implies a child's uncomplicated need for love and adulation.

17. Noël Coward, *Diaries*.

Select Bibliography

THE MAJOR WORKS OF NOËL COWARD
Play Parade, Vol. 1, Heinemann, London, 1934.
Play Parade, Vol. 2, Heinemann, London, 1939.
Play Parade, Vol. 3, Heinemann, London, 1950.
Play Parade, Vol. 4, Heinemann, London, 1954.
Play Parade, Vol. 5, Heinemann, London, 1958.
Play Parade, Vol. 6, Heinemann, London, 1962.
A Withered Nosegay, Methuen, London, 1984.
Present Indicative, Heinemann, London, 1937.
Future Indefinite, Heinemann, London, 1954.
Past Conditional, Methuen, London, 1986.
The Lyrics of Noël Coward, Heinemann, London, 1965.
Pomp and Circumstance, Heinemann, London, 1960.
Collected Verse of Noël Coward, Methuen, London, 1984.
The Collected Short Stories of Noël Coward, Dutton, New York, 1983.
The Noël Coward Diaries, Weidenfeld and Nicolson, London, 1982.

BOOKS ABOUT NOËL COWARD

BRAYBROOKE, PATRICK, *The Amazing Mr Coward*, Archer, London, 1933.
BRIERS, RICHARD, *Coward and Company*, Futura, London, 1989.
CASTLE, CHARLES, *Noël*, W. H. Allen, London, 1972.
GRAY, FRANCES, *Noël Coward*, Macmillan, London, 1987.
GREACEN, ROBERT, *The Art of Noël Coward*, Hand and Flower Press, England, 1953.
LAHR, JOHN, *Coward the Playwright*, Methuen, London, 1982.
LESLEY, COLE, *The Life of Noël Coward*, Jonathan Cape, London, 1976.
LESLEY, COLE, MORLEY, SHERIDAN, and PAYN, GRAHAM (eds), *Noël Coward and his Friends*, Weidenfeld and Nicolson, London, 1979.
MANDER, RAYMOND, AND MITCHENSON, JOE, *Theatrical Companion to Coward*, Rockliff, London, 1957.
MARCHANT, WILLIAM, *The Privilege of His Company: Noël Coward Remembered*, Weidenfeld and Nicolson, London, 1975.
MORLEY, SHERIDAN, *A Talent to Amuse*, Heinemann, London, 1969.

MORLEY, SHERIDAN, *Out in the Midday Sun. The Paintings of Noël Coward*, Phaidon, London, 1988.
RICHARDS, DICK (ED.), *The Wit of Noël Coward*, Leslie Frewin, London, 1968.

OTHER WORKS CONSULTED

ADAMS, SAMUEL HOPKINS, *Alexander Woollcott*, Hamish Hamilton, London, 1946.
ALDGATE, ANTHONY, AND RICHARDS, JEFFREY, *Britain Can Take It: The British Cinema in the Second World War*, Blackwell, Oxford, 1986.
AMORY, MARK, (ED.), *The Letters of Ann Fleming*, Collins, London, 1985.
BEATON, CECIL, *The Glass of Fashion*, Weidenfeld and Nicolson, London, 1954.
BEATON, CECIL, *Self Portrait with Friends: The Diaries of Cecil Beaton*, Weidenfeld and Nicolson, London, 1979.
BROWN MARTIN, JEFFREY, *The Screenplays of Ben Hecht*, University of Michigan, Ann Arbor, 1978.
CALDER, R. L., *The Life of W. Somerset Maugham*, Heinemann, London, 1989.
DEAN, BASIL, *Seven Ages: An Autobiography*, Hutchinson, London, 1973.
DEAN, BASIL, *Mind's Eye: An Autobiography: 1927–1972*, Hutchinson, London, 1973.
ELSOM, JOHN, *Post-War British Theatre*, Routledge Kegan Paul, London, 1979.
GIELGUD, JOHN, *Early Stages*, Macmillan, London, 1939.
GREEN, MARTIN, *Children of the Sun*, Constable, London, 1977.
GRENFELL, JOYCE, *Darling Ma*, Hodder and Stoughton, London, 1988.
GUINNESS, ALEC, *Blessings in Disguise*, Hamish Hamilton, London, 1985.
HOLDEN, ANTHONY, *Olivier*, Weidenfeld and Nicolson, London, 1988.
HUGGETT, RICHARD, *Binkie Beaumont: Eminence Grise of the West End Theatre, 1933–1973*, Hodder and Stoughton, London, 1989.
JENKINS, ALAN, *Remembering The Thirties*, Heinemann, London, 1976.
LOELIA, DUCHESS OF WESTMINSTER, *Grace and Favour*, Weidenfeld and Nicolson, London, 1961
MORGAN, TED, *Somerset Maugham*, Jonathan Cape, London, 1980.
MORLEY, SHERIDAN, *Gladys Cooper*, Heinemann, London, 1979.

MORLEY, SHERIDAN, *Gertrude Lawrence*, Weidenfeld and Nicolson, London, 1981.

OLIVIER, LAURENCE, *Confessions of an Actor*, Weidenfeld and Nicolson, London, 1982.

ORWELL, GEORGE, *Collected Essays*, Secker and Warburg, London, 1961.

PEARSON, JOHN, *Façades: A Biography of Edith, Osbert and Sacheverell Sitwell*, Macmillan, London, 1978.

PEARSON, JOHN, *The Life of Ian Fleming*, Jonathan Cape, London, 1966.

QUENNELL, PETER, *The Wanton Chase*, Collins, London, 1980.

RUSSELL TAYLOR, JOHN, *The Rise and Fall of the Well-Made Play*, Methuen, London, 1967.

STEVENSON, WILLIAM, *A Man Called Intrepid: The Secret War, 1939–1945*, Charnwood, London, 1976.

STUART, SIR CAMPBELL, *Opportunity Knocks Once*, Collins, London, 1952.

THORNTON, MICHAEL, *Royal Feud: The Queen Mother and the Duchess of Windsor*, Michael Joseph, London, 1985.

TYNAN, KENNETH, *A View of the English Stage*, Methuen, London, 1975.

TYNAN, KENNETH, *Curtains*, Atheneum, New York, 1961.

TYNAN, KENNETH, *Profiles*, Nick Hern Books, London, 1989.

VICKERS, HUGO, *Cecil Beaton*, Weidenfeld and Nicolson, London, 1985.

WARWICK, CHRISTOPHER, *George and Marina, Duke and Duchess of Kent*, Weidenfeld and Nicolson, London, 1988.

WAUGH, EVELYN, *A Little Order: A Selection from his Journalism*, Eyre Methuen, London, 1977.

ZIEGLER, PHILIP, *Mountbatten*, Collins, London, 1985.

Index

Index

Connolly, Cyril, 124–5, 165, 186
Constant Nymph, The, 72
Conversation Piece (Coward play), 88, 116
Cooper, Sir Aldred Duff, 129, 142
Cooper, Mrs Astley, 34–5, 38
Cooper, Gladys, 199, 231
Courtneidge, Cicely, 39, 250
Courtneidge, Robert, 53
Coward, Arthur Sabin (Noël's father), 11, 13, 91, 120
Coward, Eric (Noël's younger brother), 12–13, 91, 123
Coward, Hilda (Noël's aunt), 11
Coward, Ida (Noël's aunt), 14, 91
Coward, Jim (Noël's uncle), 13
Coward, Sir Noël Peirce, 1–4, 260–2
 as actor, 64, 94, 205; early days, 17–18, 18–24, 29, 37–9, 40; in films, 2, 23–4, 118–20, 165–6, 224–5; in his own plays, 39, 52, 53–4, 96–7, 121–2, 134–6, 167–9, 169, 222, 246, 248–250; stage-fright, 59
 adultery, as literary theme, 75
 ambitious, determined, 4, 28, 29, 36–7, 40–1, 45; *see also* social ambitions, *below*
 amusement, entertainment, his concern with, 27, 136–8, 196
 art, his views on, 209–11
 his art collection, 210, 220
 autobiography, 9, 80, 123–5; *see also Present Indicative; Future Indefinite; Past Conditional*
 and Cecil Beaton, *see under* Beaton, Cecil
 and Binkie Beaumont, *see under* Beaumont, Binkie
 biographies, 2; *see also* Braybrooke, Patrick; Greacen, Robert

 birth, 11–12
 his Black Book, 185–6
 as a boy, 14–15, 26
 in cabaret, 2, 172, 207–9, 215–16
 on censorship, 79
 and Chamberlain, appeasement, 129, 133, 139, 267
 character, as judge of, 71, 99
 his charm, 40, 135–7
 choirboy, 17
 cleverness, 39
 and commercial success, 87
 conformist, conventional, suburban values, 2, 67, 102, 113, 122–3, 130, 132–3, 176, 196–8, 260–1
 country-house visits, 34–5
 his country houses, *see* Goldenhurst; White Cliffs
 and critics, 86–8, 124–5, 154, 184–6, 202, 231, 234, 236, 239
 cruel, vindictive, 96–7, 248
 death, his will, 258–9
 dependency, horror of, 13, 59
 diaries, 80, 146, 222–3, 259–60
 disciplined, 2, 115, 205
 and drink, 13, 59–60
 drugs, as literary theme, 60, 65, 66, 67
 visits Eastern Europe, 139
 education, 15, 17, 40
 and 'Elvira', 151
 leaves England, 218–22
 on his brother Eric, 12
 fame, a star, 1–2, 4, 64, 97, 100, 101, 115, 207, 262, 268
 fame, as literary theme, 112, 113–14
 his family, modest origins, 3–4, 8–16, 80, 122–3, 130–1, 198
 family, as literary theme, 13, 81, 105
 and his father's death, 121

279

170–2, 179–80, 182–3, 269; *see
also Peace In Our Time*
selfishness, as literary theme, 95,
112
short stories, 8
feud with Sitwells, 48–50
and smoking, 59, 65, 119, 257
a snob, 124, 157, 221, 232
social ambitions, 33, 34–5, 38, 39,
40–1, 42–3, 50, 101–2
society, critical of, 67, 68, 77–8,
85–6
songs, 36, 169, 237
his speech, 39, 101
and sunbathing, 33, 38, 191
supernatural, as literary theme,
23, 103, 148–9, 150–1; *see also
Blithe Spirit*
Switzerland, home in, 226
and television, 216
travel, wanderlust, 7, 72, 91–2
truthful?, 27, 124
and the United States, 216–17,
220, 225; Las Vegas, 215–16;
New York, 43–5, 68–9, 79, 85,
90
in the West Indies, *see* Bermuda;
Jamaica
and the Windsors, 50, 55, 70, 176,
265
women with pasts, as literary
theme, 77–8
writing, the act of, 92–3, 213–14
and Esme Wynne, *see* Wynne-
Tyson, Esme
and youth, 53, 73–4
Coward, Russell Arthur (Noël's
elder brother), 11
Coward, Violet Agnes (née Veitch;
Noël's mother), 9–12, 13, 14,
20
marriage to Arthur Coward, 10,
11, 13

children, 11–13
relations with Noël, 14, 26, 33, 34,
37–8, 213–14
and Noël's theatrical career, 17–
18, 18–19, 20, 22–3, 29, 213–214
at Goldenhurst, 91
grieves over Eric's death, 123
in New York in Second World
War, 143, 213
old age, death, 213–14, 227–8
mentioned, 28, 39, 63, 224
Cowardy Custard (Coward
anthology), 258
Crewe, Quentin, 233
Crime Without Passion, 118
Crissa (Coward/Esme Wynne
opera, incomplete), 30
Cromer, second Earl of, Lord
Chamberlain, 61, 62, 75, 76, 79; *see
also* Lord Chamberlain
Cummings, E. E., 102
Cunard, Emerald, 101
Cutler, Kate, 61

Daily Express, 115, 158, 162, 164,
230, 247
Daily Graphic, 62
Daily Mail, 110, 164, 179, 230, 250
Daily Sketch, 129–30
Daily Telegraph, 3–4, 109, 141, 259,
271–2
'Dance, dance, dance' (Coward
song), 74
Dane, Clemence, 133, 150
Darlington, W. A., 4
Dawson, Sir Douglas, 61–2
Dean, Basil, 23, 63, 68, 72, 119, 170
Dean-Paul, Irene ('Poldowski'), 43
del Giudice, Filippo, 157
Design for Living (Coward play), 50,
75, 88, 93, 95, 112–15, 116, 130,
134, 254
film, 118